GUESTS NEVER LEAVE HUNGRY

James Sewid

GUESTS NEVER LEAVE HUNGRY
THE AUTOBIOGRAPHY OF JAMES SEWID,
A KWAKIUTL INDIAN

Edited by James P. Spradley

McGill-Queen's University Press
Montreal & Kingston • London • Buffalo

Published by Yale University Press 1969

Paperback edition published by
McGill-Queen's University Press 1972
Reprinted 1978, 1983, 1989, 1992

ISBN: 0-7735-0134-7
Library of Congress Catalog Card Number: 79-180184

Designed by John O. C. McCrillis

Printed in Canada

The cover design is from James Sewid's
family crest, the Qolus. The drawing was
made by his daughter, Dora Cook.

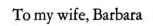

To my wife, Barbara

Acknowledgments

The research for this book was carried out under the auspices of the departments of anthropology and psychiatry at the University of Washington. I wish to express my deep gratitude to many who contributed to this project. Professors Melville Jacobs, James B. Watson, and Viola Garfield provided guidance, encouragement, and many helpful suggestions. Dr. Harry Wolcott, Dr. Gananath Obeyesekere, Dr. Peter Wilson, Dr. L. L. Langness, and Dr. Michael Crawford made valuable criticisms of the manuscript. Dr. James Oakland gave special assistance in psychological testing and analysis of the data and was a source of constant stimulation and encouragement. Mary Jahn gave invaluable editorial assistance. Joy Sullivan provided secretarial assistance and frequent counsel in preparing the mansucript. My debt of gratitude to my wife, Barbara Spradley, is greater than I can express. She was a participant, critic, and coworker at every stage of the research project.

This book would not have been possible without the help given by members of James Sewid's family. His daughter, Daisy Neel, made available to me the large scrapbook she had kept on her father's activities. She also assisted in ascertaining the dates of many events in the life of her father and translated James Sewid's names and songs. James Sewid's eldest daughter, Dora Cook, drew the Qolus for the cover and supplied a great deal of helpful information. Other members of his family answered questions, gave me pictures, and provided me with the hospitality of their homes. I owe a personal debt of gratitude to Flora Sewid, who assisted throughout the research and provided a wealth of valuable information. As a charming hostess she made my visits to the Sewid home in Alert Bay an enjoyable experience. My deepest gratitude, however, is deserved by James Sewid. His honesty, cooperation, and willingness to take time from his busy schedule contributed most to this project. This book is his life and, in a very real sense, his book.

J. P. S.

July 1968

Contents

Illustrations

Introduction

A major feature of the contemporary world is intensive contact between Western and non-Western societies. Many small tribal societies have become disorganized under the impact of Western contact. It has brought radically different customs and value systems into conflict. Psychiatric studies have shown that culture conflict is damaging to the mental health of the non-Westerner. Anthropological researchers have reported many other negative consequences of this conflict. Culture contact has often been accompanied by the breakdown of the extended family, excessive drinking, nativistic movements, anomie, population decline, and individual failure to adapt to culture change. Traditional values have become obsolete and natives do not often find Western values meaningful. The life histories of those living in culture contact situations are often filled with evidence of social and personal pathology. A current explanation to account for the failure of individuals to adapt to this situation is that they are *culturally deprived*. Like an undernourished child deprived of food, these people supposedly have an inadequate supply of culture. This explanation has been extended to many minority groups in contact with Western society who have a distinct cultural heritage of their own. While partly true, it overlooks several important aspects of the situation.

First, to be culturally deprived usually means to be deprived of values, customs, and skills important to Westerners. The ethnocentrism of such a designation is evident. It is implicit in this argument that the culture of the West is best for everyone, therefore, those with a different culture are deprived. Non-Westerners might contend that the reverse is true. Westerners do not know the rich tribal heritage, folklore, music, art, and dance which other societies have developed. They do not value extended kinship ties, native rituals, or the religious beliefs of non-Western peoples. An extreme cultural relativism which treats all values as equal may be invalid, but a naïve ethnocentrism which holds Western values as superior to all others is also untenable in the modern world. Such ethnocentrism fosters the view that culturally different peoples are culturally deprived peoples.

Second, evidence from culture contact situations does not fully support the cultural deprivation thesis. Tribal societies in contact with the West have indeed been deprived of parts of their culture. Their misery is often apparent. Their cultures are undergoing rapid change. But their problems do not arise simply from being deprived of their own or Western culture. Instead, it is the conflict between two cultural systems which overwhelms them. Their cultural environment is not too simple or restricted but too complex and conflicting. Individuals are confronted with values and customs from their own as well as from Western culture. They must come to terms with the traditional and the new cultural forms and these are often contradictory. This is far different from learning one's native culture no matter how inconsistent that may be. It is also different from learning a second culture after one reaches maturity. Generations of immigrants have demonstrated that this can be done, and while difficult, it is easier than learning to adjust to two different cultures simultaneously. Adaptation to a multicultural environment requires that individuals become multicultural (Bohannon 1963:395). Failure must be understood in terms of the difficulty of such a task. Those living in culture conflict are not necessarily culturally deprived.

Finally, the cultural deprivation thesis does not account for those who do adapt to two contrasting cultures. It is a remarkable accomplishment that a native African or American Indian can carry out a successful business enterprise, engage in local and national political activity, and acquire other Western goals, while at the same time participating with full commitment in native rituals and customs. They have become bicultural individuals. Though often overlooked, they probably exist in most societies undergoing contact with the West. They are a potential source for understanding how man can adapt to a multicultural environment, and they may also provide a necessary corrective to the idea that they are culturally deprived or that culture contact has primarily negative consequences.

James Sewid is a Kwakiutl Indian who has made such an exceptional adjustment to culture conflict. If current standards had been in vogue when he was young, he probably would have been considered culturally deprived. As a child he saw his relatives sent to prison for practicing Kwakiutl ceremonies. His early life was filled with poverty, and his home was often without the presence of a father. He had only three years of interrupted education in a segregated Indian school with a poorly trained teacher. Though he experienced the full impact of culture conflict, he has emerged as a respected Kwakiutl leader and a successful entrepreneur by Western values. In 1955 he was selected by the National Film Board of Canada to appear in a film on the achievements of Canadian Indians. An Indian Research Project, carried out by the University of British Columbia in 1955, singled him out as one of the outstanding entrepreneurs in British Columbia (Hawthorn et al. 1960:170–74). In 1964 research on his capacities and mode of adjustment to culture conflict was begun. It became apparent that, although essentially Kwakiutl, James Sewid has lived with one foot in each culture. He has developed the capacity to be bicultural, participating with full commitment in two contrasting cultures. In 1967, at the age of 53, he was the chief councillor of the largest Kwakiutl village in British Columbia. His autobiography demonstrates that individuals can adapt to culture conflict in spite of the problems.

This research project was designed to provide an autobiography of a non-Western individual who had successfully adapted to culture conflict and to investigate the complex relationship between rapid culture change and such an individual. This included the impact of culture change upon him, his mode of adaptation to culture conflict, and his influence on culture change. The life history approach formed the basis of this research. Life history studies by anthropologists have been carried out in many societies to examine the relationship between culture and personality (Kluckhohn 1945, Langness 1965). The difficulty of personality assessment in non-Western cultures is well-known. Psychological tests developed in the West may provide important data, but there is evidence that they must be used with caution (Lindzey 1961). Cultural differences require that intensive study of individuals in non-Western societies use multiple techniques. In addition to his autobiography, data on James Sewid were gathered by means of participant observation, structured interviews, psychological tests, interviews of others, and examination of secondary records related to him.

The autobiography was tape-recorded in unstructured interviews during a two-year period. The verbatim record of these interviews was transcribed and totaled nearly five hundred pages. Most interviews were held in private on fishing boats, in various homes, or while traveling. A number of structured interviews were developed from the transcribed tapes, secondary sources, and other anthropological research (Whiting et al. 1966). For example, the data revealed that James Sewid had filled a large number of different roles in Kwakiutl and white society. A structured interview was developed to elicit his perception of the behavioral requirements for each role, his own evaluation of how he met those requirements, and how others perceived him in his role behavior. Other interviews covered such subjects as the political activity of the Nimpkish band, drinking behavior, and child-rearing practices.

After most of the life history was gathered, a variety of psychological tests was administered. These included a revised Value Orientation Questionnaire developed by Kluckhohn and Strodtbeck for cross-cultural use (1961), a sentence-completion test, a self-image test, and an achievement-motivation test. Although the results are not included here, a psychologist administered the Rorschach, Thematic Apperception Test, and a number of intelligence tests.

James Sewid was observed in a wide variety of situations. These included his home in Alert Bay, British Columbia, my home in Seattle, Washington, living on his fishing boat, performing native dances, performing leadership roles in ceremonial and religious activities, supervising fishing and construction activities, and interacting with relatives, other Indians, and whites. He participated in several groups where he was the only Indian among whites. Detailed records of his activities for different time periods were made as well as an inventory of personal effects in his home.

From the start of the research, James Sewid insisted that I interview others to verify his statements. With this in mind, as well as to understand how others perceived him, interviews were held with many others. These included his wife, several children, more distant kinsmen, ministers, leaders in the white community of Alert Bay, other anthropologists who knew him, members of the Indian Department, and two different employers. A variety of secondary sources was also used for supplemental information. The minutes of the Nimpkish Council, covering about seventeen years that he was associated with it, were carefully examined. His daughter, Daisy Neel, had kept a scrapbook, letters, and notes on her father which she made available. These as well as church records, the *Native Voice* for which James Sewid was an associate editor, and personal records all enabled me to check many events which he had remembered and to encourage him to talk about other events which he had forgotten.

James Sewid's motivations for cooperating in this research centered around his desire to help his people, a sense of satisfaction with his own accomplishments, a desire for immortality, and his sense of obligation to me as a personal friend. While he perceived that the written story of his life was an opportunity to extend those achievements which had placed him in a position of being respected as an outstanding individual, he was also interested in the scientific value of the research. He accepted my interest in studying his exceptional adjustment to cultural conflict as a means toward understanding the problems his people faced. Toward the end of the project he was asked why he had decided to take part in the study, and he responded,

> I have always tried hard to live up to all the things that I have done and I think that others can learn from hearing about my experiences. I thought that if I could put my life story in a written book, then even people that I know in distant places could read about it and it might help them. That was why I thought it was necessary to make this book. (Field Notes)

His command of English was sufficient for the purposes of research, so the autobiography is James Sewid's own account. Some editing was necessary to place events in chronological order and provide grammatical consistency. Although it was difficult to determine the exact degree of change brought about by editing, it appeared to be negligible. When the final draft was read back, he responded to it as his own story and made very few changes.

James Sewid's story must be understood against the background
of Kwakiutl culture and changes which have occurred since contact
with the West. The wealth of descriptive material on the Kwakiutl
is impressive. The first descriptions were made when Vancouver
explored their territory in 1792. Franz Boas began publishing his
systematic studies of the Kwakiutl in the 1880s. His research continued for nearly fifty years and contributed descriptions of nearly
every aspect of their culture as it was around the turn of the century
(Boas 1966, Codere 1959). Ruth Benedict drew from Boas'
research to contrast the Kwakiutl with several other societies in her
book, *Patterns of Culture* (1934). Shortly thereafter another study
appeared which showed the nature of Kwakiutl competition and
cooperation (Goldman 1937). In 1941, *Smoke from Their Fires*
was published; this has remained the only other full-length autobiography of a Kwakiutl Indian (Ford 1941). Since 1950 there has
been extensive research on Kwakiutl culture change (Codere 1950,
1961), acculturation of the Kwakiutl and other Indians in British
Columbia (Hawthorn et al. 1960), Kwakiutl education problems
(Wolcott 1964, 1967), and two ethnographic descriptions of
Kwakiutl villages (Rohner 1964, 1967, Wolcott 1967). During
1962–63 Harry Wolcott did research for his ethnography in the
village where James Sewid spent much of his early life.

The Kwakiutl shared a highly distinctive culture with other
Indians living along the northwestern coast of North America. They
lived on the shores of the northeastern part of Vancouver Island,
the adjacent mainland, and the islands of the channel in between.
This country is made up of inlets, fjords, and islands resulting from
partially submerged mountains along the coast. The rugged terrain
made land travel difficult. Villages were all situated along the shores
where level land was most available. The mountains were covered
with thick forests of cedar, fir, yew, and hemlock, and they abound
in ferns, nettles, berries, and many forms of animal life. The most
important resource for the Kwakiutl was the abundant marine
life. Seaweed, clams, crabs, sea eggs, abalone, barnacles, seals, sea
lions, and many different species of fish were available. Salmon
and olachen were by far the most important. Their annual runs up
many of the fresh-water streams made them easily accessible. The

Kwakiutl lived in one of the richest natural habitats in North America so that economic pursuits did not require all of their time and energy. The abundance of natural resources enabled them to devote much of their time to the development of a complex social and ceremonial life. It also supported a large population, which has been estimated at over 10,000 in 1835.

The most important economic activities were fishing and woodworking. Traditional methods for gathering fish included trapping, netting, spearing, and use of hook and line. Salmon were caught in streams as they traveled to their spawning grounds. They were cooked in many different ways, dried, and smoked. Large bundles of the meat were then stored for the winter months. Olachen were caught in nets at the mouths of streams in early spring. They were especially valued for their oil, which was stored in kelp tubes. This oil was mixed with berries, clams, and seaweed and also eaten plain. Olachen, sometimes called candlefish, were so rich in oil that when dried and threaded with a wick they would burn like candles. While men fished, women gathered shellfish, seaweed, berries, and roots. The collection and storage of food took place during spring, summer, and fall, leaving the winter largely free for other activities.

Kwakiutl technology was based upon the abundant supply of wood. Red cedar, yellow cedar, and yew were most widely used. All of the men engaged in woodworking, but some with special training and skill became wood-carving specialists. They were hired by others to make canoes or carve masks and totem poles. By means of stone adzes and chisels and the controlled use of fire they were able to construct large canoes capable of carrying thirty or forty persons. Houses were constructed of posts and beams from cedar logs and walls and roofs from cedar planks. It required considerable engineering skill to raise a seventy-foot cedar log, weighing several tons, into the proper position as a crossbeam. Wood products were used for almost every conceivable purpose. The infant was wrapped in soft cedar bark at birth and later placed on a wooden cradle board. Food was stored in wooden containers and cooked and eaten with wooden utensils. Clothing was often made from cedar bark which was woven into a textile. Ceremonial life was centered around the display of wooden masks, cedar bark regalia, and the use of large wooden whistles. At death, the individual was placed in a wooden coffin. The Kwakiutl were highly skilled in the manufacture of all of these objects.

Kwakiutl society was made up of about twenty-five politically autonomous tribes. They shared a similar culture and spoke the same language, as well as referring to themselves as "Kwakiutl." This was the name of the tribe ranked at the top of a lineal hierarchy. Each of the other tribes was ranked in descending order, the Kweka second, Walas Kwakiutl third, Kumkutis fourth, Mamalilikulla fifth, Nimpkish sixth, and so on. The first four tribes lived together at Fort Rupert. Most of the other fifteen villages were occupied by single tribes. Tribal membership was usually traced through the paternal line, but the mother's tribe was also important. The child of a Kwiksutainuk man and a Mamalilikulla woman was considered half from one tribe and half from the other. Men lived in the village of their father's tribe while women left their own tribal villages to live with their husbands upon marriage. These rules were not strict and exceptions occurred.

In each village a series of large multi-family houses was arranged along the shore, facing the water. Some of the larger villages had as many as thirty houses and a population of nearly five hundred. Seasonal migration to other settlements located near the best fishing grounds occurred in the spring, summer, and fall. These settlements might contain several families or, in some cases such as at Knight's Inlet, groups from many different tribes living together. During the winter, a number of tribes would gather at a single village for extended periods of ceremonial activity. In those villages with more than one tribe, each had its own area and continued to be an autonomous group

In each tribe there were several ranked kinship groups called *numayms,* which anthropologists have sometimes referred to as clans. They were made up of a number of hierarchically ranked social positions. Membership in the numaym was acquired from either one's father or mother, although the paternal line was stressed. Each member considered himself to have descended from a mythical ancestor who had visited the earth and founded the numaym. This supernatural being had come wearing a certain mask and dress. These became the crests of the clan which each member had the right to claim as his own. Such crests as the thunderbird, killer whale, and raven were carved on totem poles and masks, painted on houses and other objects, and used in most ceremonial activities.

Awareness of social rank dominated Kwakiutl society. In addition to hierarchically ranked tribes and numayms, social positions in each numaym were ranked. Each position had a name which was passed from generation to generation according to primogeniture. Parents gave their highest position to their oldest son, the next position to the second son, and so forth. These positions might be in the numaym of either the mother or the father, and they could be passed on to either sons or daughters. Those holding the higher positions in each clan were the "chiefs" in the tribe, those holding lower positions, the "commoners." A person's position was largely determined by birth, but other factors influenced it. The prestige of his position was determined by his ability to "uphold his name." A chief had to conduct himself in a manner which commanded the respect of his position, and failure to do so led to loss of respect and status. The first son in high-ranking families would be taught early the importance of upholding his name.

The major institution for assuming, maintaining, and increasing social status was the potlatch, which was a complex ceremony involving feasting, singing, dancing, and distribution of gifts. The ranking chief of a numaym invited people from many other villages to attend the potlatch. The stated purpose was to bestow the children of the numaym with the names for social positions they were to assume in the numaym or one of the secret societies. After feasting and many speeches extolling the host's numaym and crest, gifts of blankets, canoes, or other valuables were given to the invited guests. A person could not assume any social position without such a distribution of wealth. The size of the gifts and the order in which they were given explicitly recognized the relative rank of each guest. The overall amount given by the host validated his own position and lowered or raised his social status. In an effort to increase their prestige, Kwakiutl chiefs went to great lengths to amass material goods and give them away. In some instances they competed with men of similar rank in other numayms in order to outdo each other. The most extreme demonstration of wealth and prestige took place when a chief destroyed items of wealth to show that he had more than he needed. An important feature of these potlatches was the display of copper shields which had been carved with the crests of the numaym. These would be "purchased" for many thousands of blankets to outgive one's rival. In some cases, coppers would be broken, destroyed, or cast into the sea as a demonstration of one's great wealth and status. While the ranking chief of the numaym was the actual host of a potlatch, all the members cooperated, many smaller distributions of gifts took place, and all shared in the increased prestige of the numaym. Giving gifts also took place on many other occasions, such as a visit from another tribe with invitations to a future potlatch. All such distributions validated the individual's rights to his position, commanded the respect of his peers, increased his self-esteem, and showed to all that he was upholding his name.

While the numayms were the most important kinship groups, the secret societies were the most important religious groups. The latter became prominent at the start of the winter season when a number of tribes gathered in one village for the winter dances. The whole social organization changed from kinship groups to secret societies at that time. The numaym names, acquired in potlatches, became taboo, and everyone used names associated with the secret societies (Boas 1897:418). Most important was the Cannibal or *hamatsa* society. Chiefs in all the tribes were members of this group or other high-ranking groups such as the Bear or Fool society. There were about eighteen secret societies. Members of each society were usually of the same sex and had similar ranks in their respective numayms. The Killer Whale society for young men, the Sea Lion society for older men, the Hen society for young women, the Crow society for young girls, and many others were arranged in rank order. The "secrets" of each society were carefully guarded by the members. The sacred winter season was referred to as "the secrets," while the rest of the year was called "profane."

The numayms and secret societies were founded by mythical ancestors who had set up a limited number of positions with their respective names. The positions were arranged in rank order within the numaym but not in the secret societies. These positions were inherited, but in different ways. Numaym positions passed from parents to children according to primogeniture. Secret society positions passed from a man to his eldest daughter's husband who held the name for his own son. In either type of group, a person could hold more than one position or positions in more than one group. Numaym positions were assumed in the potlatch ceremony; secret society positions were assumed in the winter dance ceremonies. The main purpose of both ceremonies was the assumption of inherited positions by younger members of Kwakiutl society.

The winter dances were held to initiate youths into the secret societies. Although religious in character, dramatic and theatrical aspects often dominated the dances. While most Indian groups in this area of North America practiced a very individualistic guardian spirit quest, the Kwakiutl seem to have substituted a more formalized encounter with a spirit (Spradley 1963). This encounter took place during the initiation ceremony but was actually rehearsed beforehand. The spirits which filled the woods during the winter months were simulated by whistles and masks.

At the beginning of the winter, as whistles were heard in the woods near the village, the novice would be abducted or disappear voluntarily into the woods. The first to disappear was a boy to be initiated into the hamatsa society. He was believed to be at the home of the Cannibal Spirit. During the day he would be met by older hamatsas and taught the dances of that society. At night the entire village gathered in one of the large houses, and a master of ceremonies would direct the performances of singing, dancing, supernatural feats, and other dramatic productions. The Kwakiutl were unsurpassed among North American Indians in their theatrical skill. Huge masks with movable parts danced around the fire. Trap doors in the floor enabled dancers to mysteriously disappear. Lifelike heads carved of wood and carried on top of a dancer's costume were skillfully cut from the body. Then a powerful shaman would revive the decapitated person to the amazement of the audience. The most important secret was the simulated nature of these dramas which the uninitiated believed to be supernaturally produced.

The nightly performances were for the purpose of attracting the initiates from their seclusion with the supernatural beings. After the first youth disappeared, others followed from time to time. They went into the woods or into a small room at the back of the dance house. One by one, throughout the winter, the initiates would return and demonstrate that they were possessed by the appropriate spirit. Older members of the societies would assist the novice in gaining control of the spirit. The hamatsa returned through the roof of the dance house in a simulated state of insanity. He had acquired a craving for human flesh from the Cannibal Spirit which was satisfied by biting people or pretending to devour the corpse of a human or small bear which looked like a human. The novice would be uncontrollable on his return and escape again into the woods to return the following night. He was finally tamed by the older hamatsas and would then dance and show the mask he had received. After each youth was initiated, his relatives gave away large amounts of food and other wealth to validate the initiation. At the end of the winter the spirits left the village until the following winter.

Every aspect of Kwakiutl society was linked to their interest in social status. In an environment with almost unlimited resources they limited the number of high social positions. Thus, acquiring these positions and demonstrating that one was worthy of his positions became the focus of ceremonial life. Dramatic and artistic skills contributed to this central theme. Behind these cultural features was the individual's great desire to gain the respect due his position and "uphold his name."

Contact with whites was minimal before 1849. At that time, the Hudson's Bay Company established Fort Rupert. This was the most important Kwakiutl village until around the turn of the century. Since then, Alert Bay has been the most important. The frequency and intensity of contact with whites increased, resulting in many changes in Kwakiutl ways of life. European diseases resulted in a population decline to less than three thousand by 1880. This led to confusion in inheritance patterns and competition for many high-ranking positions left vacant. Trading with whites brought increased material wealth which increased the size of the potlatch and changed its function to some degree. In 1867 an ordinance was passed which forbade the Indians to use liquor. In 1876 an Indian Act was passed which forbade potlatching and winter dancing. In 1877 Rev. A. J. Hall started an Anglican mission at Fort Rupert, which he moved to Alert Bay in 1879. With the conversion of many Kwakiutl to Christianity, native religious beliefs began to change. Many features of white technology were adopted. Power boats began to replace carved canoes; modern houses replaced many large multi-family houses. Emphasis upon the numaym began to change to emphasis upon the nuclear family. Children were sent to white schools to learn new ways. Culture conflict appears to have reached a peak in 1921 with renewed enforcement of the law against native ceremonies and an economic depression.

Since 1921 the Kwakiutl have outwardly been drawn further into Western culture. They live in modern homes on their reservations, and children attend school regularly. Many of the men are skippers of commercial fishing boats. Most Kwakiutl are of the Anglican faith. In 1951 the Indian Act was revised and no longer forbade potlatching and winter dancing. More recently the Kwakiutl, along with other Indian groups, have gained the right to purchase liquor and vote in elections. These external features often hide the very real differences between Kwakiutl and white values. Culture conflict, which may not be revealed through a broad description of cultural forms and social institutions, can be seen in bold relief by focusing on the individual's experiences. James Sewid's story brings to life the changing culture of the Kwakiutl and shows how one Indian has met the demands of living in two cultural worlds at the same time.

THE AUTOBIOGRAPHY OF JAMES SEWID

1 He Is Wealthy from Many Generations Back

I was born during the cold winter of 1913. My mother had been living with her father at Village Island and they came to Alert Bay. When I was about to be born they had to find someplace to take my mother where there would be no noise. So my grandfather, Jim Bell, made a small little tent for my mother up beside an old barn because she knew that I was going to be born. It was December 31, 1913. I was born in that little tent beside the barn. After I was born they just bundled me up and took me home to my mother's sister's house who was living in Alert Bay. She had married Ed Whanock and they had a house on the Nimpkish Reserve in Alert Bay. Of course my grandfather called all the people together right away and gave away some blankets and other things at a potlatch which was the way of my people. It was at that time that they gave me my baby names. I received my father's father's name from the Kwiksutainuk people, Owadzidi, which means "people will do anything for him because he is so respected." My mother's father, Jim Bell, was from the Mamalilikulla people and I received the name Poogleedee from him, which means "guests never leave his feasts hungry." I received the name Waltkeena which was from Chief Goatlas of the Mamalilikulla and means "something very precious has been given to us." I received the name Sewid after my father and his father, which means, "paddling towards the chief that is giving a potlatch." My father's father had taken the name James because he used to work for James Douglas, the first governor of British Columbia, and that was passed on to my father and at that time it was given to me.

My mother's name was Emma Sewid. When she was quite young she married my father James Sewid. I had an older sister but she died when she was only ten months old. My mother was from the Mamalilikulla tribe and my father was an important man in the Kwiksutainuk tribe. Just a couple of months before I was born my father was killed in an accident. A tree fell on him when he was logging. My father and mother had been living at Village Island where the accident happened and Lucy Sewid, my grandmother, was living with them. My grandmother was a very religious woman and when my father died she was all alone because my grandfather, James Aul Sewid, had died some years before. She just moved to Alert Bay then from Village Island because there was nobody for her to live with at Village Island since she had been living with my father. When he died she just left everything. She left the house and all the things in it and they just boarded up the windows and everything. She bought herself a little house, a little shack down on the beach at Alert Bay and stayed there all by herself. She was there when I was born.

Before my father had died he had begun to gather together some things in preparation for the potlatch that he would give when I was ten months old. That was the time that I was to receive my everyday names and my chief's names. I received names from the Mamalilikulla people through Jim Bell and from the Kwiksutainuk people through James Aul Sewid. Aul Sewid had an uncle who was also a very strong chief at that time and the two of them were always together. My grandfather and his uncle were so strong that nobody could pay them back when they broke a copper. They used to just refer to them as the "uncles." My grandfather had passed all his great names and positions on to my father but when he died they were to come down to me. I was the rightful owner because they could never take those names away. Those names will always be there. Chief Aul Sewid's uncle was named Yakatlnalis which means "the whale." His name was taken up by my uncle at Kingcome, Toby Willey. When my father died Toby announced that he was going to carry out what my father had started because he had been chosen to stand by me as I grew up to take all those names and positions.

So Toby Willey gave this big potlatch in favor of me when I was ten months old. He had quite a bit of money himself and everything that had been gathered for my father was given to him. All my grandparents and all my relatives at Village Island all added to this to make it a very big potlatch. Some of them gave coppers. It was going to be a great honor to my people and to my mother to receive a child in that position. That's why all my grandfather's relatives in the villages all gave something for it. Some gave canoes, some gave articles, and some gave money. They gave it all to Toby to make the thing real big. Toby was not going to just take what was coming in. He was going to put in what he can on it to make it a bigger potlatch. When everyone who knew my father was dead heard that I was born they just all moved in and helped to make it real big.

And the day came for this big do to be held in Alert Bay. They had sent out invitations some time before this. This thing goes on for a week or two. Something goes on every night, and everyone had to be given a present every night whether it was a cup or a canoe or money or something else. It had to go on for a couple weeks because there was lots to say every night. One day, when it was a very nice day in Alert Bay, all the people gathered outside. Toby Willey, the young new chief that had taken up Yakatlnalis' position and name, spoke. He held me in his arms. I was a little boy—a ten-months-old baby. He put the copper down on the ground and announced to the people: "Here is my great nephew and we are very proud to have him here. I am very proud to see him and stand by him and to be chosen to take this position to be with him. He is going to take everything. He is the rightful owner of everything his grand-father Chief Sewid owned." And he laid me on this copper, just a little bundle, and announced to the people: "This copper will be his strength." My grandfather, Jim Bell, had bought that copper for my mother. My grandmother, old Lucy Sewid, was there, and she had helped him buy that copper, and she was just full of tears. She was part of all of it. Then all the chiefs of the different villages all got up and praised me. They told everybody about this new chief that was coming up. Every chief was shouting loud with their voices. Afterward they gathered up all the stuff and put it together for me. This was all added to in order to expand it because they wanted it big for me.

That was the time that they gave me many of my names. From Chief Goatlas I received the name Yeakuqualagelis, which means "you are proud of what you have done in potlatching." I received the Kwiksutainuk everyday name Natlamutlas, which means "the other tribes all get their names and wealth from us." My father had the Mamalilikulla everyday name Glacoatlas, which was given

to me at that time, and it means "where they can get copper."
Another name I received which was one of Aul Sewid's positions
was Hanesuqwelak, which means "he always wants to share his
wealth with others." I received Aul Sewid's chief's name which
was right at the top of the Kwiksutainuk people at Village Island.
It was Maquacoatla, which means "always giving away wealth."
Lucy Sewid was part Matilpi and her brother gave me the name
Gostidzas, which means "when the guests arrive for a potlatch they
are all welcomed at his house." I also received a Matilpi chief's
name, Comanaquala, which means "he is wealthy from many
generations back." I remember that I also got the Mamalilikulla
name Lagius, which means "a very high ranking man," and there
were others that I can't remember.

During the first few years of my life I lived with my mother in
the big community house at Village Island that belonged to Chief
Goatlas, who was my grandmother's brother. Some of the time we
would live in Alert Bay with Ed Whanock, who was married to
my mother's sister. There were five or six families living in that
community house. It had a dirt floor and a big fire in the middle.
We each lived in one corner of that house and had our own fire
where we cooked most of our meals. We lived with Jim Bell's
family. When I was about three years old my mother married
Johnny Clark, who was a chief of the Tlawitsis tribe at Turnour
Island village. They were married in the Indian way. He was also
half Kwiksutainuk so I was related to him. That's why he thought
the world of me and also because my mother and he didn't have
any children of their own. He was a very respectable man and very
wise. The people used to go to him for advice on all kinds of
things. We moved to Turnour Island with Johnny Clark and
lived in a nice modern home that he had built. We lived there
during the winter, and then in the spring we would move to the
mouth of Nimpkish River on Vancouver Island to fish for the
sockeye when they were first coming in the river. During the
summer we went up to live at the cannery at Knight's Inlet. Johnny
Clark would fish and my mother would work in the cannery.

One summer when I was about five years old there was a lot of
drinking going on. We lived in a little one-room house at the
cannery. At night we used to just lock our door and we could hear

people shouting and threatening each other outside. I was really scared some of those times but of course I would fall asleep as a little boy. One night there was a fight. This man who was drunk and had been gambling and drinking for two or three nights as long as his money lasted got into a fight. He had been going around with the wife of another man who was up there with his wife and child. So this fella was drunk, he was a no-good fella anyway, and he went in the house where this woman was. I don't know whether the woman was drunk or not. She was laying in the bed with her child when this fella shot her. He first shot this woman and then he shot himself. The woman was just killed instantly. I don't know where this man had shot himself but he was still alive. Nobody wanted to go pick him up because they were scared. He was crawling around half-dead. The whole cannery was just crying, and everybody was just yelling and scared because there wasn't any policeman there in those days. All our family just went into our little one-room house and locked the door. The people were running back and forth and shouting at each other and everybody was drunk. It was a riot. When the husband found out what had happened to his wife there was really a big fight. Finally the man died. I don't ever remember my mother or Johnny Clark drinking during those days. That is when I began to think it was wrong to be intoxicated and to have too much liquor. When you do that you don't know what you are doing.

When I was about five or six Johnny Clark became very sick. We went to Village Island to be near my grandparents so they could more or less look after us. One day I was out playing and my mother was in the house with Johnny when he died from a heart attack or something. I felt very badly as a little boy even though I couldn't understand that he wasn't going to be with us any longer. When he was dressed and the blanket was wrapped around him they laid him in the bed. They brought me in and there were a lot of people sitting around him wailing and mourning for this great chief that was lost to the Kwakiutl nation. They brought me in to put me across his body four times. There were two men that held me and passed me back and forth over his body four times and then told me to put my feet against his body and kick him four times. They held my feet while I did this and an old man told me

that Johnny Clark would never think of me again now but would
go on to the next world. I thought it was just the way to say farewell
to the man I thought was my father. I was just a little boy and
didn't know that he wasn't my real father until I was old enough
to understand.

Then we all got into boats and they took Johnny Clark back to
Turnour Island and all the people from the Kwakiutl nation were
there to bury this great chief that had died. When the funeral was
over my mother walked into the nice modern home we had and
took all our personal belongings and walked out of the house and
left everything else. We were the rightful owners of the property,
the house, and the stuff that was in the house. We just left it all
and the people that were related to the chief, I think it was his
nephew, took everything and gave it away to the people. We left
Turnour Island for good after that and went home to Village Island
with my grandfather.

It was late in the summer when Johnny Clark died and soon
after that my mother and I went to stay at the mouth of the river
at Vinea Sound, as we did nearly every summer. Both of my grand-
fathers used to always go there to fish for salmon and dry it
for their own use. There was an old building there that belonged
to Jim Bell and a small smokehouse. There were some other people
and we all went together. I was just a little boy but they made a
little gaff hook for me to use and I did my own fishing right along
with the older people. There was an old man there who was related
to my grandfather who was a very experienced fisherman and
used to catch way more fish than I did. When I was near to where
he had caught a fish I used to help him put a rope through the
gills and then drag the fish down the river to where our smokehouse was.

There were all kinds of different ways of drying the salmon. My
mother and grandmother would slice some of the fish very thin and
hang them up in the smokehouse for about ten days until they were
dry. A lot of the time they would barbecue the fish first before
putting them in the smokehouse. There was a lot of work to do.
Some of the older people would cut firewood and I would carry
it back to where we were going to barbecue the fish. Then they
slit the fish almost clear through so that they could take the back-

bone out and spread the meat out flat. A stick about an inch and a half in diameter was slit at one end to hold the salmon and sharpened at the other end to stick into the ground next to the fire. Other small pieces of wood were used to make the fish stay open and flat and it was tied on with pieces of cedar bark. It took a long time to barbecue them and all this time they had to be turned and the fire had to be kept going. When they were roasted they would be hung up in the smokehouse for a few days. When the fish were ready the old people would take them down and tie them in bundles with fifty pieces of fish in each. These bundles were then put into cedar bark baskets and later we would take them to the big community house at Village Island for our food in the winter.

We stayed there for about a month and a half each summer and that was the best time of my life. I really liked to go up the river and catch some fish with my grandfather. Ed Whanock was there as well as his father and mother, old Chief Whanock and his wife. I used to enjoy swimming among the fish when they were spawning. I guess that's the reason why I love fish. I would like to live among the fish as long as I live. When I wasn't helping the older people I would make little boats to play with. There was a little canoe there and I would pole it back and forth on the river. I made a little bow with some arrows and would play with these among the bushes and in a nice big flat field that was near there. When the summer was over we went back to Village Island although some of the time we stayed with Mrs. Whanock at Alert Bay.

My grandparents, Jim and Mary Bell, had one of the front rooms in the big community house. They had about fourteen children but only four of them lived very long. Henry Bell was much older than I was, and he was the oldest of their children, and they treated him in the special way that the Indian people treat the oldest boy. Rachel was older than him and married Ed Whanock. My mother Emma was next after Henry, and Robby Bell was the youngest son and just a little older than I was. We had a good-sized room close to the entrance of that house where we would sleep. Robby and I used to sleep together in that room all the time because he and I grew up together just like brothers. At night it was very cold and there was nothing we could do when it was snowing. The fine flakes of snow would come right through the cracks onto our beds and in the morning my grandfather would come and shake off the snow. It was quite cold in there even though we had an old wood stove. We had a modern bed but I used to like to sleep on the floor the same as everybody else. There were lots of ducks that they would hunt and pluck their feathers and put them in cloth so we could lay on the feather mattresses. We had our own way of life in that community house and right across on the other side of the building lived the Hanuse family. They were cousins of my great uncle Chief Odzistales. Old man Harry Hanuse had six boys, George, Alex, Jack, Wilfred, Fred, and Dan, and we all played together a lot. He also had four girls. Alex and I were very close friends and we just did everything together.

We used to play a game like baseball where we would throw a ball at the front of the big house. One fella would hit the ball and bounce it against the house and then run while we would try to hit him. We would go down to the beach every day and play with little boats. We made little boats and dragged them in the water along the beach. All the kids in the village would be down there playing with their little boats and sometimes we would take a dugout canoe and row around in front of the island. Some of the kids would tease me about not having a father. They would say, "You got no father, your father died," and all that. I used to feel awfully bad. I would go right home and stay away from those fellas. I never used to fight back because my mother and my grandparents used to say to me that if any of those kids wanted to fight I shouldn't ever fight with them. I was told to just stay away from them. I always did that and never fought back because they were very strict with the potlatch rule at that time. They told me, "If you fight with the other kids then it is going to cost us money and we will have to give a potlatch." I remember that some of the other kids who were related to me got into quarrels with some of the others. They called all the people together right away and announced it in public what they had done and then they gave some stuff away. I remember that they gave away flour, boxes of biscuits, and a pile of biscuit dough in boxes.

In the evenings we were not allowed to go out. We had to stay home and they used to tell me that if I went out and walked along in the village the ghosts would grab me and twist me around and

twist my face. I used to be scared. At night they would build a big
fire in the middle of the house and when it was time to go to sleep
we would all sit around the fire and some of the older people
would be telling the stories. It was a big open fire and we were all
little kids sitting around it. I remember best the stories about
Tlislagila which means little Mink, child of the sun. They called the
sun Tlisla. This is one of the stories they told us:

Mink was playing one day with the other kids and the others
started to quarrel and fight with him. They told him, "We don't
want to play with you, go on, get out of here, and go play somewhere else. We don't want you because you don't have any father.
You don't know where your mother got you from." Everyone in
the village knew this and so little Mink started to cry and cry. He
went home and told his mother, "You know, mother, the kids told
me that I don't have any father. You never told me this." Well, his
mother was a very young girl, and she said to her son, "You must
sit down and let me tell you and explain why you don't have any
father on the earth. Your father is up there in the heavens. One day
I was lying down and the sunbeam came through those cracks in
the wall of the house. The sunbeam was hitting me right in my back
and that is how I became pregnant. And your father is up there."

So this little Mink was a very active little fella and he said,
"I'm going to see my father." "Oh," his mother said, "you can't go
up there. How can you go up there?" Well, little Mink told his
mother, "Oh, I'll go up there." So he started working and made
a bow and some arrows. He made thousands and millions of arrows
and began shooting them. And he shot the arrows one at a time up
in the air and each one became fastened on to the others until they
reached down to the earth. And he climbed up on these arrows
until he came up to his father. And he met his father and his father
said, "I'm awfully glad you came. I'm glad to meet you because I
had never met you before." He admitted to Mink that he knew he
had a son down there on the earth.

Then his father said, "You didn't come up here for nothing.
Don't think that you are just going to loaf around and do nothing
while you are here because we are very busy and have to watch
the universe. Everything is moving around up here and there are
different winds and these winds all change. I am going to put you

in charge of something. You are going to look after your aunts."
He meant the clouds, which were his father's sisters. "You are
going to look after your aunts and you have to be very very patient.
Don't push them around too much. Let the wind push them gently
and be careful that they do not come too close together because that
is not very good." Well, he explained to Mink how he should look
after these clouds so that they wouldn't go too close together. "All
right," said Mink, "I'll take the job." So he was very gently and
patiently pushing the clouds around because his father had told
him that if he pushed them around too much he would burn the
earth since the sun was so strong. After awhile he began to grow
impatient. He was a very impatient little fella. He started cursing
and pushing them around and kicking them around. Pretty soon
the clouds were moving faster and the sky became all clear and the
sun hit the earth and just burned everything up. They say that
that is why the rocks are all cracked and the mountains are all
cracked. It all was caused by this little Mink disobeying his father.
Of course his father found this out right away and he went to him
and grabbed him and threw him down on the earth immediately.
You know, he was fired. After he was thrown down he was drifting
around in the water and the people from the village were coming
along in a canoe and saw him floating around. They said, "It looks
like our little friend that is floating around." They recognized
him so they picked him up in the canoe and asked him where he
had been. "I was up there and the sun just threw me down because
I didn't do very well up there." That was the end of that story.

They used to tell me how Mink and Raven worked together to
make many features of the land. They told me about a little bluff
which is on Malcolm Island which was made by those two. One day
he came to Raven and said, "Let's build a bridge so that we can walk
across from the mainland to Vancouver Island." They started
working by filling up the water with rocks to build this bridge
right opposite Kelsey Bay. After working for awhile on this Mink
came to his senses and said, "I don't think we should continue, I
think we should stop right here. Some day the new generation
of people are going to use these waters here. Their boats are going
to go back and forth and if we have this bridge it will stop their
big boats." That is why they stopped, and you can see that bridge

today if it is low water. It is not really a bridge but a lot of rocks just like a reef or breakwater. So they stopped right there.

I was brought up a lot of the time by my grandparents Mary Bell and Jim Bell. Mary Bell had a lot of respect for me. She thought the world of me just like my other grandmother, old Lucy. Mary used to speak very highly of me and she did everything I wanted her to do as a young boy. If I asked her to do anything for me she would do it. It was the Indian custom to always put the oldest child first in everything they did and then the rest would follow. Since I was born to a well-to-do and very highly respected family and was the oldest son they treated me with respect. The Indian custom was all respect, and they were going to try to respect me in the same way that they would have respected my father if he had still been alive. I was just a small boy and they didn't want anybody to hurt this precious little child. They had to look after me because I was the oldest. All the others in a family are just children, that's all.

Robby Bell is just a little older than me but he's the very youngest of my uncles and my mother and my aunt. That's why they always called him just a little boy. We were brought up just like brothers but poor Robby used to be pushed aside for me and I never used to like that. If anything happened like if we were out playing and I got hurt and came in crying poor Robby would get bawled out. "Why did that happen? Why did you take him there?" and all that sort of thing. I never used to like that. Poor Robby used to just sit there and take it from my grandfather and grandmother. When we were about six or seven Robby was sent to school by my grandparents. I don't know what the law was about a child going to school in those days, but poor Robby was just more or less dumped into the Anglican residential school at Alert Bay. I wanted to go and asked them if I could but they said, "No, no, you can't go. We don't want the other kids to tease you and all that. We don't want you to go there because that place is no good. They're going to teach you things that aren't good for you." But Robby had to go to that residential school where he would live for most of the year. I never used to like to be Mary Bell's favorite among all my cousins and the other kids. I never did like this idea of being too selfish and I always liked to be treated equal with other people and I never did like to be above anybody. A lot of times I think back and wonder why they were doing that, but it has been done and that is the way it was. Another reason I didn't like not being allowed to go to school with Robby was that I knew that it was important to have an education and learn to read and write and speak English. My other grandmother, old Lucy, wanted me to go to school, and so later on I had to go to Alert Bay and stay with her in order to get any schooling.

Sometimes in the evening we would have visits from our neighbors. The old people used to come and sit around the fire, especially when they were teaching me how to be a leader of my people when I grew up. They told me all the things about my family history on both my mother's and father's sides of the family and how the Kwakiutl people used to have wars and fight among one another. They said that I must know these things from them and not just hear it from some other people. I heard from Jim and Mary Bell as well as the other older people from the village about a war that they had with the southern people on the coast. This is what they told me:

Jim Bell's grandfather on his mother's side had an oldest son who was murdered somewhere around Victoria. He would have been Jim Bell's uncle. Victoria was only a town then. Of course this boy was a very respectable young man and his father felt that he must do something to avenge his death. So he began by working very hard building some traps. It was the type of trap which uses a log and as soon as a little animal touched the string the log came down on the animal, killing him. This was the Indian way of catching these animals. Well, he got a lot of animals and a lot of fur and went and sold it. He worked for a couple winters doing this and then he went over to Hudson's Bay Company at Fort Rupert and bought some barrels of gunpowder. At the same time he called all the people together to come to Village Island and he gave a potlatch. He asked the people to go down with him to avenge the death of his son. He actually hired the people to go with him and take part in this raid against the Salish people around Nanaimo because they knew that they were responsible for the murder of his oldest boy.

There were people from quite a few of the Kwakiutl tribes that went down with him. They only used the great big war canoes and there were about thirty or forty in each canoe who were paddling. They were all supplied with guns and gunpowder. So they all went down. They had to go through Seymour Narrows past the Cape Mudge village. The Cape Mudge people are part of the Kwakiutl nation and I guess they didn't want them to know what was going on so they planned to sneak by without having them know it. They told all the people to lie down in the canoe so that just two people were paddling the big canoe. It was fair tide when they were going through so that just two people were able to paddle those big canoes. As soon as they passed the Cape Mudge village they all got up and started paddling again.

They stopped that day at a little bay on Texada Island where they decided they would camp. They pulled all the canoes up underneath the trees. They did this so that if any of their enemies should come by they won't see the canoes. One of the biggest canoes belonging to one of the tribes was so big that they couldn't pull it in far enough. The bow of this canoe was just showing at the water's edge so they took some branches and put them all around the front of the canoe to keep it from being seen. Everyone stayed back away from the shore and no one was allowed on the waterfront. They had somebody there to keep watch for anyone who might be passing by. Pretty soon they saw a canoe coming towards the bay but it was quite a ways off. They notified everybody right away to hide and they all got ready in case the canoe came into the bay. They were all hiding behind trees and the logs which were lying on the beach and that canoe kept coming right straight towards where they were. They told everyone not to shoot until they were told and this would be at the moment this canoe hit the beach. This canoe was filled with a lot of people and it came straight for the beach.

There was one Indian standing in the bow of the canoe looking at the shoreline for any indication of trouble. He was trying to point to the canoe which had been covered with branches. He thought he saw something on the beach that looked funny but the leader of the canoe wouldn't pay any attention to him. As soon as they hit the beach the order was given to shoot and they killed all those people. Everyone just jumped up and cut off their heads because they used to fight for heads rather than for wealth or land or anything like that. If you were able to get a head you were brave and had proven that you had been on a war party. So every clan and every canoe got one or two or three heads except for one canoe from the Mamalilikulla tribe at Village Island. Everyone was happy about what had happened because in getting those heads they had proven that they had done their duty and would be more respected among the Kwakiutl people.

And the canoe from the Wewamasqem clan of the Mamalilikulla tribe never got a single head, not one. This is the clan of my grandfather. Not one, not one of them got a head, and they all felt very bad about it and ashamed of themselves. So they just pulled their canoe out and began to paddle out of the bay without saying a word. Everyone was kind of worried and they whispered to one another and decided to follow them and see what they were going to do. They didn't want anything to happen to them. This canoe headed down towards Vancouver, all the time just following the shoreline of Texada Island which is quite a big island. So this Wewamasqem canoe came to Lasqueti Island not far from Texada Island to where there was a large bay. As they paddled and paddled the other canoes were following them at some distance coming along slowly. They came around a little point and saw a bunch of women eating. They had been picking berries up in the woods and were having their supper. There was only one man with them and he tried to run for his gun when he saw this canoe full of warriors but they just shot him down. Then they shot down all the women except two.

Now everybody had a head and the men of all the clans of all the tribes were happy. They took the two young girls and brought them back as slaves to Village Island. So they decided that that was enough and they figured that was all they wanted so they headed back up the coast. On the way back they stopped at the Cape Mudge village. When they landed on the shore all the people came down and said they could recognize the various heads. They all started talking: "Oh, that fella is a bad man," and "He come and raid us," and other things like that. So the Cape Mudge people invited them all to come and have a big feast before they left for home.

Sometimes we would invite our neighbors to come and eat with us and there would be about twenty or twenty-five people eating around the fire. The more people the better everybody felt, especially when we had a big family gathering. I remember most of them but especially all my grandparents, cousins, uncles, and other relatives that were around me and near me. Rachel and Ed Whanock would come up there quite often too, and I remember Ed Whanock telling one night about how the old people used to move their village up to Knight's Inlet during the spring. This is what he told me:

They didn't have permanent houses which were nailed together as they do in the villages now. All the Kwakiutl tribes were quite large and they would move around from place to place where the food was best. They knew which kind of fish would be coming in at each time of the year. They knew which month of the year they should go to Knight's Inlet and when the moon was just right they would say, "The moon wants us to get ready." This meant that everybody should start packing their things and start fixing up their canoes and getting everything ready.

Some of them would gather long pieces of kelp from the beach that had a large ball-like head on the end of a long tube. Sometimes they would be about twenty feet long and they would take them and dry them in the smokehouse as well as treat them to make them soft and pliable. They would fill these containers with olachen oil to take with them when they moved. When everything was ready they would tie the canoes together and pile all the lumber from the sides of their houses on the canoes. Then the families would get in and sometimes they would put a sail on and go to Knight's Inlet.

When they arrived at their destination they would start unloading the lumber. This was somewhere around the end of March or the first of April. The snow was still quite deep on the ground when they reached the head of Knight's Inlet. The four clans of the Mamalilikulla all had their assigned place as well as the other tribes of the Kwakiutl people. Sometimes the people known as the Bella Bella from up north would come and stay there too. The reason they all came there was that Knight's Inlet was known for being one of the best rivers for olachen and they could get lots of oil from them. When they all gathered there they used to have big feasts and potlatches. They just put their houses up on top of the snow and built their fires inside on top of the snow. As the snow melted the houses and fires would go down slowly and when the hot sun comes out in the late spring they would be right down to the ground. They would catch lots of olachen and cook it until the oil was ready and then store it in the kelp tubes or boxes.

After the olachen time was finished they would start catching halibut and gathering seaweed. The seaweed was dried in the sun until it was crisp and black and would be one of the main foods. Later on in the summer they would move to other places like the Nimpkish River to get sockeye and start making smoked fish for the winter. In the fall they gathered berries and put them up in great big boxes. Then they would go after dog salmon which would be dried for the winter. They came back to Village Island for short periods of time during the summer but it wasn't until late in the fall that they would come back to stay for the winter. Then they had lots of food and lots to eat and they would just dance all through the winter. For many weeks during the winter they would stay with the Tlawitsis and Fort Rupert people at the place where Alert Bay now is.

I used to love to sit around the fire and listen to the old people telling about the ways of the Indians. I remember very well how they would pound it into my head to know my relatives. That was very important. They used to tell me who my relatives were and why I was related to different persons in different villages. When I would go to another village I knew right away that the people recognized me as their relative. The old people would just come to me and hug me. They didn't even wait for me to say anything to them but they would just say, "I'm glad to see you because I'm your uncle or aunt or grandfather." I thought it was very important and I really took it in when I was a little boy. I learned to respect people and when I went to a strange place I was careful not to do anything that was going to hurt them or do anything that was foolish. I had to be very careful whatever I was doing because I never did like to hurt anybody. Everything I do I have to watch it because if anything should happen to me they would lose something that was valuable in my grandparents' thinking. And when I used to come and see my grandmother Lucy Sewid she used to do the same thing. She told me all about my grandfather Chief Aul Sewid. Aul means "real," and they used to call him James Aul Sewid because he worked as an interpreter for James Douglas, the first governor of British Columbia, using the Chinook language. My other grandparents also told me about Aul Sewid and I used to question them about him. They told me about the time he was at Gilford Island and the Kwiksutainuk people were massacred by the Bella Coola people from up north. This is what they told me:

Chief Aul Sewid had the position that was right at the top of the Kwiksutainuk tribe. He was living at Gilford Island village when the Bella Coola people came down and attacked them. One of the women of the Kwiksutainuk tribe had stolen one the hamatsa whistles from one of the men of the Bella Coola. These whistles were very sacred and it was a disgrace for him to lose it. When he went home to his people he told them right away that it had been stolen, so the Bella Coola came back and snuck in quietly to a little bay on the other side of the island where nobody could see them.

Some of the people began to suspect that something was going to happen and later they realized that somebody among the Bella Coola must have been friendly toward the Kwiksutainuk people and had tried to warn them. Somebody had been putting a sign near where the people went to get their water. There was a little spring at the other end of the village and they had noticed some feathers that had been placed on the top of a little tree. This went on for a couple of days before the attack and sometimes there would be something else hanging on this tree. There must have been some stranger around there that came around the village every night until the attack but no one thought anything of it.

Then the attack came very suddenly in the middle of the night when everybody was sleeping. They attacked both ends of the village and began killing the people and burning the houses down. The chief of the village usually lived in the middle of the village and that is where my grandfather Aul Sewid and his uncle, Chief Yakatlnalis, were staying. There was a man that my grandfather knew from the Bella Coola people who came in to warn my grandfather. He walked into his house because he knew where he was living in the middle of the village and told my grandfather to wake up his uncle and the rest of his family and get down to the canoes. There was a canoe ready on the beach for them. The houses on the end of the village were already burning. They burned the whole village but of course the middle of the village was the last to burn. Some of the people never woke up but slept through this whole terrible thing. Most of the women and children and men were burned to death. Some of them woke up and were alive for just a few minutes and then they died.

My grandfather and his family all got into this canoe and started paddling toward Village Island, which was only a few miles away from the Gilford Island village. Some of the other Kwiksutainuk people escaped and followed my grandfather, and some of them went the other way towards Kingcome, where they had relatives. The only thing my grandfather was thinking about as a young man was to go and ask his cousin, Chief Odzistales of the Mamalilikulla tribe, to help him go after the Bella Coola. When he got to the Mamalilikulla village that night he woke up his cousin, who was chief of the village, and told him what had happened to his people. Chief Odzistales was half-Kwiksutainuk, and right away he woke up his people and told them to get their canoes ready and they all started paddling towards where they thought the Bella Coola were going. They had already left the Gilford Island village and they started chasing after them out into Blackfish Sound. My grandfather was in charge of this group that was going after the Bella Coolas. They were heading home to the north and every time they began to get close to them they would throw a slave overboard. Of course they had to stop and pick up these Kwiksutainuk people who had been taken slaves and this slowed them down. Then they would try again. I don't know how many canoes they were using, but they were able to get back most of the slaves that had been captured, but finally they had to turn back.

When the Bella Coola could see that they were no longer being followed they stopped to camp on some island near there. They still had two slaves who were women, and one of them had a little baby. When they all laid down to sleep in the woods near the shore, one of the ladies said to the other one, "We are going to try to sneak away tonight when everybody has gone to sleep." The lady that had the baby told the other one that she was going to keep the baby awake by pinching it so that it would keep the Bella Coola from going to sleep very early. She said, "We don't have any other choice since we are going to be dead anyway. We might as well try to do something to escape."

So all the Bella Coola were sleeping around these two ladies and the baby. This little baby was crying and crying until very late that night and everybody was sleeping and snoring. These two ladies then were able to sneak out very quietly through the ring of people that were sleeping around them. They went into the woods as far as they could go and climbed way up in a tree so they wouldn't be seen.

In the morning they could see very well from where they were up in the tree. The people woke up and when they found out that the two ladies were missing they grabbed the little baby and threw it into the water, where it drowned. Some of them went into the woods a little ways and looked for the ladies, but they didn't look very long because they were too anxious to get on their way before the Kwiksutainuk people came chasing them again. So they left very quickly when it was daylight. These two old women stayed up in the tree for awhile until they were sure that they were quite a ways away. Then they came down and started working on branches by twisting them around to make a rope as the women used to do to make baskets. Then they got driftwood from the beach and made a raft and were able to get back to Village Island and tell the people what had happened.

Of course my grandfather was very young and active at that time and his relatives who were living in Village Island told him to stay there. There was nothing for him to go back to at Gilford Island since all his village had been burned and almost half of his people were dead. Some of the people had gone to Alert Bay because they were half-Nimpkish and quite a few of them had gone to Kingcome. The Mamalilikulla people gave him a location at Village Island to build a house with his uncle, and the other Kwiksutainuk people with him built their houses there too.

My grandfather was very strong in the potlatch and he and his uncle gave many potlatches traveling around from one village to another. When the first government men came around surveying his the villages he interpreted for these men since he was very good at speaking the Chinook language. He went down to Victoria one time and met James Douglas, the first governor of British Columbia, who hired him to interpret for him. There were quite a few Indians at Victoria at that time.

Now I was told that my grandfather hired the warship that belonged to James Douglas to go fight against the Bella Coola people, but I think this is what really happened. James Douglas was going up north on this big warship of some kind to do some surveying and talk to the people of the different tribes. He took my grandfather along as an interpreter. When they got up to where the Bella Coola village was my grandfather decided to pay back the Bella Coolas for what they had done to the Kwiksutainuk people.

He went ashore when they had anchored this big ship out in front of the Bella Coola village and talked to the chief and told him that he had come to pay them back for what they had done to his people. Of course, right away the chief of the Bella Coola told him that it wasn't the proper thing to do because there were a lot of white men around now and that they should make up and be friends. Then he offered his oldest daughter to my grandfather in marriage. If he would accept her and they got married he could get anything he wanted from him, all his songs and crests and names. Well, my grandfather was great on this and he accepted right away. He accepted the masks and songs and being a good composer he was able to learn some songs while he was there, which he brought back, and these have been used by his family. And he didn't accept the girl because he only wanted to marry her to get the names and other things. He told the chief that he could keep his daughter, that he didn't want her, and so he came home without her. That was the Indian way of getting more names and songs and masks. Later on he returned to the Bella Coola people and gave a big potlatch and that was when he learned most of the songs and got many more of their dances. My grandfather married quite a few times before he married my grandmother. He did this just because he wanted some songs and crests and wealth from other villages and other tribes. That is why we have names and masks and songs right up

to the Bella Bella, the Bella Coola, and the Rivers Inlet people. He
also got some from the people in the interior of British Columbia.
He just married them to get the stuff he needed and then told them
to keep the girl and he kept the masks. Some of the times he never
even stayed with the girl.

Old Lucy, my grandmother, was half-Fort-Rupert-Kwakiutl and
half-Maamtagila at the Matilpi village. That tribe is called the
Matilpi people. She was born in Fort Rupert when the Hudson Bay
built the fort there and then moved to Etsekin, which is the name
of the Matilpi village. Her older sister married a white man
and lived in Victoria. Lucy was living there with her in Victoria
when Aul Sewid came back to Victoria after getting all the wealth
from the Bella Coola people, and he married her. They had only one
child, which was my father, so I was their only living grandchild.
She used to teach me many things about Aul Sewid, especially his
songs. Here is one of his chief's songs which was to become mine:

> What are we going to do with our Chief?
> Yay-ee-Yah! Ah-Yee-Yah-Ah!
> What are we going to do with our Chief?
> Yay-ee-Yah! Ah-Yee-Yah-Ah!
> Wee-Way-ee! Wee-Way-ee!
> What are we going to do with our Chief?
> Yay-ee-Yah! Ah-Yee-Yah-Ah!
>
> The people will also come
> From the tribe of Comox
> To pay their respect to our Chief.
> Yay-ee-Yah! Ah-Yee-Yah-Ah!
>
> The people will also come
> From the tribe of Lee-Gweelth-Douk
> To pay their respect to our Chief.
> Yay-ee-Yah! Ah-Yee-Yah-Ah!
>
> The people will also come
> From the junior tribe of Matilpi
> To pay their respect to our Chief.
> Yay-ee-Yah! Ah-Yee-Yah-Ah!

They say our singing is still too weak
They say our singing needs more strength
When we start to sing for our Chief.
Yay-ee-Yah! Ah-Yee-Yah-Ah!

The people will also come
From the tribe of Tlawitsis
To pay their respect to our Chief.
Yay-ee-Yah! Ah-Yee-Yah-Ah!

The people will also come
From the junior tribe of Da-Nak-Douk
To pay their respect to our Chief.
Yay-ee-Yah! Ah-Yee-Yah-Ah!

The people will also come
From the tribe of Mamalilikulla
To pay their respect to our Chief.
Yay-ee-Yah! Ah-Yee-Yah-Ah!

They say our singing is still too weak
They say our singing needs more strength
To boast the name of our great Chief.
Yay-ee-Yah! Ah-Yee-Yah-Ah!
Wee-Way-ee! Wee-Way-ee!

What are we going to do with our Chief?
Yay-ee-Yah! Ah-Yee-Yah-Ah!
What are we going to do with our Chief?
Yay-ee-Yah! Ah-Yee-Yah-Ah!

The people will also come
From the tribe of Tsawatenox
To pay respect to our Chief.
Yay-ee-Yah! Ah-Yee-Yah-Ah!

The people will also come
From the tribe of Hah-qwa-mees
To pay respect to our Chief.
Yay-ee-Yah! Ah-Yee-Yah-Ah!

The people will also come
From the tribe of Kwa-Kewlth
To pay respect to our Chief
Yay-ee-Yah! Ah-Yee-Yah-Ah!

The people will also come
From the tribe of Nimpkish
To pay respect to our Chief
Yay-ee-Yah! Ah-Yee-Yah-Ah!

They say our singing is still too weak
They say our singing needs more strength
When we start to sing for our Chief.
Yay-ee-Yah! Ah-Yee-Yah-Ah!

The people will also come
From the tribe of A-wee-gie-nook
To pay respect to our Chief.
Yay-ee-Yah! Ah-Yee-Yah-Ah!

The people will also come
From the tribe of Gwa-sa-lah
To pay respect to our Chief.
Yay-ee-Yah! Ah-Yee-Yah-Ah!

They say our singing is still too weak
They say our singing needs more strength
When we start to sing for our Chief.
Yay-ee-Yah! Ah-Yee-Yah-Ah!

The people will also come
From the tribe of Gwa-jee-noq
To pay respect to our Chief.
Yay-ee-Yah! Ah-Yee-Yah-Ah!

The people will also come
From the tribe of Goo-bpee-nook
To pay respect to our Chief.
Yay-ee-Yah! Ah-Yee-Yah-Ah!

They say our singing is still too weak
They say our singing needs more strength
When we start to sing for our Chief.
Yay-ee-Yah! Ah-Yee-Yah-Ah!

The people will also come
From the tribe of Goos-gie-mooq
To pay respect to our Chief.
Yay-ee-Yah! Ah-Yee-Yah-Ah!

The people will also come
From the tribe of Glus-kee-nook
To pay respect to our Chief.
Yay-ee-Yah! Ah-Yee-Yah-Ah!

They say our singing is still too weak
They say our singing needs more strength
When we start to sing for our Chief.
Yay-ee-Yah! Ah-Yee-Yah-Ah!
Wee-Way-ee! Wee-Way-ee!

Sometimes in the evenings a lot of people would gather in our house to play a game. There would be two sides and the people would sit opposite each other in the community house singing their songs which went along with this game. Sometimes there would be about twenty people on each side and sometimes as many as one hundred on each side. They had seven sticks or bones for each side and one of these bones had a mark on it. These bones are placed in a bag or under a blanket and then they are shaken while certain songs are sung. One side tries to guess the way the bones are arranged after they have been shaken and if they guess right they get one of the bones. Then the other side tries and this goes on until one side wins the game. Sometimes the people would come from the other villages and challenge us in our village and they would play almost all night. I used to play this game too when I was a little boy.

They often held dances in that community house at night and they told me how the Kwiksutainuk people got those dances.

There was once a woman of the Kwiksutainuk people who had an argument with her husband and so she just walked away from

her home and her village and started wandering around. The tide
was out and she started digging clams to eat because she was hungry.
While she was digging clams a hamatsa or wild man from the
woods came down and came up behind her when she didn't notice
him. She didn't know that this man was standing beside her while
she was busy digging clams. When she looked up she started talking
to this man and asked him who he was and what he was doing. This
man made a motion to her that he wanted some of the clams that she
had dug from the beach. This lady gave him some clams and they
became quite friendly and this man told her that there was a big
dance going on in a cave up on the hillside back from the beach.

So she went up to where the cave was and when she came near
the entrance of this cave she could hear that there was some singing
going on. All the different animals and birds were in there having a
big dance and ceremony. Now while the animals were holding this
dance for many hours they would send one of their number to go
and look around outside the cave to see if there were any human
beings around who might try to barge in and interfere with what
they were doing. They had sent some animals out in the woods to
become hamatsas and they were getting ready to bring them back
to civilization. The hamatsa was up in the woods and this is what
they were doing.

So they sent a little mouse outside to look around and this lady
was outside and saw this little animal coming. She took out a little
piece of fat from the mountain goat, which she had kept to use for
rubbing on her face. She gave this to the little mouse and he asked
her, "What are you doing here? You're not supposed to come around
here." Well, this lady told this little mouse not to tell anybody that
she was there and she would give him some more fat. She did this to
keep him quiet. So the little mouse went in and made an announcement by the doorway, the entrance of this cave. He sat up and looked
around and said, "There is no one outside. I never met anybody so
we are quite safe." So the dancing started again.

So this little mouse went out several times to check and each time
the lady gave him a little piece of fat. But all the time she was
getting closer to the entrance to the cave and finally she rushed into
the main part of the cave where they were holding this dance. Now
all the animals that were singing had taken off their skins and
feathers and had transformed themselves into human beings, and

when this lady came in they all rushed to the walls where they had hung these things and tried to get them on. In their rush to cover themselves they put their skins on backwards and only partly on. They all held their heads down and were very ashamed to be seen this way by the woman. And that is how she was able to get this dance and bring it back to the Kwiksutainuk people.

In the evenings if there were any dances to be held in the village they would just come and ask Jim Bell if they could use the community house. I would just move up with the other kids to the bedrooms and just sit there watching these dances. We had big dances every winter and sometimes I would dance in them too. It was right about the time that the government had stepped in and said the potlatches and dances were forbidden. So the people had to be very careful about taking part in potlatches that were going on in the other villages. I remember we used to move around from one village to another and go to these potlatches almost every month in the winter. Village Island was one place where they never used to bother us when we were having something going on. When my relatives would put on a potlatch they would ask me to take part in the dancing.

I remember one time there was a real big do held at Village Island. It was a big potlatch given by a fellow from Alert Bay. The people came from all over and must have stayed there for ten days or more. There was something going on every night and they held it in our house. When the Kwakiutl people from Cape Mudge and Campbell River arrived on the beach my grandmather, Mary Bell, called me over and said, "There is a gas boat that has come in down on the beach and they say it is the people from Cape Mudge and Campbell River. Go down there and ask (she named somebody that was related to them) to come up and stay with us." So I ran down to that boat that had just come in and spoke to them in our language, but I didn't know just what to say because I didn't know who it was that I was looking for. So I just said as a little boy, "You are wanted up at our house. Come on up to the house." Well, the whole works came on up to our house and my grandparents had to have them all stay there. My grandmother said to me later, "Why didn't you just call the person I wanted you to call to come up?" I told her that I didn't know who it was so I just told them all to come up to our house. Well, everybody went in there and there were quite a few people that stayed there. There must have been over twenty people.

The older people used to tell me many stories which I can't remember very well, but I remember another one about Mink quite well.

There was a big gathering in Village Island and the Head Wolf had sent his sons out into the woods and they were to come in to become hamatsas. Mink had made himself a fish trap and placed it in a little stream near Village Island. Every day when he checked his trap he found that somebody had stolen the fish and damaged his trap. He discovered that it was the sons of the Head Wolf and he decided to get his revenge. He laid down beside his trap and asked his trap, "What have you caught now?" And his trap said, "Oh, I've caught a spring salmon." And Mink said, "I don't want it, throw it away." After a little while he said, "What have you caught now?" The trap said, "I've got a steelhead." And Mink replied, "Oh no, I don't want it, throw it away." And all the different species of fish were caught and each time Mink said, "Oh, throw it away, I don't want it." They claim that is why there are a lot of rocks on the beach by that little stream. They are all the different species of fish.

Finally he asked his trap, "What have you got?" And his trap replied, "Oh, I've got a double-headed serpent." Mink said to his trap, "Oh, that is very good, that is fine, that is what I like." So he took the double-headed serpent and went to his mother and asked her, "Can you come out and cut up this nice fish that I have caught?" His mother came out and as soon as she saw this fish her body became all twisted. Mink said to her, "I guess you are just very proud to be the mother of a man who is such a great fisherman." And he grabbed his mother's head and straightened it up again. Then his mother started working on this fish and Mink took the head and made himself a headgear out of it.

Now the sons of the Head Wolf, who was the most important person in the whole village, were up in the woods to try to receive their supernatural power to become dancers. And Mink went up in the woods and killed all the wolves and cut off all their heads and brought them back to his house. That night all the different animals were going in to dance and try to bring back the wolves from up in the woods. And Mink got his sisters and his mother and had them get into a canoe which was all ready on the beach. And he told his mother, "Mother, you just sit there, you are going to be the captain and my sisters are going to do the paddling. I am going to come and jump in the canoe and then we will leave." So he covered himself with a blanket over his headgear of the double-headed serpent and when his time came to come into the dance house he put the heads of the wolves on top of the blanket. The fire was low and he came in dancing backwards so no one could see him. Then he started to sing his song which had words in it which told that he had the heads of the noble men—the wolves that he had murdered. The people didn't recognize him until he came close to the fire and then everybody jumped up and they all tried to go after him.

Well, Mink ran out and jumped into the canoe with his headgear of the double-headed serpent on and his sisters began paddling the canoe. Of course everybody else jumped into their canoes and started to follow him. Mink told his mother, "If they come near you tell me because I am going to be lying in the bottom of the canoe." So they were paddling away out in front of Village Island and his mother called to him that they were getting close. And Mink just looked back and his supernatural power turned each canoe into an island. They didn't catch him. And that is why there are lots of islands in front of Village Island, according to the story the old people told me.

When I was about five years old my grandmother Lucy, who was living at Alert Bay, married an old man. I don't remember much about him but he had had a stroke and wasn't able to talk. He lost his voice and was quite a helpless old man. The old man and the old lady had a shack down on the beach at the Bay where they lived, and I would go to stay with them sometimes. This old man was very closely related to my other grandmother, Mary Bell. And about this time I went for a visit with my grandmother Lucy at Alert Bay. There was a big potlatch going on given by Spruce Martin, my uncle. He was Mungo Martin's older brother. It was the way of the Indians that if someone wanted to use a certain kind of dance they couldn't just go and use it because it belongs to someone. My grandfather owned a special dance that Spruce Martin wanted to use in this big do that he was putting on. He went in to see my grandmother to see if he could use me and told them, "He is the right boy, I want to use him because he is my nephew." Of course my grandmother said to him, "Sure, you can use him." I was only five years old then but I can remember that morning before the dance. It was early in the morning before daylight and I was to go and practice that dance with Toby Willey's mother. She was up in the woods chanting the songs that were to be used that night. It was up near the same place where I was born behind that barn, and I was so cold that she just tucked me into her arms under the blanket that she had around her. She was singing away early in that morning and all the dancers were gathered that morning getting ready to go into the big community house that night. I remember that they had a big dance that night and when I walked into that big house and danced as a little boy everybody was saying something to me.

After the dancing was over I went home to my grandmother Lucy and knocked on the door. Somebody had walked me home. As soon as I came in I asked Lucy and that old man that she was married to to sit up and beat the sticks like they do when someone is dancing. I told them that I was coming in to dance for them. I wanted to show them what I'd done in the big house. They got up and beat the wood and I came into that little shack and danced for them.

During those early years of my life I moved around a lot and was looked after by a lot of people. I was looked after by my mother and I was looked after by my mother's parents. They taught me the Indian way of life on my mother's side. They would always be saying, "Don't do this," and "Don't do that." That is all I used to hear from my grandparents and especially my mother. My grandmother Lucy used to talk to me about my grandfather Chief Aul Sewid. She told me about his position as a chief and all his different songs. She used to teach me how to sing the songs and everything else that I should know. They were all teaching me how to be a leader of my people when I grew up. Cause this was the aim of my parents, and the people who were standing around me, all my uncles from the different villages. They wanted to see me uphold my name, because this would be the beginning of our name which had been down, lost these past years when my grandfather died and my father died, and there was a gap between them. And that's all they used to tell me when I was a little boy, "Never forget that name."

2 Something Very Precious Has Been Given to Us

When I was about seven years old I left my mother and went to Alert Bay to stay with my grandmother, Old Lucy, and go to school. That's how I got my little education because I stayed with her off and on until I was about ten years old. Actually I wasn't in school regularly during the time I was with my grandmother. When I was a little boy I more or less drifted from one grandmother to the other grandmother, so that while I moved to Alert Bay I wasn't there all the time. My grandmother, Mrs. Bell, was a very religious woman and used to try in her own way to tell me to believe in God. Of course my grandmother Lucy was very religious also and she was brought up in a Roman Catholic church in Victoria where she used to live with her oldest sister who was married to a white man.

Old Lucy was living alone when I went to be with her and go to school. She was staying by herself in a little shack down on the beach which she had bought. After her husband Aul Sewid had died and then her son James Sewid died she was just lost. Her husband was dead, she had lost her only child, and I wasn't born yet when she first came to Alert Bay. I used to ask her, "Why did you come here?" and she would say, "I like to be near the church, that is my only hope, I go to church every time the bell rings." At first she had been a Roman Catholic but when she came to Alert Bay she was an Anglican. Her older sister, who had married this white man in Victoria who owned a store there, had died and her younger sister and her brother had also died. She had no choice but to go and live by herself.

I stayed with her during that time and she encouraged me to go to school and stay with school as long as I could. She could see that education was necessary. But I found it awfully hard as a young boy with nobody to turn to to support me. We used to just look after ourselves, Lucy and I. Our relief at that time was only two dollars and fifty cents a month. We had to go down on the beach, especially during the winter months and before the winter had set

in, to fill our little woodshed up and get ready for the winter. We
had about half a dozen chickens and we sold the eggs to some of the
people in the village. On Saturday when I wasn't in school I used
to go down to the big sawmill that was in Alert Bay and get old
pieces of wood to sell. There was an Indian teacher in the day
school where I went, and I would go and borrow a wheelbarrow
from him and take this wood around to different people in the
village and sell it to make a little money.

We were living right near the Anglican church and the minister
there and his wife, Mr. and Mrs. Corker, were very kind to us. When
the berries were ripe I would go with my grandmother and pick
berries for the minister as well as the Indian agent and his wife,
Mr. and Mrs. Halliday. They were very kind to us. Every now and
then they used to give us a loaf of bread or sometimes some cookies.
Sometimes Mr. and Mrs. Corker would give me some clothes that
were too small for their children and I used to be the happiest boy
in Alert Bay when I wore those new clothes. Everything else that
I had the old lady used to make for me. She used to knit me a sweater
and a little hat and make other clothes for me. We stayed together
for a long time, old Lucy and me, and she was a very religious
woman.

Robby Bell, my uncle, had already left Village Island to go to the
Anglican residential school at Alert Bay when I moved to live with
my grandmother and told her I wanted to go to the day school. The
kids in the Anglican residential school lived right there all the time,
but those kids who were living at home in Alert Bay village would
go to the day school. Every day after school I used to run to old
Lucy's house. My grandmother had some hardtack, this pilot bread
or biscuit, and she would put it in a little bag for me and I would
run up to the residential school. I would look all over for Robby
and give him these biscuits and he really appreciated it. I was just
like brothers with Robby. Everything he got he shared it with me
and I tried to do the same thing.

The Indian teacher at the day school, George Luther, was a great
friend of mine. He liked me somehow. If it was a snowy day, or if
it had snowed at night, my grandmother would wake me up early
and give me breakfast and then I would go up to the school before
anyone else got there. The school had a long stairway, and she used
to give me a broom to sweep off the snow to get it ready for

George Luther when he came. He really used to like that. He just thought the world of me and I used to go and help him make the fire in the big drum stove that we had in the school. Going to school was new to me and I found it awfully hard, especially such things as adding and arithmetic. Somehow I just couldn't put it in my head and I used to find it awfully hard. I really enjoyed school and that was the main reason I came to Alert Bay. I wanted to go to school pretty badly, and there was no school in Village Island, and that is why I started thinking about going to live with my grandmother. I enjoyed school very much but I had a lot of enemies there as a small boy.

Alert Bay was a Nimpkish village and I was half-Kwiksutainuk and half-Mamalilikulla, so that when I was a little boy in school I was an outsider. The people that were there used to pick on me all the time. They did it just because I was an outsider and my grandmother used to tell me that they did the same thing to her when she came to live in that Nimpkish village. They didn't like her to be living on their reserve because she was an outsider and they used to make remarks to her. They were doing the same thing to me when I was in school. I was the only Mamalilikulla or Kwiksutainuk boy that was there at that time. Of course the schoolteacher was a Nimpkish man but he liked me very much and thought a lot of me. The other kids used to tease me and I had a lot of fights with them. I always was pretty big for my age and nobody could ever stand up to me even if there were two of them. I wouldn't hesitate to take on two of them at a time. Sometimes I wouldn't fight them because my grandmother used to tell me not to fight. She would say, "If anybody is picking on you, you leave them alone. Don't you ever pay no attention to those people. They are doing the same thing to me."

One day there were some bigger boys picking on me and making remarks to me that I wasn't accepted there because I was an outsider. So I just let them have it. I wasn't thinking of anything else right then. I thought there was a limit for everything and they had reached the limit. Of course they all went home and complained to their parents because I had licked them all. I just went home to my grandmother but that wasn't the end of it. The parents of those Nimpkish kids came and butted in and began saying things to my grandmother which I didn't like even though I wasn't sure I understood what it was all about. They talked to my aunt, Mrs. Ed Whanock, who was also living in Alert Bay. So, as a result of this, my grandfather, Jim Bell, had to come from Village Island and give a potlatch that night in Alert Bay. The reason for giving that potlatch was because they didn't want anybody to pick on me. It was the custom of the Indians that if anybody got into a fight like that or if anybody called me down, my grandfather was not going to stand for it. So the only thing he could do was to call the people together and give a potlatch. At this potlatch he stood up in public before the people that had been making these remarks about me and told them what he thought. I didn't go to this potlatch but I knew it was being given because my mother came with my grandfather and bawled me out. She said, "If you hadn't done that and gotten into that fight your grandfather wouldn't have had to go to all this trouble and spend all this money for your misbehavior." I didn't say anything at all but just sat there and took it. I tried to avoid getting into any fights after that. Of course I went back to school and they were still picking on me.

Our little house was only about five or six hundred yards from the Anglican church and I always used to go with my grandmother on Sunday. We never missed a Sunday in church. She would get me dressed in my best clothes and comb my hair and get me all ready on Sunday morning. She would always put a little round pin on me which had my father's picture in it and then we would listen for the first bell from the church. As soon as that bell rang we would walk down to the church and sit in one particular seat. We would never go late but were always one of the first to go into the church. I remember that old Lucy used to tell me not to look around in church but just to look straight ahead at the altar. She used to say, "If you look around in church that means the devil is working in you or that somebody is whispering in your ear. Don't pay any attention to anything you hear, just sit still and look up at the altar." There were two older women who worked for the church that I came to know, Mrs. Harris and Mrs. Cook. Their husbands, Joe Harris and Stephen Cook, were leading men in the village at Alert Bay and very active in the work of the church. Joe Harris was chief of the Nimpkish tribe at that time. Mrs. Cook had been born in Seattle and was half-Indian and half-white. She was raised by the first missionary, Rev. Hall. She used to preach in the church in our language as well as interpret what the minister was saying by translating it into the Kwakwala language. Mrs. Harris used to read the lessons as well as teach in the Bible classes that were going on in the church for the older women. They were great church people and great leaders in the church. One Sunday afternoon during my first year in Alert Bay arrangements were made for me to be baptized. I had forgotten all about it and in the afternoon after church I took a long walk with Jim Bell who was visiting from Village Island. We must have been a mile or two down the road from the church when I heard the bell ringing. All of a sudden I remembered that I was supposed to be baptized and so I told my grandfather, but of course he didn't know about it nor what it meant to be baptized. So I started running as fast as I could and I ran all the way back to the church without stopping. When I got there they were just ready to put everything away. There were quite a few people who had been baptized that Sunday afternoon and they were just finishing. As soon as I opened the door to the church, Mrs. Cook and Mrs. Harris both ran up to me. They were the deaconesses of the church at that time and those two great ladies of the village were claiming me as their godchild when I was baptized. Well, they all ran towards me and they just set everything up again for the baptism. Then they all grabbed me and had me kneel down and Mr. Corker who was the minister at that time baptized me. I was still sweating from my long run down the road. My grandmother wasn't there but I don't know whether it was because she didn't know about it or whether she was out looking for me. After that I used to call those two old ladies my godmothers and they used to look out for me. Mrs. Cook would call me in her house to give me some shirts and other things that she had made for me, and Mrs. Harris also used to give me things, especially at Christmas time.

About this time my mother, who had been staying at Village Island, got married to David Matilpi. He came from the Maamtagila tribe and I partly belonged to that tribe since my grandmother Lucy was a Maamtagila. This is the reason I was naturally so close to Dave when he married my mother. They were married by Rev. Corker in the Anglican church in Alert Bay. After the wedding they had a big reception in the old day school and all the people had a wonderful time. They were square dancing and eating and all the old people were just having a wonderful time. David Matilpi was a logger and with his five brothers owned a logging camp. They would move around from one place to another. The logging camps they set up were often back on little isolated lakes. I dropped out of school for a while and used to go over to where they were living at one of the logging camps and stay with them for a while. He was a very good mechanic and could run any kind of engine. He was running those big steam donkeys they used in logging, and when I was a little boy I used to follow him around wherever he would go, and that's where I learned how to run, donkeys and engines. This was before he had any children by my mother. I came back to Alert Bay and my grandmother for a short time before school was out for the summer. That was the first year I had ever spent in school.

During the summers I just drifted from one relative to another. I remember that early in the summer I went up to Rivers Inlet with Dave, my stepfather. We put up a little tent over the bow of that little skiff that we used for fishing and would sleep there at night. We were drag seining the mouth of the river where all the fish would be. We had a long net and it was tied to a stump on the beach, and we would row this skiff letting out the net while other people would hold the net in the water. When the net was clear out and reached right across the mouth of the river we all pulled it in and dragged the fish up on the beach. During the day we fished but part of the time I would play around on the shore. One time I was going across a little creek where I had been playing and cut my foot on a sharp rock or shell. I used to go around barefoot most of the time and after I got this big cut Dave had to just pack me around because I wasn't able to walk. We came to Alert Bay later in the summer because Dave had a logging operation in the woods near the village. He was working at this with his younger brother and one non-Indian fellow, and he wanted somebody to pull the whistle on the steam donkey when it was time to pull out the logs that had been cut. It was quite nice weather and he used to pack me with him so that I could go and pull that whistle for him. At the end of the day he just packed me home because he was a very strong man and could just help me along.

In the fall I returned to live with my grandmother and started my second year of school. I went to school each day and continued to help George Luther whenever I could. I thought he liked me better than any of the others because I used to do quite a bit for him. I would go and get wood for the stove which had to be packed in from outside. I'd sweep the steps when it was snowing and wash the floor and all that. He really thought a lot of me and that's why I thought that he especially cared for me more than any of the other children. I used to do it just because I liked to be with him. He never had to ask me to do that but my grandmother used to tell me to go and help him along as much as I could. I didn't really have much else to do. In school he would put me all by myself in a little desk that was separated a little from the other kids. I was pretty good at drawing, especially the Indian designs, and every-thing that I made he would put up in front of the class so that everyone else could make a copy of what I had made. I thought that was one of the things that made the other boys jealous. It made them feel that I was better than them in drawing. The main time for drawing in school was on Friday afternoon and everyone was supposed to draw something different and then the best one was put up in front so that the younger children could copy it.

George Luther used to give us all a strapping when we were late to school. Many times I would be up in the woods by the school building a little shack with my friends and we would forget that it was time to be at school. We all rushed down from the woods and as we came running in the schoolroom he was hiding behind the door and everyone who passed would get a whallop from behind. He had a big strap and he strapped me many times. I used to be the leader of those boys who were building that little house up in the woods. We called it our "clubhouse" and I guess we were just copying the Nimpkish Club that George Luther had started in Alert Bay. I used to sneak down behind Ed Whanock's house and sneak some lumber and shingles that he had there and we used them for our little house. Each boy would go and get some stuff for building that house. We used to play there a lot. We would build a little fire and sit around and talk.

In the back of the school George Luther had set up a small pool table that belonged to him and we would go there during recess to play pool. One day I was playing pool and I broke one of the cue sticks. He came in and found out what I had done and couldn't understand it and felt badly. He sent me out and told me to go home and not to come back until I was ready to behave myself. I didn't go back to school for a week after that. Each day my grandmother would ask me if I had been to school and I would tell a lie, a white lie, and say, "I been to school." I didn't dare to tell her that I hadn't been to school so I just pretended that I was going to school each day. When I did go back to school he forgot all about it and I was good friends again with him. I was just like any other normal child. I had my bad times.

I didn't spend all my spare time with George Luther, but like any other boy I used to play and go swimming. I was always very constructive when I was a boy and never did depend on anybody. The other kids all had their toys and some of them had two-wheel and three-wheel bicycles. I suppose I felt badly that I didn't have much and I just tried to make some things that I could use and play with. Although I was poor and had no father I was able to do many things on my own. I used to make my own toys a lot of the time. There was a man who used to come to Alert Bay in a gas boat and put on silent motion pictures in the parish hall at the church. I used to go there and give him a hand packing his films up to the church and setting everything up. He used to let me in free because I helped him and this made the other boys jealous of me. One day I happened to see an automobile in the picture show and I got the idea of making one for myself.

I went up to the cannery and Mr. Chambers, who was the manager of the cannery, let me have some of the old wheels that had been thrown away. They had flat carts there with wheels on them for stacking the trays of salmon. The wheels were fastened onto a square rod which was fastened onto the cart, and when they would get worn out they were thrown out. I got a big iron and took off two sets of wheels with the rods on them to use in making my little automobile. Then I got a large wooden crate that bananas had been shipped in to use for the body. I fastened the rods with the wheels on them to this banana crate and of course the front wheels had to be able to turn back and forth. After I had the wheels on the crate I made a little steering wheel with a rod on it and I put a rope around that rod a few times and each end was fastened onto the front wheels so that they would turn when I turned the steering wheel. I got my idea for that from the gas boats that I had seen. Anything I saw I used to copy, and the gas boats had a steering wheel with ropes which fastened onto the gas motor so that it could turn the boat. I did it all myself but after it was finished my friends Bill Dixon and Arthur Shaunessey came and pushed me up and down the street. The Indians had just built a new sidewalk and the older people didn't like me running my little automobile up and down there. They used to remark that I was no good and that I was going to spoil their cement sidewalk with my little car.

I never used to buy anything to play with and nobody had to buy anything for me because I made my own toys. My grandmother had a little handsaw and an ax that I used as a hammer. Everytime she found a wooden box she would tear it up and save all the nails in a box for me. She would give me these tools and the box of nails and tell me, "Now you bring it back when you are finished with it." I would take them out on the beach beside my house and start building things there and when I came home I would put everything away. I used to make little toy boats and pull them along the beach. One time when the pile driver first came into Alert Bay I made a nice little pile driver that was just like it. I got a rod and bent it and put heavy boards on each side of it. I made a hole through those heavy boards for the rod to go through and put a rope around that rod to use it as a winch. Then I put a heavy piece of wood on the end of the rope to use as the hammer of the pile driver. When I turned the rod it would winch up the hammer and then I would let go of it and it would hammer down. The other boys always wanted to come and play with me and I started driving little piles on the beach where I was playing. I had seen a lot of steam donkeys around the logging camps and I made a small one of my own. I got some wood for a sleigh for the donkey to ride on so I could pull it around on the beach. I cut up a baking powder tin to use for the boiler and I would make a little fire in it so that there was a little smoke coming out. I put a hand winch on it with a rope and I would do logging down on the beach. All my friends used to come and work for me and we would pull little pieces of driftwood from off the beach. I made all those things by myself by just copying whatever I saw because my grandmother couldn't afford to buy any toys for me.

I was always playing with Bill Dixon and Arthur Shaunessey. We would go out on the beach or go behind the island swimming. We always used to be together. It seemed that they were the only boys that accepted me and the rest of them didn't because I was an outsider. One of Bill Dixon's parents was half-Kwiksutainuk and my grandmother used to tell me to be friendly with him because he was one of my people. We would sometimes go up to George Luther's house together, the three of us, and look through the books that he had. Most of the time when I visited George's house I would go alone.

One day in about 1922, when I was eight years old, George Luther told the kids that there wasn't going to be any school for a few days because they were going to use that room for a courthouse. The law against the potlatch had been passed and the mounted police were beginning to enforce it. The government had sent out the word that if the people would give up all their masks and coppers and their regalia and everything that they owned in connection with the potlatch they wouldn't be put in jail. There were only people from three villages who did what they were ordered, Cape Mudge, Village Island, and Alert Bay. They gave all their masks and regalia and everything they owned from the Indian way and they put it in a big building behind the Indian office. That was just full of all the masks and things from these three tribes and they took them away. And the people who had refused to give up their things were brought into Alert Bay and put on trial and they used that schoolroom for a courthouse. And some of them from Fort Rupert, Kingcome, New Vancouver, Turnour Island, and from all over the Kwakiutl nation were brought there. After some people had been tried on a certain day the ones who had been sentenced were just kept in the schoolroom and had to sleep on the floor. The mounted police would lock that place up and guard it at night. After they were sentenced they were sent down south to jail for about two to six months.

I heard that some of my relatives had been sentenced and were going to be sent to jail, so I crept around in back of that schoolroom and looked through the window. All the people were just sleeping there on the floor. I didn't realize everything that was going on at the time. Old man Whanock and old lady Whanock were in there and Herbert Martin who was a close relation of mine was in there. I felt very badly about it because they told me that they were all going to be in jail. Of course the mounted police were watching all the time and they used to chase me away from there. That was the time that we lost a lot of our masks and regalia and coppers and other wealth.

Right before the end of school each year they had a big do which lasted for several days. The Indian people from lots of the other villages would all come there and there would be lots of things going on. They used to call it the queen's birthday and it was a big day for all the Indian people. They would have games and sports and I remember watching the races out in front of the Anglican residential school. Everyone would bring their lunches and sit around on the beach and have a picnic at the same time the races were going on. They had foot races from one end of Alert Bay to the other and also canoe races. I really used to enjoy those sports days.

After my second year in school I spent most of the summer with my stepfather Dave. He was a fine man and a real gentleman. He was very very kind to me and he'd do anything for me. He was more like a father to me. He was my great friend and we were together a lot traveling and fishing and logging. He didn't know how to read and write but he was a great engineer who knew everything about diesel, gas, and steam engines. He knew how to take anything apart and put it back together again. I used to go with him when he was driving those big steam donkeys. I used to ask him, "Can I drive it?" He used to put me on the seat as a little boy and I would pull those big levers. For part of the summer I fished with him on his small gill net boat. He was a very quiet man and not like those fellows who just talk and talk. I can't remember him ever punishing me or even saying a lot to me. If I went to him and asked him a question he would just answer and that was all. But I would watch him working on engines and fixing things and take little lessons from him that way. He was a very well-liked man and I don't think he ever hurt anybody. He was a big, tall man and a strong man too. He was a very very nice man. When he wasn't working at a logging camp he would be out fishing on a seine boat. I used to go along with him on those seine boats and we used to work together down in the engine room running the engine. Sometimes I would take over and that was when I first learned to run engines on a boat. The controls to the engines were down in the engine room and they used bells to signal us what to do, like back up or full speed ahead. They didn't have any controls up on top. Dave and I were the engineers and we had to stay down in the engine room and I really thought it was great to answer those bells.

My mother stayed at the cannery and worked while Dave and I were out fishing, but we spent some time at the cannery with her. At the end of the summer everyone returned from fishing and there would be a lot of people up at Knight's Inlet cannery. It took about a week to put all the nets away and get everything cleaned up and then everyone would be paid off. It was against the law for the Indians to buy liquor, but I remember that after the men would call at the office for their pay many of them would go to the Chinese who were up there to buy a bottle. In our language they had a word for it which meant "they are going to wash their stomachs out." If you heard some fellow singing and carrying on they would say, "Oh, he's just washing his stomach out." It usually only happened at the end of the season when they had made a few dollars and they were all happy. My mother used to have a drink and have a drinking party in our little house with four or five women and their husbands. They would all be in there drinking and arguing and oh, I used to just get sick of that. She would fight with Dave and they would be arguing but the next day when they were sober everything would be all right again. They never did get mad at me when they were drinking because they had too much respect for me. I used to go in there when there was a big party and tell them off, you know, as a little boy, and they would stop and say, "Well, let's go home." I would tell the whole group, "If you're not going to stop this I'm not going to come near you. I don't like this a bit. You get out of our house because you have no business here. Go on, get out of here!" I would just go there and plead with them. I just cried my head off and I'll never forget that. My aunt was like that too and her husband who was the Indian boss of that cannery. They would have a big party since he was a big shot up there during the summer. The people would all get bootleg liquor from the Chinese. I never used to like that kind of life and that is the reason that I just didn't know where to go. The best place to go was with my grandmother, old Lucy. She was all alone and a peaceful old lady and her life was better than all of theirs put together. I still think that today.

After that summer I went back to live with my grandmother at Alert Bay. It really struck me when I was living with her about the kind of life she was living. We struggled in this world and I knew that she needed me. I knew the way she was living and especially that she was a very religious woman, an Anglican. I thought that that was the most important thing because I believed in God and I thought that it was one of the most beautiful things about our life at that time. We prayed about it every night. I used to listen to her pray. Sometimes I would be watching her while I was pretending to be asleep. She would be kneeling down at her bedside asking God to protect me, to give me wisdom and knowledge, and to guide me in all my work at school. She had a great wish for me. She used to tell me nearly every day for me to take in all that I could in school and learn it so that I could stand before my people when I became a man and preach to my people the gospel. That was her wish. She didn't actually say that she wanted me to be a minister when I grew up but to be a man that could stand before my people and tell them about the gospel. That was why she wanted me to learn in school.

When I was living with her she used to open up a big family Bible once a week that belonged to her sister. It was a very old Roman Catholic Bible that had a lot of pictures in it. She would lay it in front of me and tell me all she knew about the Bible, trying to teach me what was in it. She didn't know how to read and write but she had learned it all from the minister when she went to church. She was a wonderful old lady the way she could remember all those things. She would talk to me about it also when I came home for lunch each day and then she never failed to pray for me each night in our own language. The most important thing that she told me from the Bible was that I should be faithful to my elders. The most important thing was to respect your elders and to obey them and watch out that nothing harmful happens to them. If they say something to me I should obey them. And according to her that was the first step in Christianity. She told me many of the Bible stories and my favorite ones were about Joseph being sold by his brothers and the story of the flood. She had her own way of explaining things to me. I tried to follow what she taught me in respecting and helping the older people. There was an old blind man in Alert Bay who was related to us who would come down on the beach alone to cut firewood. I would go there and help him cut his wood by holding the other end of the saw and guiding him. I used to hold his hand and walk up to his house to help him.

I didn't want to see my grandmother Lucy stuck for anything so I tried to help her as much as I could. I remember one day there was a big scow which came in loaded with boxes of empty cans for the cannery. I told my teacher that I was going to work for my grandmother the following day and I wasn't going to come to school. I told him I wanted to go and earn a little money. I told my grandmother to wake me up at seven in the morning so I could work. I went out that day and worked all day for about twelve hours. I was wheeling one of those big trucks with boxes of cans even though I was just a small kid. There were a lot of Indians working there and they all got their pay at the end of the day. I don't know how much they got but they only gave me fifty cents for that day's work. I didn't argue because I didn't know how much it was worth, but the next day I went back to school. On weekends or at other times when there wasn't any school I used to go watch the fishing or the canning. Mr. Matthews was the manager at the A. B. C. Packing Company then. Sometimes I would work piling cans for eight cents an hour, but when I got lazy I just walked home and got a little stick I used for a fishing rod. I would go up the river and stay there all day fishing for trout. Mr. Matthews used to come and try to get me to come to the cannery and work because it was hard to get men at that time. I told him, "I am too busy fishing." And when I felt like going to work I would go and pile cans again.

While I was living with Lucy I had a little box of toys that Johnny Clark had bought for me before he died. I kept them in that little shack where we lived and would take them out and play with them. One time my second stepfather, David Matilpi, bought me a little toy steam donkey which really worked. There was a little coal oil lamp which was like a firebox and I could put water in the boiler and it would actually run. It had a safety valve on it and a little lever which I pulled to make the whistle blow. It had a little flywheel on it and when the steam began to make the flywheel turn it used to really shake. That little shack where I used to play was only about as big as one room and it was quite drafty. My grandmother used to get old newspapers from a friend and each week she would spread out clean ones on the floor to cover the cracks and keep it warmer inside. One day she was busy outside washing clothes and I was inside playing with my little steam donkey. The little coal oil lamp was burning and the steam was coming out and it was shaking while it was running. I was busy with something else when all of a sudden I noticed that the fire had dropped out of the little firebox and the newspaper on the floor was on fire. I was really scared and started jumping up and down on the fire trying to put it out by myself before my grandmother found out about it. I was able to stop the fire by myself. And there was no doubt that there was somebody unknown that was always on my side at that time and during those days when I was living with old Lucy.

During that last year I was going to school I saw a lot of my teacher, George Luther. He didn't only like me when I was in school. I knew that he liked me very much because he used to invite me to his house. He was a bachelor and since he didn't have any wife he used to invite me by. He was a very wise old man and anything I wanted to know I would go and ask his advice and talk to him. He used to stay, "If there is anything you want to know, Jimmy, you just come and see me." He used to talk to me as if he was my father when I visited him in his home. I used to talk to him about the church and about the life of our people. We used to talk about those heavy drinkers that were around in those days, awful people, and what they were doing to themselves. In those days it was a disgrace for an Indian to be drunk and you would only see a few people doing that. George Luther used to have a little bottle in his house but he never gave anything away and I never knew him to be drunk. My uncle and aunt, Mr. and Mrs. Whanock, were living at Alert Bay then and I would go visit them but I didn't talk about anything very serious with them. George Luther was the only one that really talked seriously with me at that time. He used to ask me to come up to his house on Friday nights when there wasn't any school the next day. He would ask me if we could have a little debate. He would be on the side of the potlatch and I'd be on the side of the law and he would say, "Jimmy, you criticize everything you can about the potlatch." So I would try to do this but I could never beat him. Everything that had been done in the old way of the Indians was always better and I could never win those debates. It was just the two of us there in his home doing that so that we could have something to do. We used to talk a lot about the Bible but I couldn't debate the Bible with him because he was a pupil of Mr. Hall, the first missionary, and was well trained in the Bible. He hadn't been very far in school but he would teach me many things especially about the work of the church. He was the person that really encouraged me to teach my people in our own language about Christianity. If we were not talking or having a debate we would be at the organ where he would start playing and I would sing for him. He was the organist for the church. He would teach me how to sing and what little I learned about music I learned from him. And he liked it because I really took a personal interest in everything that he was doing.

When the fishing season came around near the end of the school year I had to go to work. That was in 1924 and I was only ten years old. I had been out on fishing boats before but this was my first job on a fishing boat where I was a member of the crew. The gill net boats that some of the people used in fishing were quite small and there was only a couple of crew members. Some of the older men were running seine boats at that time and there were about six men on the crew of those larger boats. I worked for Ed Whanock during that season, cooking and washing dishes on his seine boat. He was a very nice man and very respectable. He was a very successful fisherman and one of the first Indians to own his own seine boat. He was the first man that ever gave me a job. I was mostly washing dishes and used to get two dollars a week. When we came into Alert Bay I lived with Ed and Rachel Whanock most of the time. They had two girls about my age and I had played with them a lot when I was in school. They both died about that time and they wanted me to come and stay with them. They pleaded with me to come and stay with them and I felt that I should because they had lost those two nice girls. They always felt that I was part of their family after they lost their two daughters, and Mrs. Whanock was more or less like a mother to me.

I didn't go back to school or to live with old Lucy after that summer. That was the time that I began drifting again. I used to live with my mother for a while and then I would take off and live with my aunt and then I would go up to Village Island and live with Jim Bell for a while. At about that time Dave had a logging operation over at Sointula on Malcolm Island. I went and stayed with him and my mother for a month or two. I felt very close to Dave at that time and I worked together with him in his logging. I used to just love to run engines. What I wanted to be most of all then was an engineer. He would go out each day to run those big steam donkeys and I followed him around wherever he went. I would help him put the tubes in the boiler of those big steam donkeys. It was about that time that my brother and sister were born, David and Mabel Matilpi. I liked to go to where Dave and my mother were staying so I could be near my brother and sister. I really felt proud to have them but it bothered me to see my mother spanking them. She was a very quick-tempered woman. I didn't like the way she used to treat my younger brothers because I had a lot of love for them. I used to like to get away because I wouldn't stand for it. It made me feel better if I was away from it.

There were a lot of Finnish people living at Sointula and I came to be very good friends with some of those Finnish boys. There were about three or four of them that I used to play with. We used to wrestle and jump and have contests lifting big stones on the beach trying to beat each other. We would go camping down on the beach together.

I came back to Alert Bay and stayed with Ed Whanock for a while after being at Sointula. I played soccer with the other boys a lot of times while I was there. One afternoon I came in after playing soccer and felt very tired and my body was aching all over. The next morning when I woke up I couldn't hardly walk or move around and this lasted for two or three days. After about three days I had a dream one night in which Toby Willey's mother came to me and told me to go up in the woods and bathe in some water. She told me in my dream to find a stream or a little pool of water and take a bath and then rub myself down with hemlock branches. I was to do this four times. So as soon as I woke up that morning I got out of bed and was more or less crawling up the hillside into the woods because I was still very sore from playing soccer. I finally found a little pool of water and I took my clothes off and started bathing, using some hemlock branches to rub myself down. Right away I felt much stronger and the aches I had felt seemed to ease off. I only did it twice even though I had been told in my dream to do it four times. It was a strong belief of the Indian people that everything had to be done four times. After the second time bathing and rubbing down with branches I felt so much better that the pain was gone and I was back to normal again. Soccer was the most important sport to us then and I always tried my best.

During this time of my life I ran around most of the time with my uncle Robert Bell. I went up to Village Island and stayed with my grandparents for a while and Robby and I did lots of things together. We used to go hunting with older boys in the village. There was a little trail through the woods to a bay where the geese would come in the fall of the year on their way south. I wasn't allowed to carry a gun because I was too young, but we would follow along after the older boys and we would get quite a few geese. Sometimes I would go hunting for ducks with an old man. I would row the canoe for him and we would pile branches over the canoe so that it just looked like a drift log. We would sit there and drift along until some ducks came by and then he would shoot them.

One time Jim Bell had been out fishing. He hadn't caught anything and was getting hungry so he came in and beached his canoe. Robby and I ran down to the beach and jumped into the canoe and paddled over to the end of the island. We had some Indian hooks on the end of long lines and we let them down and then put a little buoy on the end of the line with a little flag on it. After we had two or three lines down we decided to go back to the village and play around for a while and then come back later and check our lines. Before it got too late we paddled back to where our lines were and began pulling them in. We pulled one line up and there was only a small halibut on it. We thought we had lost the other line until we saw it quite a distance away so we rowed over to it and started pulling it in. I started pulling it and discovered that there was something heavy on it. Robby said to me, "Just pull it up and I'll hit him." As it came nearer the boat we could see that we had a great big halibut. As soon as I lifted his head up Robby hit him in the face. You weren't supposed to just hit him in his face but at the right spot on his nose so that he would be knocked out. Well, that big halibut really went wild and splashed around so much that we had to get into the bottom of the canoe. There was so much water coming in from his splashing that we were almost sunk. So I said to Robby, "Just let go of the line." As soon as he let the line go that halibut ran away and when he touched the bottom the line stopped going out. So Robby and I figured that we should tow him to a little island that wasn't far away. When we got to the island I went up on the beach and started to pull that thing in. When it was close to the surface I ran up the beach a ways and Robby was ready there with a little ax and chopped him in the head and killed him. Then we had an awful time trying to lift him. We didn't know how to do it but we pried with our oars until it was up on the beach and then we tipped the canoe until we could just slide it on and we finally made it. We were very happy and rowed to the village and shouted to the old people to come down and look at what we had caught. They were all happy about it when they came and saw what we had done. It was a big halibut that weighed almost two hundred pounds or more. Three or four of the women started butchering it and cut it up and made thin slices of meat to dry in the sun. Old Gordon, Jim Bell's grandfather, came down and asked us, "How did you get him in the canoe?" So we told him how we had towed him to the island and chopped his head with the ax and how we managed to get him on the canoe. "Oh," he laughed, "you will never get any more halibut. You will never get one again because that is not the right way to kill them. If you tow them onto the beach you will never get any again." That was right because after that we tried and tried but we never got any more.

The next year when I was about twelve they started a little school at Village Island and I went there a little when I was staying in that village. Miss O'Brien was a missionary and came there to be the district nurse. She had a little house down at the beach on a float and the teacher would stay with her. I used to go down to her house and visit them every night and look at all the magazines and books they had there. I really liked to look at books. They were nice old ladies and would hold church there at Village Island and I used to go every Sunday morning and evening. I had a friend in school there by the name of Peter Fred. I used to pal around with him and go to school with him but he was a mischievous boy. When the teacher wouldn't be looking he would run out of the school and off into the woods and the teacher would run after him. There wasn't a day that he stayed in school all day. I always stayed in school because I liked to go to school. I remember we used to have a drill where we would raise our arms up and down in time with music from a little gramophone that our teacher played. It was about that time that I got a little gun, a little 22 shot. I used to take a little boat and go around by myself and get some ducks. I was really independent. I was able to move around and had freedom to go wherever I liked to. That was one of the happiest times I had at Village Island.

That same year when I was twelve I started running an engine on a seine boat by myself for the first time. My grandfather was in his last year as skipper before he retired and I ran the engine for him. It was only a twenty horsepower engine but it was so big I could hardly turn it over. I used to use a big bar to get it started and he used to come and help me. That was on the seine boat called the "Sunrise," and even though I was only twelve and our crew was pretty weak we were catching fish the same as the other boats. I worked like a man and tried to be one. I used to stay down in the engine room and watch how the engine worked because I was so interested in engines. I never thought I would be a skipper even though sometimes I would ask my grandfather if I could take the wheel. If we were going through a nice big channel he would let me take the wheel and sit beside me telling me where to go and how to go through that channel.

My grandfather retired after that fishing season and the next year I fished for a while with Ed Whanock and then I started running the engine on my uncle Henry Bell's boat. Henry was my mother's oldest brother and quite a bit older than me. He was a very successful captain and I fished with him for a long time during the summers after that. I was a teenager then and after the fishing season I would go with my friends down to Vancouver. Since most of the boats were owned by the packing companies we had to take them down for the winter, and since I used to run the engines I had to go down with the boat. Sometimes the boys had a room in a hotel and we would stay there for a few days. One of the boys would usually buy a bottle and if they gave me a drink I would take it. I would always take a drink when I went to Vancouver with my friends but I don't ever remember getting drunk. I knew it was wrong and that if I was going to drink too much I would get drunk and then I wouldn't know what I was doing.

I came back to Alert Bay from Vancouver and stayed with Ed Whanock again. I used to go out in the evening with the other boys to a dance or something. Sometimes somebody would steal a bottle from somewhere and bring it to the dance and pass it around and everybody would just drink it out of the bottle, a little bit each. We would dance until three o'clock in the morning sometimes but my mother didn't like that. She would be worrying and when I came home late she used to talk to me and say, "You know that I don't like you to be like that. I don't want you to stay out late. I want you to come home at regular hours. I heard that you fellows were drinking there last night and we don't want that." I wouldn't talk back but I just held my head down while she talked to me about it. And the old lady, my grandmother Lucy, heard about it and told me, "You will have to quit that." If my mother or grandparents ever heard anything that I had done that wasn't right, or if they heard the other people talking about something wrong that I had done, they would get after me and talk to me. They were really strict with me because they wanted me to grow up and be the leader of the people. I know they were stricter with me than with all the people that were around me because I was in line for those high positions of my grandparents and to become a hamatsa. They were more or less polishing me up all those years—more or less like polishing brass and everybody knew me and everybody would see me. I was recognized by the people because they had been witnessing me dancing whenever my grandfather or my uncle gave a potlatch. In those days when I walked into the hall and all the people were there, my relatives and all the respectable people of the village, it seemed to me that everybody's eye was on me. If I went in there half-drunk and did something foolish then I would never forgive myself. That is why I used to be very careful what I did because the minute I did anything wrong my mother and grandparents would hear about it. I guess that somebody would go and tell them because our village was so small. I never did like to hurt any person.

And that's when the big day came. It was late in the fall and I was going on fourteen. My grandparents had been up on a little creek at Vinea Sound drying salmon and had just come home that night to Ed Whanock's house in Alert Bay where I was staying. I had been out late that night to a dance with my friends and when I came in I lay down on the couch. That was when I heard Jim and Mary Bell talking about me to Ed and Rachel Whanock and my mother and stepfather. One of them was saying, "You might as well go and see her parents because I think he should get married because we don't want him running around like this." Then I heard my mother say to my aunt, "It's getting to be pretty dangerous now for him to go around with his friends." I lay there and pretended that I was sleeping and pretty soon my grandparents walked out. So as soon as they had gone I got up and said to my stepfather, "Let's go take a walk. It's pretty warm in here." I used to be very good friends with him and we were just like pals. "All right," he said, "we'll go for a walk." When we got outside and were walking along the road I asked him, "What was going on in there? I heard the people talking about me." "Well," he said, "you're going to get married." "Well," I said, "I can't get married! I'm too young!" "Oh, that's all right," he said. "We'll look after you. I think it is the best way for you, to get married now, because if you're not going to get married now you might go haywire." "Well," I said, "who is this girl anyway?" And just then we happened to be passing by the house where Moses Alfred lived, and David said, "It is the girl that lives here." I didn't know what to say. I used to see her around the village but I didn't know her.

Well, it was the Indian custom for someone to go to the parents of the girl and ask their consent. That is where my grandparents had gone that night when they walked out of the house. So I just waited for the answer that this girl's parents would give to the old people who went to talk with them. I was careful after that not to listen anymore because I didn't like to butt in on what was going on. A few days after that I was alone with my mother, just the two of us, so I said to her, "I hear that I'm going to get married. You know that I'm too young to get married." "Oh, no!" she said. "Don't talk like that. We want you to get married. You are going to marry Flora Alfred. It has already been arranged with her parents and it's all right. Now you have to go and see the minister so it can be announced in the church and published in the band." "Well," I said, "I don't think I should get married. It isn't that I don't want to get married, but what am I going to do if I have children?" "Well," my mother said, "we'll look after you some."

After that I went to see my old grandmother, Lucy. She had already heard about it. I went down to her little shack and asked her for a cup of tea. She used to make me wonderful tea. I went in and sat down and said, "Well, they say I'm going to get married." "Yes," she said, "I heard about that and I think it's a wonderful thing. I would really like to see it. I want to see you get married and have children before I die. There is nothing better that I wish to see than your children before I go." Well, that is what made me kind of give in. I didn't want to get married but of course I had no business to my own personal opinion. I had no business to try and argue or anything like that because I knew that the older people knew what was right for me; that's what I figured. I never did like to argue with anybody that was older than me but I always liked to respect what they said to me.

It wasn't long after that that we began to get a lot of opposition from some of the other Indian people. There were quite a few people who wanted to marry Flora Alfred. A lot of these families heard about me getting the best of them and they tried everything to stop it. They went to the Indian agent and told him that I was too young. They even used the Indian way of fighting by using witch-craft. When I was younger they used to tell me to be careful what I did and not to spit on the ground or leave my coat or hat behind when I went to a strange place or a strange home. I never did believe in that but I noticed that some of my shirts had a little piece cut off of them and that my blanket had a hole cut in it. I didn't know what it was until my mother saw it and right away she knew what it was all about, but I didn't think anything of it because I didn't believe in those things. Of course my grandfather and my uncle and my stepfather were all standing by me and they wouldn't allow anything to happen to me. And when my uncles in Fort Rupert and Kingcome heard about this they all just moved in. They wouldn't allow anything like that. They thought it was the right thing for me to get married to Flora Alfred. They all looked upon me as the young boy who would some day be the inheritor of the name of my grandfather, Aul Sewid. They were all looking on me as the rightful owner of all the things that he had so they thought we were doing the right thing. That is why they were all doing their share to help us along as much as they could. So those people who were opposing it didn't have a chance. I didn't know what my wife's family were thinking. It wasn't any of my business to know whether they were saying, "He's a good boy," or "He's the right type of man for our girl." I didn't know and I couldn't talk for them.

Well, I went to Mr. Comely, who was the minister that came after Mr. Corker, and told him that I was going to get married. He didn't say anything. A few days after that the Indian agent, Mr. Halliday, who was a good friend of ours, saw me on the road and said to me, "You come into my office." He was kind of mad. When I went in he bawled me out as an Indian agent. "You know you are only fifteen years old, not even fifteen years old. You can't get married. You have to be seventeen years old." "Well," I said to him, "How did you know my age? I am seventeen years old." That was the biggest white lie that I ever told in my life, because I didn't want to disappoint my parents. I already knew what they had to go through with all the people that were discouraging them. He said to me, "How are you going to look after yourself?" I told him, "I can look after myself. Don't you worry about that." I guess he figured he was going to have to give me relief or something. I was thankful that I wasn't like that. Anyway, nobody else would stop me because I wasn't like that. If I knew I was doing the right thing I was going to push it. It had always been my policy since I was a little boy that if I made up my mind then I was going to do it and I was not going to turn back. When I thought that it was all right with my grandparents and my mother and my aunt then it was going to be all right with me. I wasn't worrying how I was going to live and all that because I had struggled with my grandmother for what little we had, sometimes only fifty cents a day.

After it had all been decided we had to wait for three weeks while it was announced in the church. My grandfather had given some money to Moses Alfred in order to make them believe that we were going to go through with it. During those three weeks my grandparents told me to go and help my wife's parents with whatever they were doing. I went and helped them chop wood and went up the river with their family to help them get some fish. It was the Indian way for me to show that I was really going to go through with it. One of the main reasons that my relatives wanted me to marry Flora Alfred was because of the high positions that her family had as well as the Indian wealth that went with those positions. I heard about other boys who would be going around with girls who were not their equal. Sometimes the parents of those girls wouldn't do for the boy's parents who were well up in society, and they wouldn't match. My relatives were looking at the wealth that Moses Alfred had against the wealth of my family. When a boy chose his own girl because he loved her and had been going around with her it didn't always work out. His family wouldn't care too much for that girl and just look down on her because of her low position. Sometimes after they were married the girl would just take off because she was not welcome in her husband's house. You couldn't blame her for doing this. I thought that was bad and I didn't like that.

I understood that my grandfather gave some money to Flora Alfred's relatives because the aim of my relatives was to get the masks and the things like that for us. They wanted to see me uphold my name, as I said before, because this would be the beginning of our name which had been down and lost these past years when my grandfather died and my father died, and there was a gap between them. That's why they were all pushing for me to uphold that name again. And that's all they used to tell me when I was a little boy, "Never forget that name because some day you will use it." There was an old chief up at Fort Rupert who was Flora's great-uncle and he was putting in a lot of his wealth for me when we got married. It was the custom of the Indians at the time a couple got married for the girl's father and other relatives to transfer a lot of their positions and masks and dances to her new husband and then he could pass it on to his children. That is the same way that I had gotten some of

Jim Bell's names and positions. They were given to my father when
he married my mother and even though he died they came on down
to me. Well, this great-uncle of Flora's, Chief Odzistales, was half-
Kwiksutainuk and half from the Fort Rupert Kwakiutl people. The
reason he happened to use the name Odzistales was because that
was a Kwiksustainuk name. Since my grandfather, Aul Sewid, was
a Kwiksutainuk man, Chief Odzistales knew him and was related
to him. When Aul Sewid was alive he gave a potlatch one time
and asked Chief Odzistales, who was a young man, to be his head
dancer, since he had no children then. He could be the head dancer
for my grandfather when he used that feather dance because he was
related to my grandfather. Well, that was why Chief Odzistales felt
so happy upon my marriage to Flora, because he felt that I was the
rightful man to own everything that he had. So he gave us all his
masks and dances and it all came to me.

The day before I was to get married in the church there was a
big do where Moses Alfred transferred all these things over to my
grandfather, Jim Bell, to hold for me. Ed Whanock had a seine boat
then so he went around and invited all the people in the Kwakiutl
nation. He invited the people from Fort Rupert and Kingcome and
all the different villages to come to Alert Bay for this big do where
I was going to be married in the Indian way. On the night before
the wedding in the church they held this thing. I wasn't there and
didn't even know anything about it. I wasn't old enough to go there
and make a speech. My mother and grandparents and all my other
relatives were there. All the chiefs and the prominent men of the
respectable villages were there at Moses Alfred's house and I was
married in the Indian way. I heard about it later, that everything
was given to me in a big chest that had all the masks and other
regalia in it for the cedar bark dance. And all that stuff was given
to my family.

The next day I was married in the Anglican church by Rev.
Comely. It was December 20, 1927. We had a big wedding in the
church and the parish hall was full afterwards for the wedding cake
and everything. I'll never forget that I had a little stiff collar on
that was size thirteen and I was only thirteen years old at the time. I
was going to be fourteen in just a few days and Flora had just turned
sixteen so she was two years older. That was the best Christmas

present I had in my life just five days before Christmas. The day after the wedding in the church my grandfather gave a big potlatch for all the people who had come to Alert Bay. He didn't call the people together because it was against the law to give a potlatch, but he just went around to the houses and gave money and other things to the people in honor of me. And my mother gathered up a lot of dishes and pails and other utensils and called the ladies together in my wife's house and gave these things away in honor of my wife.

After I got married it was the Indian custom that I couldn't return to my home at Village Island right away. That is why they kept me in Alert Bay even though I wasn't aware of it at the time. My wife's parents just asked us to move in and they gave us a nice room up-stairs in their house. It was like an apartment with a little kitchen and everything. During the next couple of years while I was living with them they were gathering together all kinds of stuff to give away when we finally went to Village Island to live. They wouldn't have dared to take us home to Village Island right after we were married because I was different from any ordinary man who would go right home to where he came from. I was a respected man and they treated me different from any other person because I held a big position and a high name. They all respected me that day. About a week after we had moved in with Moses Alfred my wife got the measles and two or three days after that I got them. That was the wedding present I got from my wife.

About the first of April the next year we went up to the cannery and my wife worked there with some of her relatives while I was out fishing. I worked some on Moses Alfred's boat but mostly I ran engines for my uncle Henry Bell. In the fall I visited my mother and David, who were living at Turnour Island, and I went up to Village Island for short visits. We continued to live most of the time with Flora's family at Alert Bay. Flora had a bad leg that was giving her a lot of pain so I took her down to Vancouver to have it checked. We went to Dr. Codrington and he X-rayed her. After he had looked at the X ray he just walked away and looked out of the window in his office and asked her, "Why didn't you get this fixed up when you were a little girl?" She said to him, "Well, my parents didn't know any better. I guess they figured when I got well that

that was all there was to it." I don't know what had happened but she got hurt when she was a little girl. He didn't tell us what he saw on that X ray but he told her, "If you can't stand that pain maybe I could do something to help you." We went back to Alert Bay and she was able to get along okay.

My brother, Gordon Matilpi, was born about that time and I felt very proud to have my brothers and sister. I used to play with them and take them out whenever we were up at Turnour Island or whenever they came to Alert Bay to visit. I used to ask my mother if they could come to Alert Bay and stay with us for a while, which they did. I used to like them to come around all the time.

Mr. Comely was the minister of Christ Church for about a year and a half after I was married there. I used to go there almost every Sunday and I thought a lot of Mr. Comely. Mr. Prosser came when Mr. Comely left and he really influenced me a lot. He was just a natural minister of the gospel. He came from England and he had never seen the Indians before, but he just liked to put himself in the place of the Indian people and see how they lived. He learned the Indian ways and would barge right into someone's home and sit there and eat the Indian food. He would go to the people and not just wait for the people to come to him or to his church when he rang the bell. He actually went to the people, not only in Alert Bay but he would go to the other outside villages. He used to go to Village Island and Turnour Island and spend a couple days or a week with the people. He would just walk right into the house that he wanted to stay in and say to the people, "I'm going to stay here." Sometimes when he visited the people it happened that they were having lunch or supper. He would just walk right in and say, "That's all right, I'll get a chair." It didn't matter what they were eating, he would just dig right in, even if they were eating Indian food. He was working among the Indians and I guess he figured that he had to go all out to win the people. He invited the kids into his home sometimes for parties. He was a good man and the people liked him very much and I used to go and talk with him lots of times.

During the next summer I was drag seining with Moses Alfred over on the Nimpkish River. My wife had had one miscarriage during our first year of married life and was now expecting again. I don't know when she went into the hospital, but when I came home that weekend our first baby had already been born. I was very very happy like any father would be. It was the first time in my life that I had a child. The first thing I did was to go and see my grandmother, Lucy, and tell her about the baby. My mother's parents were in Alert Bay at that time so I went and told them about it. They were all happy. Then I went to the hospital and went in to see my wife. I had been wishing for a boy to be the oldest one but I was very happy with this baby and we named her Dora Georgia. She was born on July 9, 1929. My mother was very happy too and she was very willing to help us look after our child. I'm sorry to say that she used to like to have one of my children, but I never did let anybody have my children because I liked to look after them myself even though Flora and I were too young. I was only fifteen years old at that time.

Moses Alfred's house wasn't completely finished and I had to do a lot of work for the old man helping him finish it up. He wasn't much of a carpenter and I helped him finish the upstairs. I also used to fix his boat and go and overhaul his engine. I was well prepared to do that because I had learned a lot about engines by that time. Flora's mother was very strict with us while we were living with her. She had been very strict with Flora when she was a little girl and I guess that was still in her mind even though she was married. If we wanted to go to a picture show in the evening we would have to sneak out of the house and the old lady would be waiting for us when we got back and she really bawled us out. I guess she wanted us to stay home and tend to business since we had the responsibility of being parents and she felt we should stay home and look after our family. When we got back from the picture show I used to wait outside and tell Flora to go in first and she would get bawled out from the old lady.

There was a little house in the front of Moses Alfred's house that they gave to us as a wedding present but Flora's uncle was living in it at that time. I was working in the field up behind the residential school with him and so he would wake me up every morning. I didn't have an alarm clock because I couldn't afford one, so we fixed a fishing line that went up to our room upstairs in Moses Alfred's house and tied a lot of tin cans onto it. In the morning Flora's uncle used to come and pull that string and wake me up and I think that it woke the whole house up. We didn't get wages for working but we worked in order to get our relief check. I was getting three dollars a day and I really worked hard. I wanted to fulfill my promise that I wasn't going to depend on anybody. After that job was over I went out halibut fishing for a little while, and then I used to go out and get beach logs and cut them up for the house so we would have firewood for the winter. It was at that time that they tore down the old sawmill in Alert Bay and they hired a lot of Indians to help them tear it down. There were about thirty of us working and they asked me to act as straw boss, sort of the foreman, and I was running a little tractor pulling the timbers down. I was only about fifteen and there were lots of older men, but I was working five days a week and some of them only worked one day or they would just come for a couple of days and the crew was changing around. They wanted me to stay on every day because I was doing the work satisfactory.

3   Paddling Towards the Chief That Is Giving
a Potlatch

When I was sixteen my grandparents and my wife's parents had gotten enough stuff together so that we were ready to go home to Village Island. They had gathered some money and dishes and furniture together which they put on Moses Alfred's seine boat and they took us home. They called it the Indian custom of "taking you home." My grandfather called all the people from the different islands to come to Village Island for this big potlatch that was to be given in honor of me. When we arrived there my grandfather got all the people together and announced that I was home. Then they gave away some money, dishes, big pails, furniture, and some bedding. My grandfather was the main person that was arranging for that ceremony and I didn't take an active part in it because I was only a teenager. That was his glory and even though it was in my honor it wasn't up to me to give it. The people who were taking part in it were the chiefs and the other responsible men of my village and all the people they had invited from the other villages. After that we settled down to our new life in that village.

I was glad to be back at Village Island. That little village of about two or three hundred people was where I had spent most of my early life and I felt like it was my home. It was to be my home for the next fifteen years. In the fall of the year when the fishing season for the cannery was over I would sometimes be lucky enough to get a job in some logging camp for a couple of months. A lot of times I never bothered to look for a job because in November and December there just weren't any jobs around. I would just stay in Village Island and gather food to live on or work at things around that village. In January and February I used to go with some of the other people to dig clams on some of the other small islands near there where the clam digging was especially good. There were some buyers who would come around and buy the clams we had dug but we would always keep enough for our families to eat. Sometimes I would go out fishing for myself in my spare time for dogfish and halibut. I had a friend who owned a little plant in Victoria where they processed dogfish liver for the oil. He would send me some great big 45-gallon barrels and I would buy dogfish livers from others who were fishing and send them down to Victoria on the steamboat.

Moses Alfred had given us a little two-room house that he owned in Alert Bay and when we moved to Village Island we floated it over and made a place for it right on the beach. Most of the houses there were up on a bluff that was fifty or sixty feet above the water. There was a little trail up from the beach to these houses which were placed in a long row all facing the little bay which was in front of the village. David Matilpi helped me float that house over and get it set up. Miss O'Brien, the Anglican missionary, was still there at that time and she had a little house on a float down on the beach near ours. Another missionary had come with her to be the schoolteacher of the little school that they held in that house on the beach. Miss Nixon was her name, and she was the same teacher who had been there when I had gone to that school for a couple of months before I was married.

The minister in Alert Bay told Miss Nixon to have a little confirmation class for some of us at Village Island who were interested. There were two or three of us who used to meet with her to study the catechism and church creeds. She taught me all that I was supposed to know in order to become confirmed in the church. When we studied the Ten Commandments she used to emphasize that we should live up to our marriage. She talked to us about all the different sins of the world. She warned us about drinking and said that if we were out getting drunk then our families were going to be poor and pretty soon our wives would lose their respect for us and we would lose our friends. That was part of her teaching, and she used to ask us to ask her questions about all those things, which we did. She was a great old teacher. When I was ready she told the minister in Alert Bay to get ready for my confirmation when the Bishop came to Alert Bay. When the time came there was a special service held at Christ Church and I was confirmed by Bishop Schofield. There were quite a few of us who went through it from

St. Michael's school as well as the various villages. We went up to
the altar two at a time and the Bishop laid his hands on us and we
were confirmed. I didn't feel anything special and I can't remember
too much that went on, but it was then that I began to feel that I
should have more responsibility for the work of the church. Miss
O'Brien was quite a wealthy woman from England and most of the
time she used her own money in all the work she did for my people
at Village Island. I always used to do all I could to help those two
old ladies.

One of my closest friends was Simon Beans. He was married to a
girl who was my wife's aunt, and I was always very close to him.
They were married just one year before us and when they came to
Village Island they were both strangers to my village. That is why
we were so close to them, and we would always be together visiting
in their house or they would come and visit us. Simon was a very
close relation of mine and so we were very close and I did all I could
to give him all the advice he wanted. He was very helpful to me also
in everything I did. Robby wasn't married yet and he used to stay
with us in our house down there on the beach.

During those winters at Village Island the people from other
villages used to come and invite us to go to a big potlatch somewhere. When they arrived to invite us there were usually twenty
or thirty people who came and sometimes as many as fifty. It was
customary when they arrived in our village to invite them up to
have a big feast and give a small potlatch. We gave them a meal
and then the leading men of the village would give some money
away to the people that had come to invite us. I used to take part in
that with what little money I had. I would gather up all I could and
give it away in order to take part in what was going on because
they looked upon me as a leader of the Kwiksutainuk people who
were at Village Island. I was taking the place of my grandfather
and my father and they looked upon me to do this whether I liked
it or not. A lot of the time my mother would give away things and
give me money to give away because it wouldn't be right if I didn't
do it. If I didn't take part in that giving, then when the people went
home they would talk about me and things like that. Sometimes I
would be up in the woods working and I wouldn't even know that
it was going on. Then my mother or my grandfather would give

something away for me and mention my name that I was the one that was giving it.

The people didn't respect those young men who spent all their money on drinking and gambling and weren't able to give anything when the other tribes came to invite us to their village. There were two or three people in Village Island who used to make home brew and drink and play cards all night. One day after they had been at this the Kingcome people came and called all the Village Island people together. There were about 150 people that came into Jim Bell's big house when he called them. Jim Bell and others gave some things away and then he stood up and made a speech about these three fellows who had been drinking and didn't have anything to give away. He named them right in front of all those people and then said, "What's the matter with you? Why don't you do something for these people who have come to visit us? I thought that's why you were playing cards all night, to make all kinds of money. Why don't you give something to these people? You are an awful disgrace to this village. What would you do if we weren't here? People would just come into this village and nobody would look after them!" That was a strong speech to get from a man that was so respectable, and those three fellows didn't open their mouths. They just sat there and held their heads down almost between their knees. If it had been a white man talking to them they might have just said, "To hell with you," or something like that, but not to such a respectable Indian. It was the Indian custom in those days that if they argued back that would have cost them money. In those days there were only a few people who would get drunk every weekend. Jim Bell would take a drink once in a while or he might just "wash his stomach out" at the end of the fishing season, but that was all. It was a disgrace in those days for an Indian to be drunk, and nobody wanted to have anything to do with a drunk Indian who was just falling and staggering down the road. It was a big disgrace to be seen in such a condition by your father or mother or grandfather or uncle. All the time they would have been praising you as a young respectable person and if you got drunk it meant that that they would have to call the people together and give a potlatch to make up for that disgrace. The people were very proud in those days and there were some great men among the Indians. They were so great and so respected that nobody could do anything to shame them. They were great and everything they did was the best, and they would call the people together and give really big potlatches. They were really big and the people just came together and would be happy because there was lots to eat and all kinds of articles and things to take home.

Around April every year we would move up to the cannery at Knight's Inlet and stay there until October or November. Some of the people stayed at Village Island, especially the older people. I stopped in there a few times during the summer when we were out fishing. When we arrived at Knight's Inlet we would settle our things into these one-room houses the cannery owned and begin our work. The first thing I did was to work repairing the nets and getting them ready for the fishing. There was a lot of building going on up there and the manager used to move me around. I would work on the pile driver, which was used to repair the wharf. He used to ask me to work with the contractor who had come up from Vancouver to build a new addition to the cannery. Sometimes the freight boat would come in to pick up the canned salmon which was left over from the previous year and still stored in the warehouses. The manager used to come and see me about getting the boys to go and load the canned salmon. Sometimes we would start loading at 7 or 8 at night after we had worked all day in the net loft. We would work all night loading and then go home for breakfast and then right out to our other jobs. Sometimes this happened for a whole week and we hardly got any sleep at all. We were getting paid for it but it wasn't much since we didn't ever get overtime pay or anything like that. I used to like it because it was during the depression and the more hours you worked the more money you made. That was the way I felt about it. I had to do it because I had a family to support.

Around June we had finished all the work on the nets and the other work around the cannery and our boats started coming in. They were all company boats that were kept in Steveston during the winter and a man delivered them to us at the cannery. As soon as Henry Bell's boat came in we loaded the net and other things on and then went to pick up our crew in Alert Bay and the other villages. I was running the engine for him. I used to love that job. After we picked up our fishing license in Alert Bay we would go out fishing from June to October. Although I was the engineer on Henry's seine boat I used to try everything. I would put one of my friends down in the engine room and go up on the wheel and make a "set." There are many different ways to make a set, but in all of them you have to let the net out where you think there might be some fish, and then when it is out you circle around and get the other end of it. Then the bottom of the net is all pulled together and you have to pull the net in and get any fish you have caught on board. If Henry Bell was going to have his supper or take a little sleep he would say to me, "All right, Jimmy, you take over." I would watch and if I saw a fish jumping, I would make a set. Sometimes he wouldn't tell me to do that, but if I knew that he was busy eating or sleeping I would just go up there and do it. I used to do about everything on the boat. I was a real handyman and would man the nets, do some cooking, splice the ropes and lines, and work in the engine room. There wasn't anything that I didn't do on his boat. There was no control for the engine in the pilot house so I had to stay down in the engine room most of the time, especially when we were making a set. Henry would be ringing the bells which signaled me to back up, kick ahead slow, and go ahead full speed. Unless someone else was down there the only time I went up was when we had made a set and were pulling in the net. Then I would work on deck with the rest of the crew. I used to like working in the engine room because that was my job.

Every weekend during the fishing season we returned to Knight's Inlet for supplies. We had to get fuel, oil, water, and coal for the stove on the boat. If there was any damage that had been done to the net we would repair them when we came in. While I was out fishing Flora would be working in the cannery. Her job was to put the salmon that had been cut up into the cans and these would be stacked on a tray. She was paid for how many trays of canned salmon she did each day. When I was home on the weekends the ladies were usually free and so we would all go up the little river there and have a picnic. We would fish for trout and the kids would all play around and swim in the river. Sometimes it would take us six or seven hours to get back to the fishing grounds so we usually left early on Sunday morning.

One winter not too long after we had moved to Village Island we were staying in Alert Bay and our second baby was born. I don't remember what was going on at that time but I don't think I was working, except for a few odd jobs. Just after that boy was born I went into the delivery room at the hospital to see him. He was born on December 9, 1931, during the depression, and we named him Eugene Daniel.

George Luther was still teaching in the day school at Alert Bay and I used to see him and talk with him. One spring he decided to build a new house and so he tore his old house down and started to build a new one. There were some people trying to build this house for him and they couldn't even put the foundation posts in, so they had to go to Village Island to get me. My wife's father came up in his seine boat to get me and he asked me, "I wonder if you can come and help the old man? He is building a house." Moses Alfred was related to the old man, George Luther. "Well," I said, "I'm going to go up to Knight's Inlet in five days time because the cannery is opening up then." Well, I decided I might as well go and do something anyway to help him out. I came to Alert Bay and in five days I put the posts in, the sidings on, the windows in, the partitions on, and the roof on. Of course there were four or five guys helping me do this, and I was just instructing them. I was just cutting the lumber. We had no plan for building that house but I used to talk to George Luther and ask him, "What shape roof are you going to have? How many rooms are you going to have?" and all that. He just told me what kind of roof he was going to have and all that. I used to work until it was dark because I wanted to do all I could before I left. While I was away they did the inside work but I helped some more when I was back in Alert Bay. When it was all done George wrote me a nice letter and thanked me for what I did building his house. He was very pleased with his house.

One time, during those early years at Village Island, my grandfather came to me and told me once again that he was going to put on a big do and it was going to be the last one. And he told me, "I want you to be my top dancer," because that is what they called it. The highest dancer had to be the oldest son or the oldest grandson because it would be a disgrace to him if he took one of the younger ones. And I told him, "No, I don't want to be the one. I've got a lot of cousins, why don't you take one of them?" And he said, "Oh, no, that's not allowed. You have got to be the one." Well, I just figured that I shouldn't do it because I already had a couple children and I guess I was afraid of the law at that time. It was against the law to have potlatches and put on those dances and I didn't want to break the law. I always liked to be on the right side of the law ever since I was a little boy.

Well, all the people got together right away and Jim Bell announced to them that I didn't want to go through with it. Well, the people all said to him, "You can't have anybody else, it has to be him. He is going to have to go through with it. He is the rightful owner of that dance that was given to him when he married Flora. That is the dance that was given by the great chief Odzistales." Well, I didn't have any sons old enough to take the place of the top dancer so I had to do it. Anyway, I gave in. It was the time to open that big chest which had all the regalia and different dances in it that had been given to me by the Fort Rupert Kwakiutl when I got married. My grandfather had been holding all those things for me and it was up to us to take them out of that box and perform those dances. It was time for me to become a hamatsa.

In our Indian way we had lots of important names for the positions in the clans of the various tribes of the Kwakiutl nation. During the winter time the people used to put on their dances, and there were also important names and positions for the groups of people who had the right to those dances. There were lots of different dances, and some were for people of low positions and others were for people who were in high positions. The highest dance group was the hamatsa or Cannibal society. In order for a person to become a hamatsa he had to have the right to a name and a position in that group given to him from his ancestors or his wife's ancestors. Then there was a long ceremony to go through in order to really become a hamatsa. I had seen many of these at Village Island when I was growing up, and all the leading men of the other villages would come there and a young man would become a new hamatsa. The older hamatsas were only the men in the highest positions in all the tribes, and they would teach these young men to go through this ceremony and help them to become hamatsas. It was a very important position and that was why Jim Bell wanted me to go through with that and all the other people that were around me. That ceremony would go on for two or three weeks and the people would come from all over the Kwakiutl nation. There was one man who would be the master of ceremonies and he would tell the different people when to do their dances. There were always other new dancers for the other groups which were not as important as the hamatsa, but everything started with the hamatsa and that was the center of the whole winter ceremony. I had already become a dancer in some of the other groups when I was younger. The first time I became one was for my uncle Spruce Martin when I danced for him in Alert Bay when I was about five years old.

As soon as I gave in and decided to go through with it my grandfather sent word out to the other villages inviting them to come to our village. The day before everyone arrived I was supposed to disappear into the woods and go and seek the supernatural power of the Cannibal Spirit. I lived up in the woods for about ten days. In the early days they used to stay up in the woods for three or four months. My grandfather had been out that long when he first became a hamatsa. On the day that I disappeared into the woods I left all my clothes in the village and just dressed in some hemlock branches that were put around me. Some of the older hamatsas were up in the woods and they all began to blow on the whistles which were supposed to be the voices of the supernatural beings in the woods. Although I disappeared into the woods I didn't actually live up there all the time. Alfred Dawson was also a new hamatsa at that time and one other fellow. We would go out in the woods all day and then sneak back into our houses at night. In the morning we would leave before anybody was up so that nearly everyone thought we were out in the woods the whole time. My grandfather told me to go up in the woods in the morning and bathe in a stream or pool of water because I would need the strength to dance at night. We used to just walk around in the woods and never go near the village because there were lots of things going on there. They were dancing and giving potlatches and all the other things that were part of that winter ceremony. They hired a couple of my close relatives to stay with me at all times to be sure that nothing happened to me while I was walking around up there in the woods. I used to ask them to bring me something to eat, but although they brought our lunch up there they didn't give us much to eat. They wanted me to

reduce and thin down by fasting. So every morning I took a cold
bath and rubbed myself down with branches where nobody could
see me. It was winter time but that was supposed to make me tough
and feel light so I would be ready when the day came for me to
come back to the village and dance. Sometimes during the day I
would come into the village and show myself to the public for a
minute or two and then rush back into the woods. All I had around
me was the hemlock branches and when I did this all the different
kinds of whistles would be blowing. They all had different tones
which imitated the raven and geese and all the different birds of
the woods. In the early days they really lived up to this ceremony,
and when they were in the woods getting the supernatural power
they didn't eat hardly anything and became very light and thin. I
didn't feel anything special when I was up there.

The day after we disappeared into the woods the people started
arriving from the other villages. They used to take two or three
canoes with little gas motors on the back of them and tie them together to make the trip. As the people came into the village they
had their regalia on and would start singing. All of their dancers
were ready. Then the Village Island people all went down on the
beach and as soon as the people got out of their boats they performed some dances for these visitors. Then all the people came
up into the village, and they had woven a long piece of cedar bark
and all the people held onto it and formed a big circle all the way
around the community house where the dances were going to be
held. They walked around and around the house holding onto this
cedar bark which formed a big ring. Then they laid it down on a
large canvas and a special man cut it into pieces for all of the
people to make smaller rings which they put on their heads. The
hamatsas all got theirs first and then all the other people. The dance
connected with the hamatsa is called the "cedar bark dance," and
when it began later on all the people put these rings on their heads.
Then my grandfather gave a big feast for all the people and gave
some things away.

Every night the people were all called into the big house where
different dances were performed. They did these dances each night
in order to bring back the new hamatsas from the woods. While
we were in the woods we were supposed to become wild men and

they were trying to bring us back to civilization. At night after the dances were over the hamatsas would all stay in the big community house and eat and sleep there. It was at this time that all the retired hamatsas would come and teach me how to dance and the new songs. They kept all of this a secret and nobody else could watch except the retired hamatsas. It was awful hard for me to take because they just sat there watching me dance and if I made any mistakes they told me to do it all over again. They didn't like the way I was doing it. It was really something for me to learn because I had never been through it before and didn't know what I had to do. The people teaching and watching me all knew because they had all been through it before. It was very important to perform that dance exactly right and not to trip and fall when you were doing it. And they told me that when I came in I was to pretend that I was fierce and wild. In every dance I was supposed to just run around like I was wild.

My grandfather hired singers and composers for the songs that were sung each night. There were singers from all of the other villages. They picked all the best singers and they were getting paid every night. The most important singers were paid a couple of dollars each night and the others were paid a little less. These singers all knew my songs which had been given to me from my grandfather Aul Sewid as well as some new songs that had been composed for this particular time. My grandfather had hired three or four composers to make up these new songs and teach them to the singers. All these new songs were telling the history of my father's side of the family and my mother's side in our language. During the dances each night while I was out in the woods, these singers were singing other songs while certain men were beating on the drums and beating the sticks on a long wooden log that was partially hollowed out. They were saving my songs until I came back from being with the Cannibal Spirit.

Finally the night came when I was going to return and all the people from all over the Kwakiutl nation were giving their dances. They started about 7 that night and it went on until about 3 in the morning. Each tribe and clan and family had their own songs and different kinds of dances. I was watching through a crack in the wall from a little room in the back of the big community house where I was hiding. No one knew I was there except the hamatsas because everything was a secret, but I'm telling the truth now. And I watched as all the different dancers came in and did the feather dance and the ladies did the paddle dance. They stood in front of the singers and made motions like they were paddling a canoe. Others did the salmon dance and the ghost dance and many others. Nobody could ever do a dance that did not belong to them or to one of their relatives. If one of the leading men wanted to have a particular dance done for him he could only do it if one of his relatives had a right to that dance and then he could call them in and have it done. Some of the dances that were done had a lot of clowning in them. And they were doing all of this to attract me and the other new hamatsas to come back to civilization, which wasn't so easy.

I had been told to watch for a particular dance which was going to be the last one at the end of all this dancing. They warned me that when that dance came I had to sneak out of that little room and go up on top of the big house. I saw someone talking to my stepfather, my grandfather, and Ed Whanock from that place where I was hiding and knew that it was time to go up. It was important for them to help me get up on the roof because in the early days that was when your enemies would do something to cripple you while you were climbing up. Of course we all have enemies and I had heard about this sort of thing happening at those big dos. They would try to do something to you so that you couldn't come out or so that you might come out crippled, and this would disgrace your family and the chief who was giving the ceremony. I had to come out a perfect man in perfect health. So I went out to the back of that house and put only my hemlock branches on around my body and on my wrists, ankles, and head. I had nothing on but branches. It was a cold winter night and the snow was falling. Dave Matilpi held the ladder while I climbed up and then stayed there so that no one else could come up. Ed Whanock was up on the roof and he had several of the hamatsa whistles with him. Ed knew the exact spot where I would remove a couple of the boards on the roof and go in. I was waiting up there patiently for my time to come and I was very cold. So then a certain dance came in that was the cousin of the Cannibal Spirit, which was my dance. This person began dancing and every time he jumped he held his head up and shouted, calling for me to come. On his third time of jumping and calling he was right in the middle of the house and we removed a couple of the boards and Ed Whanock began to blow this whistle.

As soon as the people heard this whistle they knew I was coming. All the dancers got behind a great big curtain at the end of the house and they all stayed there until I came in, no matter how late it was. Everybody was looking up because they heard this whistle and the master of ceremonies quickly told everybody to get up. And everybody got up and there was a lot of commotion and it was just as if everybody was panicky. Ed Whanock held my legs and I lowered myself halfway into the house and showed half of my body to the crowd. I was making the hamatsa noise and I could see all the people standing up and swaying their hands, which is the way they would greet one another. Some of them were chanting and beating with the sticks and there was a terrific noise that I heard up there. I had a strange feeling when they received me that night as I was hanging down through the roof. They were all chanting the songs and swaying their hands. I don't know how to express it, but it was a wonderful feeling to see all the people swaying their hands at me. It was something that I was going through that not many persons could go through.

Then Ed and I moved over to another spot and removed some of the boards and I went through again. The people were all down there chanting and about thirty or forty people were beating the drums and sticks. It was out of this world what they were doing, and I can't express how I felt. It made me feel funny, made me feel out of this world, everything that was going on in there that I could see down below me in the big house. Then we moved to another place and at this last one there was a rope tied to the big log of the roof and that is where I slid in. And all the hamatsas from the different villages were there with a big strong blanket to receive me. I jumped onto this blanket from the end of the rope and I'll never forget that when I came through my mother was crying. She just cried and cried because I guess she thought it was so real that I had come back to civilization again after I had been away so long.

My grandfather had picked a group of prominent young men from all the different villages and paid them to look after me during the ceremony. They all came right close to me and didn't allow anybody to come near me while we began to go around the fire in the center of the big house. At the far end of the house from the door was where the singers sat and the people who beat the drums and the sticks. All of a sudden when we came near that end of the house I broke away from those boys who were with me and went under a place in that end of the house and disappeared again. Right away the master of ceremonies got up and told everybody to sit down. When they had quieted down he said, "He does not altogether like to come with us or to come near us. It is a good thing that he came and showed himself to us so that we were able to see him again. We wish to see him again tomorrow and to have him visit us. I'd like to thank you all for what you have done tonight." And then everybody went home and slept for a little while except for the hamatsas.

That night after they had gone out I came back to work with all the retired hamatsas putting up the screen. During the previous nights several good painters had been painting a figure on this big wooden screen. Sometimes these screens were made out of cloth but mine was a wooden one. They painted the form of a man on it and in the stomach of this man they had a little round door through which I would come when I was to dance. It took about three hours to get this screen all nailed together and the branches all put around it. It had to be placed at the end of the house. All the hamatsas were there working together to get everything ready. The Kwakiutl tribes were strong in those days and they really worked together. That is where I learned what it meant to have unity and work together. Some of them would be sleeping for a while as others took care of the fire, gathered branches, or worked on the screen. Every time somebody was going to pound a nail a group of them would pound the sticks and make the hamatsa cry so that it would drown out the sound of pounding. When the pounding stopped they would stop making noise until someone began pounding again. When everything was ready we all slept until daylight. Then we all got up and went into the woods after breakfast to our place where we practiced the songs and dances. It was a secret place and nobody could come there except the hamatsas. This was the second day of my return and we all got ready for that part of the ceremony.

Then the master of ceremonies notified one particular man to go around to all the houses and call everybody to come to a big field there in the village. It was about 8 or 9 in the morning and this was the time when I was supposed to come in on my own. Then they formed a big procession with all the people doing their dances as they approached the big community house. When they got to the house they all went in one at a time and did their dance and then sat down. I was supposed to be the last one to come in. When they were ready I came in just wearing the hemlock branches and also the large hamatsa mask. They referred to that mask and the others which would be used for me as "my children." Some of the masks had large beaks on them and these were clapping together and making a loud noise as we came in. There were about twelve to fifteen boys with me that had been hired by my grandfather. They were real strong boys with blankets around them and no shoes on. They had been picked to look after me each time that I came in and especially before I was tame. Well, as I came in that morning I didn't dance in the right way but just stamped and ran and pretended that I wasn't completely ready to be with them there. I danced for a little while and then I would just go wild again, which is the reason they call it the wild man dance. Oh, it was really a man-killer. There were two of those fellows pushing me while I ran and danced and I would just run away with them hanging onto my arms, pulling them along. And all the time I was going around, the hamatsa whistles were going and the singers were singing and others were beating the drums and sticks. Then I disappeared by running in behind the big screen that had been made especially for me. Then they told all the people that they could go home until that night.

That night as all the people gathered in the big house the whistles were being blown slowly and gently all the time. They were never supposed to stop. I was hiding behind the screen on that special night. It was going to be another big night for me because they were going to try to tame me. Then the door of the screen which was in the stomach of the figure opened up and I came out to be the first dancer of the evening. All the trained singers were lined up outside of that door where I came out and they were singing my songs. They knew all the songs both new and old that told the history of my father's side and my mother's side of the family. I had been told that when I came out I should never stop moving but just to pretend that I still didn't want to dance until they finally held me down. I didn't have any cedar bark on but only the hemlock branches, and I went running around the big house in the wrong direction, doing a few dance steps and then stamping and running again to show that I didn't have any sense. Then the master of ceremonies gave the order to the boys who were with me to try to hold me down. When they tried I just jumped up and ran around again. Finally they just really pushed me down and held me down on the dirt floor.

Then as they were holding me down a specially chosen retired hamatsa who had blackened his face came out with a long pole. This pole was about ten feet long, and they tore an old blanket in strips and tied them to the end of this pole. They dipped that end of the pole into some water so that when they set fire to the pieces of blanket it would just smoke and not burn. He held the stick over the fire until the blanket pieces began to burn and it really started to stink. They call this *nueelqual* in our language. Then he came over to where these boys were holding me down and sitting on me. All the whistles were going and the people were beating the sticks all the time. He took this burning rag which was smoking and smelling and swung it over my head one time. As soon as he did this I jumped up and gave my hamatsa cry and started to try to move around again. When they got me down again this fellow ran over and put this burning rag over me again and this time I became a little less wild. On the third time that he put it over me I didn't move too much and just pretended that I was getting weaker. It was part of the play that I would keep weakening each time that they put that smoking rag over my head. On the fourth time I didn't move at all and then the whistles became very faint. This man then threw the pole into the fire and all the retired hamatsas began to make their cries and came down around me making noise with their rattles. Then the whistles stopped and it was finished. They took off all the hemlock branches and put brand-new cedar bark on me that had been made by the experts.

Then I began to dance in the proper way while they were singing my songs. I was not quite tame so that after one or two dances I would run around a little again. Then some of my relatives who had been picked came out and danced some of those dances and showed some of the masks that belonged to me and had come in that chest when I was married. All the time I was dancing those boys who were looking after me stayed right close to me. They sang four of my songs and on the fourth one, when I got over near the door, I just disappeared out of the door and left those boys standing there. They all began to push each other and cry out, "What happened to him?" Then they blamed each other real loud and said, "You shouldn't have let him go." One of them ran out after me and came back in a couple of minutes bringing my beautiful brand-new cedar bark. He brought it into the center of the big house and announced: "He is not quite ready to come to us yet and he is gone again. We have to expect and hope for the best." That ended the hamatsa dance and then all the different dances began. They did the swan dance and the ghost dance and many others until about 10 or 11, when everybody went home. As they were coming out of the big house to go home they could hear the hamatsa whistles way up in the woods. Those boys who were picked to be with me had come up there and were making the noises of the birds and then everybody knew that we were up there for something.

Just before daylight on the next morning I came in on my own free will with my mask that somebody had brought to me in the woods. I went behind that screen and stayed there all day until the big ceremony began that night. On this night I came out with the cedar bark on and danced many of my dances. I was the first one out and danced for a couple of hours. I was very tame then and was being very careful not to make any mistakes. The fourth night was the last one and I had to dance again for about the same length of time. They sang about eight of my songs that night. Each of these last two nights after I had danced the others all came out and danced too. All the masks and songs and dances that I had received from my ancestors were shown on those nights. Before any of those dances would be shown the master of ceremonies would announce where I got them from and tell everybody that I had a right to them. Some of my relatives came out and did different dances in my honor that they owned. In the early days the big chiefs had large dances because that showed what great men they were. That was why I used many dances, even some my grandfather didn't own but some other relative did, because my group of dances had to be large. Some of those dances were the ones that my grandfather Aul Sewid had received when he married into the Bella Coola people.

And when everything was completed on the fourth night they called everybody together to give us new hamatsas a bath. In my language they called us, "They're going to give you a bath." It wasn't really a bath in water but they used a great big circle of branches that was about five feet in diameter. All the chiefs were holding this ring of branches and I had to step inside of that circle and they rubbed me down with it. While they were rubbing me down it was the custom for them all to say something to me about my character. Some of the things they said were kind of like teasing me. I was the first one to be put through those branches and they told me to behave and to be kind to my friends and all sorts of things like that. I had to stand on my right leg all the time through that and then I stepped out. Right after the bath ceremony there was a big do and Jim Bell gave a lot of stuff away. He gave away money, clothes, shirts, pails, dishes, pots and pans, and many blankets. He gave it to all the people that had been taking part in the ceremony. The chiefs from the different villages received some expensive gold broaches and bracelets and he gave them more than the other people. Those hamatsa positions were all in me then and I felt that I was honored in a high position because that was a very high dance. You had to be an honored and a respected man to go through that kind of thing and not very many people went through that. After that I had the right to do that hamatsa dance any time I felt like it and to take part in any ceremonies where some other young man was becoming a hamatsa.

Just a couple of days later, before any of the people had returned to their villages, we heard that a sergeant of the mounted police was coming up to Village Island to investigate what was going on. They had heard about our dance there and that a young man had been put through it, which was against the law. That was why they sent this sergeant all the way from Ottawa. All the chiefs of the different villages were still all together when this mounted police came in. He told us, "I have been sent from the government to investigate what was going on in this village and I'd like to see what it is that you were doing." He demanded to see it that night, so we put on a good show for him. The dances we did were all mixed together and not in the right way we had been doing them. I was dancing with a fool's mask on along with a group of masks. The mounted police was standing to one side of the house while the big dance was going on and one of our people was interpreting to him what it was all about. And he asked him, "What is that dance there?" referring to me. "Well," he said, "he is supposed to be a person who doesn't know anything and just imitates anything he sees. We call it the fool dance because he is supposed to be a man that doesn't know anything." Then this mounted police said, "Oh, you people are all wrong. I think he is the smartest dancer in the whole works. He can dance any dance." Well, I was just giving it all I could. I was so strong that I was able to dance with that heavy mask on for over an hour.

When the announcer said that the ceremony was over the mounted police said, "I'd like to see the young man that went through this thing. I'd like to see him dance for me tonight because I was sent here to investigate this young man. I want him to dance with everything he had on, all his masks and everything. I want him to do it just like the way he did it last week." He was referring to me and the people named my name to him. Well, the chiefs of the village all come and looked for me and found me in the back of the big house and they said, "You have to come out and dance. The mounted police wants you to come and dance for him." So I got all my stuff on and the others who were dancing my dances and came out and started dancing. After I came out my masks came out and danced. At the end he got up and thanked the people and said, "It was a wonderful dance. I really enjoyed it. I can't see anything wrong with it." After that he went back to Ottawa. That was part of my becoming a hamatsa and it was a good thing they didn't lock me up.

My old grandmother Lucy was getting quite old and so she wasn't able to come to Village Island when I became a hamatsa. She was awfully happy that I had two children, Dora and Eugene, and I used to take the kids over to her and visit her whenever I could. She used to say to me, "Whenever you talk to your children, talk gently and never talk rough. If you talk rough to them they are going to be like that. You have to be very gentle and show them your love and kindness. That is all they need." She was getting too old to walk even as far as the church and so she would go to a little Pentecostal church that had started up in Alert Bay right next door to her house. I used to go with her once in a while when I was in Alert Bay but I didn't think too much of their ways. Shouting, crying, and jumping around were just not my way of worshiping God. Old Lucy told me that she didn't like it either. They used to force her to stand up and testify and she told me she never liked that. She used to tell me, "God is everywhere and you can quietly speak to him. It doesn't matter where you are, you can always turn to him, especially in your troubles. He is ready to help you." That was her belief and that was always my belief.

About that time on one of my visits to Alert Bay the district nurse came and told me, "I think you had better stay with her. She is geting pretty weak now but she is up and around." I went in to see her and said, "I'd like to stay with you tonight. I don't want you to be alone and I'd like to look after the fire." "Oh, no," she said, "I want you to go home to your children and your wife. I'm not alone because Somebody else is looking after me. I don't want you to worry about me. You'd better go home." So I had no choice. I had to walk out, which was really hard because I felt that I should stay. My wife's mother and aunt went there the next morning and found her kneeling down at her beside where she was praying. She was dead. She must have been praying when she died. She was a very kind and humble woman. I just don't know how to express it. That was in 1932 and she was about 71 years old according to the records in the Indian Office, but I figured she must have been close to 100.

The year after old Lucy died we came to stay in Alert Bay for a little while in July. Eugene was a year and a half old and beginning to walk. I felt very proud of my oldest son. One day when I wasn't home he fell and must have hurt his back. My wife woke me up that night after midnight and told me that he was crying and crying and wouldn't stop. It seemed to me that he had a lot of pain so in a few hours when it started to get light we took him to the hospital. Well, he didn't live through that day but died in the afternoon. That's all I can remember because it was a sad day for me. I felt awfully bad. It really broke my heart as a young man of only about twenty years. It was quite an experience. It was a dark day and I just don't remember anything. It was awful and I can't even describe it now. It was just as if I was going through darkness and I think it really shortened my life. I just had Dora and Eugene at that time and didn't think of my other children coming. My wife was really lost without that boy. That was a terrible experience for us. My wife blamed a lot of strawberries that he had eaten that day, but according to the doctor he had spinal meningitis as a result of his fall. We didn't have much money at that time and there were people in Alert Bay kind of looking after us. My wife stayed there while I went out fishing, and just a month later Louisa was born. My wife stayed there with her family until the fishing was over and then we went back to Village Island for the winter with just our two girls.

4 Where They Can Get Copper

In November of the next year, when I was 21, Mr. Matthews came to me when we were closing down the cannery for the winter. He said to me, "Jimmy, I'm going to give you a boat next year. I want you to be the skipper on the 'Annandale' which is the best boat our company owns." Mr. Matthews had been the manager of the cannery as long as I could remember. He was there when I started working for the company as a crew member with my grandfather Jim Bell, I had been running the engine on Henry Bell's boat for about nine years. So the next spring when the fishing season began I went out fishing as the skipper of the "Annandale." I was worried just like any other man would be when I started out on this new job. I felt awfully alone because all of the years before that I had been fishing under my uncle Henry Bell and my grandfather or some other skipper. I always felt that someday I would have the responsibility of being a skipper. I was very anxious but I was willing to put all my mind to what I was doing, and it didn't take me too long to overcome that feeling of being alone and being so scared. I used to pray to our Creator to help me as I went out the first thing in the morning. My old grandmother Lucy had told me that before I did anything, no matter what it was I was going to do that day, that I should always look up to my Maker to guide me. I believed her quite a bit. I thought it was very important to look up to somebody who would guide me in my work because I was young and inexperienced.

I left Knight's Inlet and went over by the mouth of the Nimpkish River where I made my first set. As soon as we had made that set someone came and told me that my wife had just had a baby. She had stayed in Alert Bay because she was expecting a baby, so right away I came in to see her and that little boy that was born. I felt awfully happy that I had a boy again. We named him Harold Robert. Mr. Matthews happened to be in Alert Bay at that time and he was happy that I had caught a few fish and that I had a boy, a

son. When he was a few weeks old I took Flora back up to the
cannery to stay in that little shack which was just a little bigger
than one room. The bed and the stove were all there in the same
room where we stayed. I remember Bobby used to cry because it
was so awfully hot up there in the summertime. My wife would take
all his clothes off and let him just lie naked in his bed and then he
would be all right and stop crying.

My grandfather had retired from being a skipper quite a few
years before that, but that first year I was a skipper he wanted to
come with me. So I thought that I would put him on because I
knew he was going to be a great help to me. I used to ask him
questions about the tides and where the best place to fish was. Well,
he got sick one night on the boat and I took him into Alert Bay the
next morning to the hospital. He died in the hospital just a few
hours after that. I felt very bad because I had been so close to him.
I had lived in his house when I wasn't staying with my grandmother Lucy as a young boy and he had more or less raised me
with my uncle Robert Bell, although he never adopted me legally.
He was a very quiet man and a very kind man. He was very soft-
spoken. He didn't have any education whatsoever but was brought
up in the real Indian customs. He was a very respectable man in my
village and had belonged to a very high society on both his mother's
side and his father's side. I felt pretty bad when the old man died
because I felt closer to him than anybody. He had been the first
Indian skipper for the A. B. C. Packing Company for which we
worked. I had fished under him lots of times and we had often gone
drag seining together. When he was raising me I don't remember
him ever punishing me, but if I did anything wrong he would just
tell me quietly why I shouldn't have done it and all that. I didn't
feel there was any point in dragging all the people away from the
cannery and fishing, so it was mostly all the family who came to
Alert Bay for the funeral. We had a very good funeral for him in
the church. My mother and my uncles and all my relatives were
there.

After that I went back to fishing on the "Annandale." It was very
difficult to be a good skipper and I worked awfully hard. I had a
very good crew at that time and we were almost the top boat in
the company that first year. Before the end of the fishing season I

went into the cannery office to get a small advance on my money. I asked for $5, and Mr. Matthews came out of his office and asked me, "What are you going to do with $5?" "Well," I said, "I want to pay for a C.O.D. parcel that has come for me." And he said to me, "You better come into my office, I want to talk to you." So I went in. "Jimmy," he said, "when are you going to start to think like a man? If you are going to come in here and ask me for $5, when are you going to come to your senses and think about buying yourself a net and getting yourself a boat? You know that the Yugoslavians and the Italians that are working for us all have good boats and you fellows don't have anything!" "Well," I said, "I haven't got any money to pay down." Oh, he really bawled me out. "That's it! How are you going to have money if you just throw your money around? You have a lot of nerve to come in here and ask for $5. It is about time you thought about your family. You are never going to be a man if you are going to start drawing out your money before the end of the season. That's the time you should get it and go home with plenty of money. I think it is about time now that you save up so that you can have your own boat and have your own net, and then you will have something to show for it instead of being like these other fellows that haven't got anything left at the end of the season. They just draw it out as fast as they make it." Well, that really made me think. Mr. Matthews was the kind of man who was very strict. The fishing week used to close at about 5 or 6 on Friday afternoon for the weekend and then it would often take five or six hours to get back to the cannery from the fishing grounds. If I came in at 5 or 6 he really got after me for wasting my time. I must say that I learned quite a bit from him and I thought he was a very fine man and good in his way. He was the man that taught me what responsibility really means to a person.

I fished as skipper of the "Annandale" for four years and did very well. Our company always kept a record of how much fish each boat caught during the year and we all knew at the end of the season which was the high boat. The top two or three boats were referred to as "highliners." I don't know how high I was, but I was doing fine. I was about average for the boats that were going out, but I was above some of the old-time skippers who had been fishing for that company for many years. I had worked with many of those

skippers and some of them were very easygoing, nice men. They
didn't push their crew too much and they didn't rush. They didn't
seem to care too much but just took things easy. I had worked with
those kind of skippers in my earlier days. Then too I had worked
with skippers who were really going to go after the fish. They
were really hard-working men who were rough and didn't have
mercy on their crew. They didn't slow down at all, especially if
there were any fish around. They just set and set and set and worked
hard. Some of the crew would be complaining, and the skipper
would just be rough with them and tell them that they must set
again because there were fish around. And that was the kind of man
I was as a skipper. I didn't know how my crew felt about me. I didn't
want to be mean to them or anything like that but it was just my
way; I liked to work fast and I'm still like that today. If a fellow was
slow or seemed lazy and didn't take any interest in what I wanted
to do I really went after him and told him to smarten up or else.
Being a skipper on a seine boat means you are responsible for firing
men and when they are family men that is quite a responsibility.
The captain is the man that is going to be responsible for their
families. I had to work hard in those days and I had a lot of trouble
with my crew. They were drunk all the time and I didn't like it so
I fired some of them. I was pretty tough at first. We would go
ashore into Alert Bay and they would get a bottle and start to drink
and then they came on board drunk and would have to sleep it off.
I had no alternative except to fire them and get another crew to
take their place.

I had some very good crew members also. Some of my crew
would bring a lot of books along, and when they came aboard they
would go down to their bunk and read until we made a set. Then
they came out and worked until the fish were all in and then they
went right back down and read. As the skipper I would be up at
the wheel for twelve to fourteen hours a day looking for fish. I
really thought that some of the crew could come up and help. I
really appreciated it when some crew member came up and would
see some fish jumping and tell me. When we came in on weekends
there was some work to be done around the boat like getting fuel
and groceries and coal for the stove. It was a lot of work for one
man to do but I used to do it all alone. We used to burn three or

four sacks of coal a week and I used to put them on my back and take them to the boat, which was an awful messy job.

I always checked the tide the night before we went fishing and decided on a place that I thought would have a lot of fish. When we let out our net most of the time we timed it so that the tide would bring the fish into the net, so I had to know the time when the tide would change. Then the next morning I would get up before daylight and go and take our position at the fishing grounds. There might be several boats there already and so we would have to wait until our turn came up for the good spot. When our turn came we would usually try to make an open set. I put two good men on the skiff and they would take one end of the net and row to the shore and find an old stump to tie the net to. It was important to have two good men because I couldn't be there watching them and they had to know how strong the tide was and where it would be good to tie up. I knew that when they had tied onto a big stump we had to stay there for fifteen or twenty minutes to allow the fish to be brought into the net by the tide. If the tide was too strong and they tied onto a little log, then when we began to pull the net around with the boat the log would come down and the fish would get away. There are a lot of mistakes that can be made in catching fish, and I have seen other boats set around a much bigger school of fish than we set around and they didn't get as many fish as we did because of some foolish move they made.

Well, after the net was tied to the shore I would stand up at the wheel and watch for the fish. Our net would be strung out in a large half circle. I could tell by the way the fish jumped which kind of fish were coming into the net. I always watched for the herring to jump because the salmon feed on the herring and this meant that they were there too. The herring come in large numbers and they are quite small and lots of them would be jumping at the same time. There are all different species of salmon: spring salmon, sockeye, coho and pink salmon, dog salmon (which are chums), and steelhead. The sockeye is the most expensive and has nice red meat which is very rich. I always liked to catch a lot of sockeye. A coho salmon is a lazy jumper; he comes right up out of the water and makes a loop, diving in head first. A dog salmon jumps at an angle, sort of on his side. Dogs are real strong fish, as well as sockeye, very strong. We always refer to a fish jumping as a "finner." We would all be watching for fish to jump near the net and when somebody saw a finner breaking the surface of the water he would holler to me up on the wheel.

Right away I would begin to move the boat slowly around in a big circle back to the shore where the two men in the skiff would be waiting. When we were close enough they would come out to the boat in their skiff with the other end of the net. I usually used a net that was about 150 feet in width so it would go down pretty deep. The lead weights along the bottom would make it go right down and the cork floats along the top kept one side at the surface. As soon as the men in the skiff got back to the boat we would take the two ends of the top of the net and pull them over the rail on the side of the boat. The net would then be strung out in a large circle from the side of the boat. The next thing to be done was to pull in the purse line. That is a smaller rope which goes through small metal rings which are fastened all along the bottom of the net where the lead weights are. It would take about ten minutes to pull the purse line in and that would close up the bottom of the net. It was very important to purse up the net quickly so that the fish wouldn't go out under the net. One or two of the crew would be banging on the water to scare the fish back into the net and keep them from coming out underneath the boat. They used a long pole with a metal plunger on the end of it or a piece of rope with a piece of wood on the end. When these were splashed on the surface of the water the noise would keep the fish in the net.

We had to work fast to get the net pursed up and I had to keep after my crew. If they didn't work fast or some of my crew got lazy I had to get very strict with them. I would give them orders to work fast and not make any mistakes. Sometimes the purse line would get tangled in the net or something else would go terribly wrong with our setting so the crew had to know what they were doing. Sometimes I would have to get really mad when everything went wrong. Of course you couldn't expect everything to go smoothly everyday. When something went wrong that is where the captain had to be because he was the responsible man. He was the man that had the brains in order to produce a lot of fish and to know what to do when something went wrong. He had to be the

man that bossed his men around to do everything right. A lot of
captains would boss their men but not get right in and pull in the
net themselves. I was always down there on the deck doing most of
the work most of the time because I had to see that everything was
just right. I would go there and pull in the purse line or the net
especially when we were tangled up. If there was somebody there
that didn't know how to do it it would be worse. I liked to do that.
A lot of times we would set on top of a reef and we knew it was
there but thought the tide was good so we could do it. Then all of a
sudden the net would hook up and we would have to try and get it
off. Sometimes it was awful difficult and we tore our net all to
pieces.

In those days we had to do all the pursing of the net by hand and
then pull the net in by hand, which was a big job. It was quite a few
years before they installed power blocks on the boats which made
it much easier to pull in the net. Once the pursing is all done we
could relax a little because we knew that the fish were all in the net.
On the back of the seine boat was a large platform which was
called a "seine table," and it is on a swivel so that it could be one
way when the net was going out and then we could turn it to the
side of the boat when we were pulling the net in. After the net was
pursed up we turned the seine table sideways and began to pull the
net in, stacking it neatly on the seine table so that it could be let
out easily on the next set. It was a hard job to pull the net in and all
five of my crew would be working at that and I would sometimes
be helping them. I liked working fast and efficient at all of this
because I wanted to get those fish into the hatch and make another
set. Especially when I could see some fish jumping around I wanted
to work fast and try to make more sets while it was daylight because
that was the only way to get more fish.

I didn't really care whether all the men were fast workers or not
because I knew I couldn't find all fast workers among the five men
on the crew. Since a lot of the time I couldn't be down on the deck
I usually tried to have one good man who was a fast worker and I
would tell him to look after the most important jobs on the deck.
The other men would have to listen to him because he was more
experienced than the rest of them and naturally they would. Of
course he wasn't going to boss them around because they all had

their own jobs. I remember that a few times I had some trouble-makers on my crew who just thought they were going to bully the crew around. One man I had used to get mad at the crew when they didn't do things the way he was telling them. As soon as I found out what this man was like I switched him around so that he had to work at a job where he would be alone and would mind his own business. I had to watch those men because sometimes they weren't very good in their work. Some of them would think they knew what they were doing and would be pulling the purse line in too fast or making some other mistake and the fish would be going right out of the net. That was why I always stood around and watched when they were pulling in the purse line and the net. That's how I worked my crew.

When the net was up to where we could see the fish we would start to scoop them out of the big net with a smaller hand net and put them into the hatch. That was called "brailing the fish." Later when the boats were equipped with a power block we used a pulley and winch to pull this smaller net up after dipping fish from the large net. In those early days it all had to be done by hand and if we had a pretty good catch it would take several hours to get all the fish into the hatch. After all the fish had been brailed we brought the net all the way up onto the seine table and then I would go look for another place to set. And it was a wonderful feeling when we got a good catch and especially when we got the hatch loaded up. If the fish were coming through heavy we sometimes made as many as fifteen sets in a day. Sometimes we moved around when we figured the fish should be good further up or further down. In the early days we didn't have a radio telephone so that the other boats couldn't notify us of other places where they were catching lots of fish. We would have to take a lot of chances when we made a move. It was awful risky at times and I usually never moved when the other boats were moving but would just wait for the next tide. Sometimes I missed and the fish didn't come or I didn't catch many because of my own mistakes.

Many times I made a set and didn't catch any fish at all. I would feel awfully bad. Some days I never got anything because of being in the wrong place or getting snagged or having engine trouble. If the net caught on the bottom and got snagged and torn we would have to spend a lot of time mending it. Sometimes after working for most of a day mending the net we would come out late and make a set and find that it was too late or we were in the wrong place and there would be no fish. It made me feel awfully bad not to make anything at all for the day. That has happened a lot of times. There are many times when we were out fishing that we would just be traveling or waiting for our turn to make a set. Sometimes we would drop anchor and have to wait a long time and the boys would be reading or playing cards. While we would be waiting I might be mending the net or doing some work around the engine room or splicing a rope or something. I usually had work to do around the boat. Sometimes when we didn't see any fish jumping we would make a "blind set," which meant that we set in the same way but we didn't see any fish jumping at all before we closed up the net. Other times we might not be able to find a good place to tie up on the shore and we would just make a "round set" out in a channel without tying up at all.

Toward dinner, at the end of the day when it was getting dark, we would go to where the packer was anchored and transfer our fish. We might have to wait for other boats to unload and that would keep us there until midnight or even 2 in the morning. They would weigh our fish and then ice them down while they were loading them onto the packer. A lot of times we only had about an hour or a couple hours sleep before going out again the next morning to make some more sets.

At the end of the summer the company would figure up how much the total earnings of the boat were and then after they deducted for the fuel that we had used they would divide up the money into eleven shares. The net owner got one and a half shares and the boat owner got two and a half shares. The captain would get two shares and each of the crew would get one share. The expenses for food were shared by all the crew members but any expenses on the boat such as repairs were taken care of by the owner of the boat. I had been using a company boat and net at the time and I lost the company net during my second year as skipper. I was fishing near Barnard Pass in the Johnston Strait and set quite near to a riptide. The tide was coming from two directions and where they met there was a big whirlpool. We set on one side of that big whirlpool and as soon as we had finished making the set I ordered the men to purse up full speed because I knew we were in trouble since we were drifting toward the riptide. The boat only had a small engine on it and we didn't have enough power to close our net fast enough or we could have pursed up before drifting into that riptide. The net started to go down and it began to pull the boat over so that water was coming over the deck. I told the men to slack off and let the purse line out. They let go of it and it was just going out like a bullet. I told them to try to hang onto it when it was all the way out but they couldn't stop it and everything was just torn apart and each end of the net was pulled from the boat. We lost the whole net. We ran around there for about three hours waiting for the tide to change to see if the net would come up again but nothing ever came up. I felt awfully bad because I thought I was going to get fired. I had already had two big snags before that which tore the net quite badly. That net was almost brand new and worth about $2000. I went back to the cannery and told Mr. Matthews that I felt ashamed of myself because I had lost a good net like that. "Well," he said, "that's all right, we'll make another one. We have lots of web." He didn't seem to care. It cost the company a lot of nets to train me.

After I had been skipper for a couple of years Mr. Matthews gave me a chance to own my own net. I didn't have to pay anything down on it but I was able ot pay him back within two years. It was a $1700 seine net, but since that meant I got one and a half shares from the net it paid off for me to own it. I was the first Indian up at that cannery to own his own net. The other skippers were all using company boats and nets.

In 1936 there was a strike in order to try to get better prices for the fish. We were all tied up in Alert Bay with our boats. They stopped everything and the company wouldn't give us any more groceries for our boats. Flora was up at the cannery and I didn't know how they were looking after the women up there. They didn't want the boats to move around but to just stay tied up in Alert Bay. We were all out of grub and all the men were getting kind of panicky. We weren't allowed to go up to Knight's Inlet to see our wives and children and we wanted to know how they were getting along. They finally settled it but we didn't make hardly anything at all because we had been tied up nearly all season. During the winter months some of the leading men called a gathering to talk about forming an organization on the coast. Chief Billy Assu from the Cape Mudge people was speaking our language while he talked to that meeting and encouraged all the people that were there to come forward and make up their mind for forming a fishermen's organization. George Luther was one of the ones who was really pushing it, and we formed the Pacific Coast Native Fishermen's Association. George Luther was elected to be the secretary of that association. I learned a lot about negotiating for the fish prices after that from George Luther since he used to ask me to sit in when they talked to the cannery people.

In the winters of those years that I was skipper on the "Annandale" there wasn't much to do so we stayed in Village Island most of the time. There were a lot of potlatches in our village as well as in some of the other villages but we had to be very careful because of the law at that time. Whenever a new hamatsa was dancing for the first time I would go there and help teach him what he was supposed to do. One of the most important things we did was practicing all the old songs. When I would go to a really big do at another village where a lot of the tribes gathered, the speaker for the ceremony used to call me in and say, "We are glad to see you, Jimmy. We welcome you, because we would like you to learn these songs, because we aren't going to be here very long to assist you when the time comes for you to lead them on your own." I used to like it whenever I had time, especially the singing. There was one old man named Jolof Moon who was the greatest composer I had ever known. Every tribe had their composers and singers but he was the leader of all the singers because he knew the songs of all the tribes. We used to get together before the big night when everybody sang all the songs in order to try to bring the wild man out of the woods. Since each tribe came in the order of their rank we had to know which songs would be sung and in which order. Old Man Moon would tell me to put down the first two words of the songs that he wanted to sing which belonged to the person dancing. Then that night I would sit real close to him all the time and he would ask me, "What is the first line of the next song?" And I would tell him and he would start singing right away. That was very important to him to have them in the right order and not to forget any of them so he always used to look for me. I didn't blame him because if he made a mistake the hamatsas would not like that.

One winter about this time my stepfather, David Matilpi, came to Village Island to invite the people to a big do at Turnour Island. Dave was a Maamtagila and he was getting ready to have his nephew Jimmy Wadhams become a new hamatsa. Dave had been loaning things out for a long time getting ready for this big potlatch. He had married my mother and Jim Bell had given one of his hamatsa positions to him and he was going to have his nephew take it. Everybody was expecting it because Dave was one of the leading men of his village. Jim Bell had about ten hamatsa positions and Dave was proud to have gotten one of them from the Village Island people to give to his nephew. When I arrived in Turnour Island to stay at my mother's house Jimmy Wadhams had already gone out in the woods. The whole village was quite busy and something was going on every night.

It was very important for me and the other hamatsas to be there because I had gone through that and could teach any of the new ones. All the different groups from the different dances were having their own gatherings and getting ready for the ceremony. I spent most of my time around the big fire in the big house where they had the dances every night. During the daytime all the hamatsas would be singing and dancing in order to practice. Some of the time we were teaching the new hamatsa how to dance. That's where I really learned how to sing the songs, especially the new songs that the new hamatsa was going to have. I never used to care about that. I used to sit and listen because I didn't think it was important. Of course they had a lot of good singers like Mungo Martin and Jolof Moon and some others. They are all dead now. Sometimes during the day they had a big feast. All they did was eat at those great big feasts. They would go out and get a big hailbut and put it in a great big pot and everybody would come and eat. I had the right to be in that house during the day and at night after the big do was over because I was a hamatsa. I had gone through that before and it was in me. I was a hamatsa and that is the highest society and therefore we were entitled to go into the big house.

When Jimmy Wadhams came through the roof of the house on

his first night I was down below dancing and cooperating with all the retired hamatsas. All of Dave's relatives danced because they had the right to. Then that night after it was all over we worked late getting the screen put up and all the branches around it. We had to be careful again to drown out the noise of pounding the nails into that screen. I often thought of the Bible days when we were doing that. They claim that when they built King Solomon's temple they did all the chipping and everything many miles away so that they wouldn't make any noise when they were building it. It was so sacred because it was God's house and nobody was allowed to make any noise. And then when everything was over Dave gave a lot of things away to all the leading people and after a few days we went back to Village Island.

Village Island was a Mamalilikulla village but there were also some Kwiksutainuk people there ever since the massacre by the Bella Coola from up north. There were also a lot of Kwiksutainuk people at Gilford Island. I was the only one who had positions in all four of the Mamalilikulla clans as well as in the Kwiksutainuk people. The chief of the village had been Mary Bell's father who had a high position in the Temltemlels clan. There were lots of chiefs in the village but he was looked upon as being the speaker of our village. The chief was usually the one who had the highest position in the highest clan of the tribe. My great-grandfather's name was Goatlas and he had been recognized by the government as the hereditary chief of that village. When he died he left three sisters and so the oldest one gave a big potlatch and assumed her father's position, but the government wouldn't recognize her but instead recognized another man, who was at the top of the Wewamasqem clan. Jim Bell was in the second position of that clan. So this man became the chief when Goatlas died and then his son became chief when his father died. He was the chief at that time.

There was a lot of timber on our reserve there and so the tribe decided that it would be a good idea to have our own logging operation instead of selling the rights to the timber to some other firm. We thought we might employ our own people by doing that but it didn't work out. The chief was the one who was running that logging operation but his brother was the one that was a very good logger and more or less the brains. His brother was a hook tender and a high rigger and a very good logger. Of course I was running the steam donkey to pull the logs out of the woods and then boom them up in the water, and a tugboat took them to Powell River. It was awfully hard in those days to get somebody to run the steam donkey. I was the only one who knew how to do that. I would get up real early in the morning in order to get there by 7 and steam up the donkey. I used to get there one hour before everybody else. At 8 the other boys would come and go up to the woods and cut down the trees. When they were ready to be pulled out they blew a whistle and I would operate the controls on the donkey to pull them out. I had an elderly man working with me as a fireman and two or three others who would unhook the logs when they were pulled out and pile them up.

On Saturday I used to go for half a day to do some repairs on the donkey, like cleaning the tubes. It was a lot of work on that steam donkey. It wasn't like a diesel which could be worked on whenever it needed work. On the steam donkey you had to keep things in good shape. If there was anything to be done on the machine I had to go over it and fix it myself to be sure that I had it going. Everything had to be in order. Well, the chief and his brother were fighting all the time and his brother finally quit. We knew that he knew more about logging than any of the boys that were up in the woods. So the boys that were working, especially the boys that were close to him, felt that he should be brought back into our logging operation. They wanted him rather than his older brother, who just walked around and didn't do anything or know anything. I didn't know what he was there for. So when the younger brother came back in the chief quit. It was better that way and Henry Bell took over to kind of be the boss. We owed money to the man who sold us the donkey and we tried to pay all our debts. We carried on for a few years after that.

It was somewhere around that time that I began to feel that it wasn't right to have these potlatches. When the people were invited to a potlatch they would be gone for ten days or two weeks and it would spoil it for the people who had jobs. I was busy logging and since I was so busy I didn't attend some of those potlatches. That was the downfall of the villages that started anything. I thought a lot about why I should give up the logging operation and go to a potlatch. We wouldn't be producing any logs during that time so I began staying right in the village even though the other people went. A few of the younger people would stay with me but about 80 percent of our people would go to the potlatch. The way I looked at it, it was more important to be on the job. I thought it was all right if it was a free time but not when there was a job to be done.

I used to come to Alert Bay to visit my relatives and my wife's relatives quite often. When we were there we would go to St. Michael's residential school to see the picture shows that were held there. The principal of that school was Mr. Anfield, who came right after they built the new school. The boys and girls were all there together in the new school and not separated as they had been before. Mr. Anfield was a great worker for the church. He used to come up to Village Island and visit and help Miss O'Brien sometimes and I knew that he liked what I was doing. I was helping Miss O'Brien in any way that was good for the village and especially the church. Sometimes during the summer I would go out and catch a lot of fish on the "Annandale" and bring them in and give them to the school. The minister at Christ Church in Alert Bay was Mr. Oswald Hodgson then, and he was a very good man. He really cared for the people, especially the young people. He used to go around and talk to the young people and of course he asked them to come to church. He would get acquainted with them and then invite them to have a little gathering in his house. Sometimes I would go there for a big supper with about ten or fifteen boys and afterwards we would wash all the dishes for him because he was a single man without a wife. After supper we had a big party with games and things like that. He would have a party for the young couples also and Flora and I went when we were in the Bay. He was doing all that he could to help the young people and the way I saw it he was thinking about the young people more than anything else. He worked awful hard to get the young people, even the young girls, to go to church. He used to go visit my wife's younger sister Nora whenever she wasn't in church. He would go to her and tell her, "I missed you in church last week. Don't miss again. I'll see you next Sunday." He was that kind of man. He didn't just let it go and say to himself, "Well, I don't know what happened to her. I guess she doesn't want to come or something." He would actually go and talk to the people and then they would come and he used to have a big congregation.

In March of 1937 we went to Alert Bay and our next child was born. It was just a month after my friend Mr. Hodgson had died and so we called him Oswald Alfred Hodgson after the minister. I was working at Village Island then in our logging camp and we had gone to Alert Bay because my wife was expecting. The following year, in November, Daisy was born. We had five children then and most of them had been born during the depression. I often felt bad that we couldn't get more for them but on two or three dollars a day wages it was pretty hard. At the same time, the way I felt was that we were in a place to pay more attention to our everyday life with our children. We happened to live in a very isolated little village with no stores or television but only radios. There was nowhere to go so our whole life was lived right there especially in the winter time. Miss Nixon was teaching school and Dora and Bobby had already started going. They would go to school and then come home and help me to do some work. I'd be on the beach working, chopping wood, and they would come and pack the wood into our woodshed even if they were only five years old. If I got some fish they would go down on the wharf with me and help bring it in. Even when we went up to Knight's Inlet cannery they used to help in the same way.

Flora did most of the work to take care of the children when they were real young, but I helped her when I could. Her aunt lived with us during some of those years and she was a big help too. I took care of them myself sometimes when they were little, like changing their diapers or feeding them when they cried. One thing I always liked to do was get up early in the morning and get their breakfast. I never stayed in bed in the mornings because I never liked to sleep late. I would always get up and cook for them in the morning and then I would wake Flora up and she would get the older ones dressed before they went to school. I didn't mind seeing her sleep in. When I was a young boy I remember seeing old Jim Bell and other old men cook and they used to take care of the babies some too. I also used to get up with the babies at night, especially if Flora wasn't feeling well. I would go and heat some milk and feed it to them.

One of the hardest jobs was washing clothes and I used to help Flora with that. With our first babies we didn't have any washing machine or anything like that. When we were at Alert Bay we would get up early in the morning and go over to the Nimpkish River and make a big fire. Then we would heat the water in a big pot and wash the clothes by rubbing them on a board. When they were all washed we would hang them out in the trees and stay there most of the day until they were dry. In Village Island we had to pack the water by pail from a well. It was a lot of work packing the water because we didn't have any water piped into our houses. I've seen the other men washing clothes too.

Flora had learned a lot about taking care of children from her mother and aunt and also because she had looked after all her younger brothers and sisters. She had gone to the residential school for a while but got out of there by telling them that her mother needed her to help look after her brothers and sisters. At Village Island the missionary and district nurse, Miss O'Brien, used to get all the mothers together and tell them how to look after babies. She had a hard time teaching them to let the babies cry. Flora was told that if we picked up the kids right away when they cried that it would spoil them. We used to try but we couldn't usually take it so we would just pick them up right away or get them a bottle to quiet them down. When we learned the ways of the white man we found out that it was good to use a soother, which was a little round thing with a rubber nipple on it. And then we were told later that it wasn't good for the children to use it because it would cause their tonsils to get bad.

We had different ways of punishing the older children at that time. I didn't want any child to boss me around and I knew it wasn't good for them to allow them to act that way. I used to send Dora to bed without any supper or make her stay in the house to play. I spanked my children some but I remembered how old Lucy had told me to be patient and speak gently with them. If they ever did anything wrong when they were small I would spank their hands. Sometimes I would get a stick and spank them behind. We felt that too much spanking would just make them meaner when they grew up. They didn't learn everything right away and I felt that you had to allow them a little time and just keep at it. Sometimes if they were bad I would just ignore them and not talk to them for a while. Another thing we did was to tell them about the *Tsunuqua* that were up in the woods and would get them if they weren't good. Sometimes we would scratch on the walls to pretend that the Tsunuqua were coming and Bobby and Dora used to be scared, but we stopped doing that later on and the younger ones weren't scared of that. We also used to tell them that God was always there where they were, seeing everything they did and that they would have to be nice if they wanted to see Him one day. At that time the main way that we used for punishing the children was making them stay in and not allowing them to go out. I think we learned that from the teacher in the school because they used to do that there. We were much more strict with our kids in those days.

I felt that we were raising our children kind of in between the Indian way and the white way. I didn't know too much about the ways of the non-Indians, especially how they teach their children and all that. What they had taught me as a little boy was still in my mind and I knew what was right and wrong. I felt that was what was so important, that they know what was right and wrong. Because we had a large family and there were lots of other kids in the village, they usually played with other children. If any of my children ever had a fight with other children I punished them because I wouldn't allow that. There was no doubt that they would fight in school or when they were out playing but when I heard about it they would be punished. If I saw one of them starting to fight I would stop them right away. Even if somebody was picking on them I would tell them to keep away from those kids. That's what I had been taught and I would tell them, "Don't let anybody pick a fight with you. Just walk away from him. If anybody tries to bully with you, just get away from him." I had done that many times myself, and people used to make fun of me because they thought I was a coward and all that. I know that the white man doesn't like that. They don't want to be called a coward. They have to roll up their sleeves and go at it even if it is with somebody who is twice as big. You might be cut up and be all black and blue but you are still a hero according to the way that the white man thinks. In the Indian way, if a child got just a little scratch from fighting there was going to be a lot of money involved. I never gave a potlatch when they got into fights but I would just get after them.

Many times when I would be working on the beach with the kids playing around, one of them would fall down and get hurt and I would go right to him and take him into the house and fix his wound. If they were doing something and asked me for help I used to do what they wanted unless it was something they could really do for themselves. If I knew that he knew how to do it but wanted my help, then I wouldn't help him because I felt that he had to learn in his own way. I felt that I should show them how to go about doing what they wanted but not always help them. I always felt it was good for them to have little jobs to do. I always told them that my job was endless and gave them different things they had to do. It is good for every child to do work. It didn't matter if it was going to be real hard for them; it was good for them to be taught how to work. I wanted my children to grow up to be successful and have a good life. I felt there was nothing in the world better than that they should be successful, especially in their work, and have good jobs and good families.

5 He Always Wants to Share His Wealth with Others

In 1939 Mr. Matthews gave me another boat called the "Frank A. M." It was 41 feet long, which was a little smaller than the "Annandale," but it was a faster boat with a bigger engine that was only five years old. The cannery had bought it from an Italian skipper who had been using it for a few years. I really felt as any good skipper that I had to catch lots of fish in order to build myself up and have a good name in the company that I was working for. If a skipper didn't produce the way he should the manager would ask him to step down and give his boat to another person. If a skipper was a good producer then the company would do everything they could to help him along. I was learning through my experience of being skipper what it took to be a good captain. It was important to know a little bit about navigation. I didn't know too much about it because I didn't have any education in navigation courses, but I had an idea about it. I could use my compass if I knew where we were and I could measure the chart out in my own way. I had to be very careful about the tides, which I was becoming very familiar with. Most of the time I just looked at the water to tell the direction of the tide and when it was going to change. All the tides are different and I knew them all—they were all in my head.

In my own personal experience every skipper was different. They all had their own way of doing things. For instance, when I put my net together it was different from a lot of those other skippers. A lot of them used shallower or deeper nets or nets with lighter lead weights on them. It depended partly on the size of the boat and the power of the engine. And some of those skippers when they tied up on the beach and made a set would just stretch their nets out and wait for the fish. The way I did it was different. I really liked to catch fish. I didn't just stretch my net out and wish that we were going to catch fish. When I saw a fish jumping I knew that I was going to get it because I knew how to get it. I had seen many skippers making a set when I was waiting behind them for my turn. Four or five schools of fish would go into the net and they would just hold it wide open and never even put a bag to it. That was how they pulled the ends together to close it up some so that the fish would stay inside of it, because as soon as the fish hit the net they would try to get out of it. I had seen skippers make a foolish set and not get very many fish when they could have. Then I would go in after them and make a set and two or three schools of fish would go into my net and I would get way more fish than they did.

Sometimes a good skipper has to take risks. I did this many times if I thought it was worth it. I knew I was going to get my net ripped up but still get a lot of fish. If there was a reef or a bad snag near where I set and the tide was just right I could often make out all right, but if it was a bad tide I wouldn't try to take those fish. A lot of skippers take bigger risks and they lose the whole works. It was important to know where the snags and reefs were and I was learning all that. There were times when we had ripped our net and spent a whole day mending it. Sometimes I knew where a snag was and if there were a lot of fish there I would take a chance. I did this a lot of times and got away with it by watching the tide and being careful not to drift onto the snag.

Some skippers liked to purse fast and some liked to purse slow. That is when they are pulling in the purse line and closing up the bottom of the net. I would always watch that very carefully from the side of the boat. If the tide was no good or there was an under-current or back eddy I would tell my men to purse slow. It was very easy for the purse line to be lifted up by the undercurrent and the fish would go underneath it and out of the net. We would lose everything so I had to be very careful and watch it. If the tide was good I would tell them to purse fast and the quicker the net closed up the more fish we had swimming around inside the net. A lot of skippers thought that if they open set for a long time they were going to get more fish, but that is not the way I saw it. Some people made a bad mistake by being open too long and they would lose everything that they had inside their net. There were many things that I was learning from my own experience being a skipper. That first year that I was skipper on the "Frank A. M." I was up among the highliners, which meant that I had one of the top boats in the amount of fish caught.

The Indian agent at that time was Mr. Todd. He was just like a father to me and he used to call me in and talk to me about starting up my own business, especially buying a boat for myself. He said to me, "You are young and you can prove to your company that you are willing. You are a good fisherman, Jimmy, and I'm sure they will do everything they can to help you." Mr. Todd was just like a father to me and he talked to me as if I were his son. And I took him up on it. So I went to Mr. Matthews, the manager of the A. B. C. Packing Company that I was working for. I asked him how much he would expect me to pay down on the boat if I bought it. "Well," he said, "we could accept maybe $500. You could have the boat for $5000." That was very cheap in those days. "Well," I said, "I haven't got that kind of money, but I will get it." I thought very seriously about where I was going to get $500 to put down on the boat. The only way that I could think of was to try to get a partner to go in with me, so I came to Alert Bay to see my friend George Luther. He was still teaching school there. I asked him if he could come in with me as a silent partner to buy the "Frank A. M." He was very interested and came down with me and looked at the boat and asked me what I thought of the engine. I told him, "That's a perfect engine and it is going to last a lifetime." I knew because I had been running engines for a long time. Somehow he had a lot of excuses and said he wanted to build himself a new home and he wanted to buy himself a new radio. I figured he was kind of scared to go in with me on it so I went to see my uncle, Robby Bell. He was also fishing for the same company and was skipper on one of the company boats. Robby had always been part of my life and so when I had this chance to get into business I felt that I wanted him to come in with me on it. I asked him, "Do you want to come in with me as a partner and buy the 'Frank A. M.'?" He said, "Sure, I can do that with you." So I asked him to get $250 and I would get $250 and then we could give the company $500 for our down payment. Well, it was up to him and I didn't care whether he got it or not or where he was going to get it. Well, Robby came to me and said that he couldn't get any money. "Well," I said, "that's too bad. You have to have the money if you want to come in with me." He told me that he still would really like to buy that boat with me and he was sure glad that I had asked him.

I only had $100 in the bank and so I came to Mr. Todd and talked to him about it. He said to me, "I understand you are looking for a partner to buy a boat. I could give you some money and go in as a silent partner." So I told him that if Robby didn't come through with the money that maybe I could fall back on him, but since I had already told Robby to try and raise the money I would wait to see what happened. So I went to see Mr. Anfield, who was the principal of the residential school and a good friend of mine. I told him that we would like to borrow $400 from the bank but that we needed somebody to cosign for us. He was good enough to do that without asking us any questions. He knew that I was married and doing well in my fishing. I will never forgot that time that he did that. It was a big favor to me as an Indian because other people didn't trust the Indians. So we got a loan from the bank that summer for $400 and were supposed to pay it back by October. It was in 1940 that we bought the "Frank A. M." and signed an agreement with Mr. Matthews to pay the rest of the money for it.

I stayed on as skipper of the "Frank A. M." and really did well. I used to fill it up every day and sometimes twice in a day when I was really working hard. The war had started then and there weren't many men to run the packers so that we had to travel a long ways and sometimes we hardly got any sleep. My wife was working up at Knight's Inlet cannery and our five children were staying there. She made about $200 that summer and I borrowed $150 from her and was able to pay off my part of the loan at the bank by the end of the summer. The next summer the share for the boat was almost $2500 because I was really producing the fish. I think that I was the highest boat in our company fleet that year among the Indians.

The war was getting very critical at that time and the government asked the Indian agents to make a report of all the available men in the different agencies. Mr. Todd called me in one day and asked me some questions so he could fill out a form on me. He asked me, "Jimmy, what can you do if you should go into the Army?" "Well," I said, "I don't know. I know that I can run any kind of engine and I can look after a boat. I'm also a carpenter." So he put many things down on that form and sent it in. It wasn't very long after that that I got a call to go and get my checkup. I was to report to a certain place inside of two days, so I told my manager at the cannery about it. "Jimmy," he said, "I don't think we can let you go. We need you. You are a good fisherman and you will do just as well here as over there. You can produce lots of fish and they need them over there as food for our soldiers. I guess we will have to write a letter for you." So he wrote a letter because he could just look at my record on the fish tally to see that I was really producing a lot of fish. That was why he didn't want to let me go, because it was awful hard to get good captains at that time.

After the fishing season was over I decided to move my house from down on the beach to the bluff where most of the houses were in Village Island. I hooked a cable up to that house and used a steam donkey to pull it up and when we were moving it up the cable broke. That little house just slid down the bluff and was all smashed up. So we didn't have any house and I had to tear it all apart and build a new one. Since my family was getting quite large I decided to build a bigger home so I had to buy some lumber to have enough. I went over to Telegraph Cove to get the lumber on the "Frank A. M." A friend of mine had a sawmill there. When I built that modern home I wanted everything in it like running water, electricity, and an inside toilet. None of the other homes had these things at that time. I got most of my house built that winter but we still lacked a lot of those things that go in a modern home.

Shortly after I finished building that house, Mr. Harold Sexton, the Archbishop of British Columbia, came up to our village to visit Miss O'Brien. He came to our little church on Sunday and we had a service with him. Before the service I told him I would like him to come and bless my new home. So he announced it to the people during the service and after it was finished he led the people through that little village and they all went into my house and we had a short ceremony there. The Anglican church has a special ceremony for opening the house and he made the sign of the cross in the floor there with his staff and performed that ceremony there.

I used to have a lot of dreams but one or two kept coming back to me. I think I dreamed them many times ever since I was married and I used to talk to my wife about them. In one of them I dreamed that I was going to some very wild country and when I got there I met a wild beast such as a lion or tiger that was trying to harm some people. I would go there in my dream and just tear that animal apart and if the people were suffering or drowning in the water I would just go there and save them all. At other times I dreamed that I was in a strange country and there would be about twenty or thirty people trying to harm me. When they came at me I would just grab them and throw them all over the place and nobody was able to harm me. I dreamed about these things a number of times and I used to sit and talk to my wife about those dreams. I never did learn to understand those dreams.

One time when I had been over to Telegraph Cove to get some lumber my friend had asked me if I wanted to buy a little diesel light plant. There was no electricity in any of the isolated villages then. I told him I'd like to buy it but that I didn't have any money. He wanted $300 for that little five-horsepower engine and the five-kilowatt generator that went with it. I brought it up to the people of Village Island but the chief and some of the leaders didn't want to have anything to do with it. Miss O'Brien had her own home there then, as well as a little rest home where the people could go when they were sick. She used to clean all the little lamps in those two buildings and fill them up with coal oil every day. That was another reason why I wanted to buy that little light plant, because I knew it would be a great help to her. The chief was a good man in his own way and in the Indian custom, but he wasn't the right man to look upon as a good leader to improve the living conditions of the people. The way I saw it, he was lacking many things and he never tried to do anything about trying to live up to the progress of the modern world and to try to keep up with it. He was just satisfied with what we had. I was an altogether different person. I was a young ambitious man and wanted to live in the best way. Some of the other people couldn't see it my way either but I decided to go ahead with it anyway. I had a few boys on my side that were with me and I told them, "Let's do this thing anyway. I'll borrow the money and maybe when you fellows get some money you can pay me after awhile." The shares were about $50 each and I talked to Miss O'Brien and asked her if she would like to buy a share. She was very glad to help and so I borrowed the rest of the money and went over to Telegraph Cove in the "Frank A. M." and bought that light plant.

I really had to work hard to get that thing fixed up. I had to pack lumber and sand and get some wire and other things that we needed. Most of the time I was doing it alone and had to work long hours. I used my own boat for getting all the materials and never charged anyone for doing that. It was on my own and I knew it was good for the village and especially for our new home. We got some cement and made a foundation for the engine and generator and then on my own I bought some lumber to build a little shed to cover the light plant. Then when the plant was finished I wired all the houses of those who had come in as shareholders. Jack Hanuse helped with the wiring of the houses and his house was one of those we wired. Besides him and Miss O'Brien there was Simon Beans, Henry Bell, Robby Bell, Alex Hanuse, and Sam Charlie that came in with us. And after I had wired all their homes we put up some street lights along the path between the houses. And that was a big night when we started that engine up. Miss O'Brien pulled the switch and all the houses lit up and the street lights and the little rest home which had six patients in it all lit up and she was very happy about it.

After it was going we formed a little company for the light plant because we had to have somebody to look after it and go around and collect a few dollars for the fuel. So we got together and I put it before the meeting that we had to have this. Nobody was just going to say that I was it because it was up to the shareholders to appoint the man that was going to chair this company for a year and then the next year we would change. Well, all the boys said, "We want you to be elected. We think that you are the man that can really run this thing because after all you put a lot of work into it. This thing is going now and we want you to keep on year after year." Well, I didn't ask to be elected because I knew it was going to be hard and quite a responsibility. I fixed a string to the switch on the engine and ran it into my bedroom, and every night I would just pull that string to turn off the lights in the village. I don't think the chief of the village liked the idea of my being elected chairman of that little light company. He didn't see it the way I saw it and some of the other people too couldn't see it my way, but we were the first isolated village that ever owned an electric light plant in the Kwakiutl nation.

I was doing a lot for the people in Village Island at that time. I used to build houses for my people there when they started building modern homes. I used to go and help them and never ask anybody for pay or anything like that. If somebody had to fix their boat I would go and give them a hand. If they wanted to come to Alert Bay I would take them on the "Frank A. M." when I came once a week to get groceries. There was a small wharf in front of the village where I would come in when it was high water. When the tide went out the water was not deep enough for a seine boat and it was dry land right out to some little islands nearby. I used to take my boat out almost a mile to anchor it and every time I wanted to see my boat I had to get a little rowboat and row out. I would go out a lot of times during the winter months and pump it out or examine the ropes. At times it was very windy there and not a very good place to anchor my boat. I felt that we should build a wharf around the end of the island from the village where the water was quite deep. We talked about it with the people and they were in favor of doing something to have a wharf built. Ed Whanock and Moses Alfred were visiting Village Island when we decided to build it and they thought it was a good idea and said they would give us advice. We weren't doing any logging ourselves at Village Island anymore so I went over to Turnour Island village, which was about seven or eight miles away, and asked David Matilpi if I could borrow his steam donkey. He loaned it to me and we were going to pull out some timber from our Indian reserve and tow it over to Telegraph Cove. The sawmill there was going to cut half for us and they could keep half. I put that steam donkey on a float and towed it over to Village Island and we started to pull the logs down to the beach. The whole village was working together helping except for the old people, who couldn't do much. They used to just stand around and watch us and they really enjoyed seeing the ambitious young people of the village doing something at last. So we boomed the logs up on a boom and towed them over to Telegraph Cove and they cut them up for us.

When the lumber had been cut up they delivered it to us on a big scow. Most of the people were away from the village at a potlatch in Kingcome when the scow arrived, so I went down and told them to just throw the lumber overboard. The tide was going out and there was no danger of it floating it away. They were able to get all the lumber unloaded and push the scow out from the village before it was too dry. Then I worked there for quite a long time trying to get the lumber up to where we were going to build the wharf. Flora was helping me with a little hand winch. I would go down on the beach and wrap a cable around those big timbers and then we would pull them up on the dry land so that they wouldn't float away when the tide came in. It took a long time because we were all alone and nobody was helping us. Then when the people returned to the village we all worked cutting some pilings and building the wharf. When it was built everybody enjoyed using it, especially the people from other villages who would come to visit us and tie their boats up there. The Indian Department never helped us with that wharf but we built it all on our own.

George Luther was still the secretary of the Pacific Coast Native Fishermen's Association and I used to travel with him when he was bargaining over the fish prices. I was interested in taking part in anything that was good for the people and especially the fish prices. We would travel between Port Hardy and Alert Bay and discuss the fish prices on the steamboat with the canners. We would go to Port Hardy and meet the steamboat and then we'd have a meeting on the boat before they dropped us off in Alert Bay. That was the way we used to negotiate the fish prices. We had to come to some agreement with the canners before we hit the wharf in the Bay because we'd all be dumped off there. I didn't know too much about it but George used to ask me to come along because he wanted to teach me and train me.

In 1942 the Native Brotherhood of British Columbia held a convention in Alert Bay. The Indians in the north had formed this organization but the Kwakiutl were not in it because we had the Native Fishermen's Association. At that time the president of the Native Brotherhood talked to all the people and the leading men of the Kwakiutl nation about why they wanted to form the Native Brotherhood in our area. We had a banquet every night and he was preaching to us that the Brotherhood was the answer to the Indian problems in British Columbia. It was decided at that meeting to amalgamate the Native Fishermen's Association with the Brotherhood. I was young and didn't know too much but I used to go to all the meetings and listen because I was very interested. So one day during that convention two old gentlemen, Eber Clifton and Alfred Adams, who were leaders in the Native Brotherhood, asked me if we could go somewhere and have a talk. They asked George Luther if we could meet up at his house so we went that night and stayed there for a long time talking. I'll never forget that night. Those two old gentlemen were sitting on each side of me and I'll never forget one thing they said to me: "You are the man we are looking for. You are the kind of person we are looking for. We have been watching you and you have been coming to the meetings every day and we know you are interested. You are young and someday you will go into the doors of the Parliament Building in Ottawa. We won't live to see it but that day will come when you will sit around a conference table with the members of the Parliament and talk to them about the Indian people and their problems." In those days not too much had been done about the Indian problems, such as the land question, because the Indians were just fighting among themselves and all split up. The government had just told them that they wouldn't allow the Indians to come and talk to them when they were so divided.

At about that same time Oswald began to get sick. He was outside one day playing football with the older kids and Flora noticed that he kept falling down and was having trouble getting up. She brought him in and he was having trouble with his speech and sometimes his face would just kind of twitch all over. The water at Village Island wasn't very good and Flora thought that might be what was making him sick, so Flora and the kids dug a new well behind our house so we would have better water. It didn't seem to help too much and so we took him in to the doctor at Alert Bay. Flora also thought it might have been caused by the other kids scaring him too much. Well, the doctor told us to put him to bed for a few months, and then Flora took him back and the doctor said it was time for him to go out and rough around with the other kids. He was to play rough with them and wrestle and play football. After that he seemed to be okay.

Flora was expecting another baby that summer, but she worked up at the cannery most of the summer and when she wasn't feeling good enough to work she would sometimes have Dora go in and pack cans for her. Dora had worked in the cannery off and on to keep Flora's place ever since she was about eleven years old. When she wasn't taking her place in the cannery she would take care of the younger children while my wife was gone all day. One weekend late in October just before the baby was born I had a dream. I dreamed that there was a little baby coming down on a cloud from the sky and it came down right where I was standing. It was a little baby boy, and when it came down I grabbed that baby boy. I remember when I woke up I said to my wife, "I think we're going to have another little boy because I dreamed about a little boy coming down from the sky laying on a little cloud." A couple weeks later while I was fishing near Steveston her time was getting close so the manager of the cannery hired a little fish-packing boat to take her to Alert Bay. She went to the hospital there and sure enough, there was a little boy born. He was born on November 6, 1942, and we named him Alvin George. That was also the best year I ever had on the "Frank A. M." That was to be my record catch for one season. I put in over 100,000 fish that year and the share on the boat was just under $4000. As soon as the fishing season was over and we had been paid off, Robby and I went in to the manager and paid off our agreement on the "Frank A. M." We were the first Indian skippers working for that cannery to completely pay off our boat.

I was doing well in my business and making progress in the things I was doing for that village. I began to feel though that it might be a good thing for our little village to amalgamate with some other village that wasn't so isolated. I knew for a fact that the more people there were in a village the happier they would all be. We were so isolated from the doctors and stores and I felt that it wasn't up to the nurses and doctors and stores to come to us. It was up to us to go and find a better place to live and enjoy life much better. The most important thing was the young people so that they would be able to go to school a full term. The school at Village Island was run by the Indian Department and we used to have that schoolteacher for three months a year. One year I pleaded with the teacher to stay for another month. I went over to the Indian Office at Alert Bay and pleaded with the Indian agent to keep her on for another couple months. He told me that he had no authority to pay her for another month and that they had spent all that was allowed. So I went to the schoolteacher and asked if she would accept $50 to stay for another month. Money meant a lot to me because I didn't have much. She gladly accepted the $50 to stay for another month. So the next month Simon Beans paid her $50 to stay for another month. That's how hard it was for me and my family to live in a place like that.

I thought if we could put some little industry there it would have been good. It was my ambition to build a little clam cannery and a fish cannery and a cold storage plant there. I thought that if we had our own little processing plant and could smoke cod and clams we could sell them all over the country. It would have been a good little industry for the people to work at. Of course there was opposition to my ideas from some of the leaders of that village, and they figured I was just trying to boss the chief around. He wasn't progressive like I was.

The next year I was top boat in our company and the fish prices were very good because of the war. A friend of mine, James Jamieson, owned a 275-acre farm on Cracroft Island and he decided to sell it and move back east. So I bought this farm from him because I was thinking about putting in a little freezing plant there to freeze clams. The best clams on the coast are right around there and so I thought it would be a good place to have a little processing plant. There were only about 5 acres of that farm cleared and there were about seventy fruit trees there, so we had our own plums and apples and cherries. There were five small buildings and during the last part of that summer, while I was out fishing, the whole family stayed there along with my wife's aunt and uncle. There were a lot of tame deer and they would come to the house and the kids would feed them out of their hands. The kids really had a wonderful time there. There was a little smokehouse where we smoked fish and with the fruit trees and the garden we planted they had plenty to eat. There was a big field for them to play in and I made a big swing for them. I would come in on the weekends with fish to smoke and while I was there if it was low tide we would go out and dig clams. Dora was about fourteen years old then and she would go beachcombing with Flora's uncle, old man Roberts, or cruise around in a little gas boat that belonged to him. We only stayed there during the summer or for a few days at a time in the spring when we were digging clams. That winter after we bought the farm my wife had another baby. She went into the hospital at Alert Bay and just before Christmas had a baby girl and we named her Lucy Mary. When she was born we had seven children.

Norman Corker was the manager for the A. B. C. Packing Company then and I went and talked to him about buying another boat. I had seen him around Alert Bay when I lived with old Lucy, because he was the son of Rev. Corker who was the minister then. I also knew him when he first came to Knight's Inlet cannery to work as the tally man. I went to him about our business and what was the best thing to do. It was near the end of the war and I had talked to Robby about buying another boat, since we were both doing very well. I had been high boat for the company for several years and I thought it was good for us to work together. We had grown up together in the big house at Village Island and I always used to think of him as a brother. He was a very capable man who was a good fisherman and was one of the highliners. He also was a good carpenter and he had helped me building my house and I had helped him with his. So in November of 1944 we bought another seiner called the "Adele M." It was a 47-foot boat which was the sister to the "Frank A. M." It had the same kind of engine, an Atlas Imperial Diesel, which I used to overhaul myself. We had saved a lot of expenses on the "Frank A. M." by doing our own work on the engine or any woodwork on the boat and that was how we paid it off so fast. We paid $12,000 for that boat, which was pretty cheap, and Robby was skipper on it while I was working on the "Frank A. M." That winter we got in on buying clams and we did it for four or five years after that. It was a good winter job. I would be on the "Frank A. M." and start at Alert Bay and go around to the other villages and buy clams from all the diggers and then end up in the evening at my farm. We would transfer the clams to the "Adele M." at the farm, and some boys we had hired at union wages would take them down to a cannery at Redondo Bay just behind Cape Mudge Village. Then the next day I would go back around to the villages buying clams and arrive back in Alert Bay that night. It kept us busy for quite a while during the winter. When the clam buying was over I went to work for a logging company that was logging the timber off the Village Island reserve. It hadn't worked out too well for the people to do their own logging there so they sold the rights to this logging company. I was running the little gas donkey for them.

Mr. Todd used to come up to Village Island quite often and I used to help him quite a bit when he came. He would come to my house and we used to talk things over. Although we had a chief there he didn't like to go see him because he felt that he could get more out of me than him, so he would come and see me and I had a lot of ideas. He knew that I was really working for the people. I wasn't just talking about what I was going to do but I liked to just go ahead and do the things that I thought were good for the people. When we had built the wharf several years earlier I didn't wait for anybody but just went and borrowed my stepfather's donkey and started to work right away. He had been talking to me for about two years about moving to Alert Bay. He used to say, "Jimmy, you should come and move here. I will give you the best location and you can go up on the Industrial Reserve and choose whatever ground you want." The Anglican church had set aside five hundred acres of land there for any Indian in British Columbia who wanted to be progressive. That reserve was open to anybody who wanted to come and transfer there as long as they were able to meet certain requirements. They had to have been a pupil of the Anglican school, to have been married in the church, to have no use for the potlatch, and to promise to try to live a good clean life. There were already a few people from other villages who had moved onto that progressive reserve. Mr. Todd always used to think that that was the best place for a young man like me because it had been set aside for the progressive people. So he would ask me to move there because he thought I could be a great help to him if I was nearby. I thought a lot about what he had said.

So one night early in January of 1945 we had a meeting at Village Island to elect new officers for our light company. There were still only eight members who had electricity in their houses and we used to pay about a dollar a house each month to help pay for the fuel. If we got behind because some of them hadn't paid I used to just go buy the fuel and pay for it myself. A lot of the people from the village were at this meeting, and when I was elected chairman of the company the chief got up and said many things that I don't like to remember. He felt that I was against him. Some of the people didn't agree with the way I liked to improve the village. I liked to work and improve it so it will be a nice little village to live in, but some of them thought I was trying to change the way of life of my people. I suppose the boys elected me because they felt that I was the man that ought to be on there at all times because I started that thing. I borrowed the money and I was the engineer and it was situated behind my house. I would start it each morning and pull the cord running to my bedroom at night to stop the engine. Everything worked fine. So I got up and walked out of the meeting and went to my home. And that was the time that I made up my mind to leave Village Island.

While I had been in the meeting the boss of the logging camp that I was working for had come down to my house looking for me. So I went and looked for him to see what he wanted. I had just been promoted from running the steam donkey to go up in the woods and do high rigging and rope tending. When I found him he said to me, "We are starting another logging camp up behind Alert Bay. How would you like to move to Alert Bay and run my camp there? You would be the foreman." He never had to ask me again. I said, "I'd be glad to. I'll leave the first thing in the morning." So I picked out the best men we had in Village Island to come with me to operate that camp at Alert Bay. We left and started working there and I was really working hard in order to produce enough logs to satisfy our boss. I wasn't just bossing the other men but worked right along with them. My wife happened to be in Alert Bay at that time, staying with her parents, so I just stayed there with them.

On the following Sunday it was a nice day and so in the afternoon I went for a walk with my wife on the trail that went through the Industrial Reserve. I asked her if we could take a walk and while we were walking I asked her, "How would you like to live here?" She asked me, "Why do you ask this?" "Well," I said, "I know we have a beautiful new home in Village Island that we have just completed and that it will be hard for you to leave it. But if you would like to move here I would like you to tell me. I don't want to do it without you saying so. I have been thinking that what I'm doing in Village Island is not approved by some of the people there. I like to improve that village but I've been thinking that if they're going to like to live that way then I'm not going to stay there." "Well," she said, "Whatever you want to do is fine. I'll do as you please, anything that is best for us. It's up to you." So I told her, "I don't think it is good for our older children, Dora, Louise, Bobby, and Oswald to be brought up in a place where they can only go to school for a few months a year. I think the main reason we should move is for their education and if we moved here they could get more. We have been moving around too much. We go to our farm, we go to Knight's Inlet, we go to Village Island, and then we come here. We have got to stop this." So I made up my mind to move to Alert Bay and live on that Industrial Reserve.

Mr. Todd was away at the time that I made up my mind, so I couldn't talk to him about which part of the reserve I wanted to live on. It was a funny thing though, when I made up my mind everything had to go quick. I'm not going to wait for anything. My wife's father had one acre of ground in that reserve and he told me I could have half of it. There was a bulldozer that happened to be there working for the logging camp, and so I asked him to come and bulldoze the ground to make it level so I could start building a house. So I started building my house right away. I went over to Telegraph Cove and got some lumber and started getting ready to pour the foundation in. I hadn't told anyone at Alert Bay that I was leaving but I sent word quietly to my uncle Henry Bell that he could buy my house if he wanted it. That house had cost me over $3000 and I sold it to him for only $800.

Before that house was even built I sent my wife over to Village Island to get some of our stuff. I didn't want to go because I found it awful hard to go, especially to see my close relations there. I didn't have the nerve to go back. I thought I should go but I felt very badly leaving the people I loved very much. It was hard to leave that place, especially with what I had done in a very short time. I'd built that village as a progressive man. I had built the power plant, the wharf, and a nice home for ourselves. It really hurt me to move. So I said to my wife, "You go back to Village Island and get what you want out of our house. You don't have to get everything. Just leave anything that's not good enough to move. Don't mention to anyone that we are moving and don't talk to anybody. You can hire a couple of the boys to go with you on the 'Frank A. M.' "

So she went over to Village Island, and when she landed Simon Beans and Jack Hanuse met her at the wharf and went to help her move some of the stuff out of our house. They moved out some of the smaller things and nobody thought much of it, but when she had them move the piano out which Miss Nixon had given her it made Simon Beans wonder what we were doing. So he asked her, "Why are you moving all this big stuff out like the bedding and piano and all that furniture?" So my wife had to tell. "Jimmy told me to come and get all our stuff. We are not going to come back. We are selling our house here and we are going to live at Alert Bay." I'm sure that he was really hurt when she told him that. There was no doubt that he talked about it to the others that night. The other boys must have felt very badly about it too because about three months after that a lot of them started moving to Alert Bay. Simon Beans was the first one and then all the Hanuse boys moved and then some others. I would say that within a few months nearly 50 percent of my people moved here from Village Island. The other people felt bad also and Miss Nixon was crying while they were loading those things on the boat.

When Mr. Todd came back I told him I had decided to move onto the Industrial Reserve. Alert Bay at that time was made up of three sections: an unincorporated village at one end where the white people lived and all the stores were, the Nimpkish Indian Reserve, and the Industrial Reserve where the St. Michael's Residential School was. These three parts of Alert Bay were right next to each other and stretched out along the waterfront. Mr. Todd showed me a book which had plans in it for different houses and I found one that looked like it would be a nice house for a large family. I got the main idea for the house from this book but I changed it around some. I had worked with contractors up at the cannery and had been familiar with blueprints, so I made plans on paper as to the size of the house and the rooms and where the electricity was going to be and everything else. I had learned some of this from looking at plans of boats and how they were built. It was similar to building a house. Then I had had a lot of experience from building my home at Village Island and helping others build theirs. I started building it about the first of March and got the basement done and the shell put up and the roof on. Then I boarded it up and went up north to go fishing.

Some of the waters up north were strange to me but I could check the charts and make my way pretty well. I had an echo sounder on the boat then which would tell us how deep the water was and that was a big help. At the start of the season I went to each of my crew who had fished last year to see if they wanted to come back with me again. I usually gave my old crew another chance each year to come with me. So they all came and we went out fishing, but I had some trouble with some of them. I had been the high boat in our company for a couple of years and wanted to stay right up there so I really worked hard. I put my mind to what I was doing and I never wasted any time and stayed out on the fishing grounds as long as I could. Some of the other boats would just take off whenever they wanted to. We were allowed to make our first set on Sunday evening at 6. That was the time that the whole crew had to be alert because there was a lot of fish around then, and sometimes if we made a good set the first time on Sunday night we would have made it for the whole week. It used to be very important to a good skipper who was trying hard and catching a lot of fish to make a good set on Sunday night. Well, that summer a few times when we came in for the weekend some of my crew would just drink all weekend and then walk aboard my boat with a hangover from Saturday night and they weren't any good to me all day Sunday. Sometimes I would have trouble finding them on Sunday morning or getting them down to the boat on time to leave. I wanted to leave early in order to get a good position and be able to make a set right at 6 o'clock that night.

Well, I'd had some trouble getting one of these fellows there on time and when he came I was talking to him and he started to argue back. The engine was running and it was windy and when I talked to him I shouted at the top of my voice. I knew that I couldn't control myself but I made sure that he heard what I had to tell him. Maybe I shouted that way because it was so noisy and windy on the boat. Well, he argued back and tried to tell me that he was right and so I told him he was wrong and just kicked him off. I used to have to change my crew around a lot because of fellows like that. I used to find it hard to have my relatives on board as crew members because sometimes they depended too much on me. That's the way I saw it. They didn't like to take too much responsibility because they figured that the old man was up at the wheel and they would just go down and sleep. I thought it was much better to have a strange man. I found that if I had my relatives sometimes they didn't care. I would talk rough with them too but it didn't matter how rough I talked to them, they would just think that I was no good and that was all there was to it. They weren't all that way because some of them were very good workers.

Right after I kicked this fellow off my crew I met one of my Yugoslavian friends on the wharf who was the skipper and owner of his own boat. We started talking and I told him that I had kicked this fellow off and I had to get a new man for my crew. He said to me, "Jimmy, your people are not very reliable. Why don't you get some of our people? There are a lot of Yugoslavians in Vancouver." "Well," I said, "I don't know who to get." So he told me that he was going down to Vancouver and he would get one for me. A few weeks later he let me know about this fellow he had brought up with him and I picked him up on the wharf, a Yugoslavian fellow named Mike Lazich. He had some little kids of his own who stayed behind in Vancouver with his wife. He was a very humble man and I found him to be very reliable and a good worker. Alvin was just about three years old then and he would come on the boat fishing with me like all of the kids had done. I used to see Alvin when he would get up and he would go in to Mike who was cooking and say, "Come on, cook, you cook me bacon and eggs." He would order him around and Mike would just sit him down and cook his breakfast for him. We did very well that year again and I was top boat for the company among our Indian skippers. Some of the other Indians fished for a couple of other companies but I was above the top boats for those companies too.

After the fishing was over I came back to Alert Bay and began working on my house again. I used to work from 7 in the morning until midnight just nailing away and then I would just about crawl home. Everything I did was by hand because we didn't have any power tools. I built everything there was to that house, except the electricity, because everything was inspected in that village. I knew a little bit about electrical wiring but it was different from Village Island where we had our own light plant. Sometimes some of the boys like Simon Beans would come and give me a hand for a couple of hours. Mr. Todd used to come down in the evening when he had finished his supper and sit down and watch me work. Flora used to bring me some sandwiches and stuff like that about 6 and I would eat right there and then start all over again and work until midnight. When I was building the fireplace he came and lay down on the floor and watched me putting the bricks in. When it was built up through the first floor he came upstairs and lay down and watched me. He used to say, "Jimmy, I sure like to watch you work," because I was just packing the bricks and everything by myself and usually nobody was there helping me.

One day late in the fall he came to me while I was working there with Simon Beans and my wife's uncle. He didn't want to say what he had to say in front of them so he asked me if I could go and take a walk with him. There was a little trail from the house but no road then, so we walked up there together. "Well, Jimmy," he said, "I have bad news for you. I thought you should be the first man to know about it. The government in Ottawa wants this particular reserve to come under a band of people and not be a separate reserve. Since the Nimpkish people are close by they are going to give them first chance to have you amalgamate with them. If they don't want to accept the people in this Industrial Reserve then maybe we can go to the Mamalilikulla band and see if they will accept. You know yourself, Jimmy, that you people come from all over this agency and some of you are from outside of it."

It didn't take me long to answer Mr. Todd when he said that to me, because right from the beginning when I first moved from Village Island the people who already lived there looked upon me as a leader of all those people. Some of them were from Turnour Island, Village Island, Kingcome, and Fort Rupert. There were people from all over the Kwakiutl agency as well as other parts of British Columbia, because that Industrial Reserve belonged to all the Indians in British Columbia. Anybody could have come there and that was what was in the back of my mind. I was really active and felt that if other progressive Indians wanted to move here we could build a real wonderful reserve. I knew that I was going to do it without the help of the Indian Department. I knew that if a man stood on his own feet it could be done and if I could train my people like that and everybody stood on his own feet we could be much better off than the other villages.

Well, I told him right away, "I will not go for that!" He asked me why and so I tried to explain it to him in the little knowledge of English that I had. "I moved here because I thought this was a shelter for a person like me. I know that I was having a difficult time in the village where I came from with the people who liked to do things in the old Indian way and were not progressive. And I think that the people who moved onto this reserve before me and after me chose a wonderful place to come because it is much freer here than where we came from. I understood that we were to be protected by the law here and we were to be helped in anything that we would like to do. Maybe I am too late now. If that is going to happen then I would like to move out of here." "Well," Mr. Todd said, "I just thought I'd tell you, Jimmy. Think about it. Don't say anything about this to the other boys for now." Then he went away.

Then about a week later he came back and talked to me again and tried to get me to change my mind. So we talked and I told him, "You know why I came to this reserve. I liked to work and improve things at Village Island so we would have a nice little village to live in there but some of them didn't agree with that. Even though it hurt me to move away from there I did it because this property here was separate from any other reserve and was for the people who wanted to pull away from their own reserves. This reserve was put aside for progressive people that want to advance in life with modern homes and things like that, which I think is very good. If you let us live here on this five hundred acres I am going to make something out of it. I'm going to start some industries and maybe have a little sawmill here as well as our own barber shop and cooperative store. It has been in the back of my mind to start up some things like that for the people, so that their money will come back to them and not all go down to the white end of town where the stores are. All the stores and businesses and anything we want to buy are all in that end of Alert Bay and nothing comes to our end." Mr. Todd talked to me every week or two after that but I kept telling him that I was against amalgamating with the Nimp-kish people.

The ministers at Christ Church in Alert Bay were changing around every few years. When I moved the minister was Mr. Roberts. He was a very good minister in his own way and he did a good job. He was a white man but was married to Emma Kenmuir's daughter, who was half-Indian and half-white. Some of the minis-ters who came before him were altogether different men. Some of them were the kind that used to just ring the bell and sit in the church and expect the people to come. I didn't think much of them because I didn't think that was right. I thought the right approach was to go and visit the people. If you have a friend you have to go and visit him and he has to go and visit you. That's the way friend-ship is. If you don't visit your friends then you are going to lose contact with them. Pretty soon, if you don't visit your friends or even your relatives, you just drift away from them. First five years go by, then ten years, and then twenty years pass and you don't see them. The first thing you know, even though you are relatives, your children and their children grow up and they don't know that they are related. I am speaking as an Indian because that is the way the Indian feels about it.

At that time some of the leaders in the church, Mr. and Mrs. Harris, Mr. and Mrs. Cook, and George Luther, got up a special gathering for me. Mrs. Harris and Mrs. Cook were my godmothers and very strong leaders in the work of the church. I remember that Mrs. Harris used to stop me on the road and ask me how the fishing was. I would say, "It's real good. I got a lot of fish." Then she used to say to me, "We are praying for you all the time. I pray for you every time you go out there so that God can supply you with all your needs." I'll never forget that. I thought a lot of her for saying that to me. At that special gathering one of them got up and said: "We are all very happy to see that you have moved to Alert Bay because we need you. You are the person that we have been wishing would come here to take up our work that we have been doing these last few years." I had been trained and I looked back and realized that my parents and my grandparents were all gone and I moved towards the church away from my grandparents and towards those people who were carrying on the work of the church. They weren't going to live very long after that and all the work of the church was to come on me, just one man.

At that time I was appointed by the minister to be the rector's warden. The leaders in the Anglican church were the rector, the rector's warden, and the people's warden. Then there was a committee of ten people who carried out the business of the church. My job was to work together with the minister as well as sit in with the church committee. Whenever the rector was away I would step in and take over the services in the church. It was quite difficult for me to do that the first time because I couldn't speak very good English like I should. I found it pretty hard. The first time I ever spoke in the church I had to speak half-Kwakwala and half-English. There were half of my people in there and I explained to my people that I had to do it in order to get used to what I was doing there standing before my people in the church for the first time. I never forgot that my grandmother, old Lucy, used to tell me to take in all I could in school and learn so that I could stand before my people and preach to my people the gospel. That was her wish and I wished then that she could come for one minute and see. Before I would get up in the church and preach I would read the Bible at the place I thought I would talk about. I looked at it in the Bible and prepared it but I couldn't write it down. One of the first few times I tried to write it down but I lost my notes, so from then on I just put it in my head and when I got up there I just started preaching. I never forgot what I was going to say. Quite often I talked about loving one another and working for the church and for one another. I was a great believer in unity. I believed we should be united in everything we did, especially in our Indian village, so that we could work together in order to build a better place for all of us to be worthwhile to live in. That was always my ambition.

It was at that time too, when I first moved to Alert Bay, that I started conducting the Kwakwala prayer meetings on Friday nights. It was started many years before that by Rev. Hall, who was the first missionary to come to Alert Bay. He started this but he didn't want to run it himself. He wanted the Indians to take the greater part of it and to hold it in their own language and to take turns preaching every Friday night. That was why they called it the Kwakwala prayer meeting. I had gone to it before when I happened to be in Alert Bay on Friday nights and George Luther, who was conducting it then, would ask me to sing a hymn in our language. They used to like very much to hear it in our own language. The old-timers who went to the first Anglican school here had translated many of the anthems into the Kwakwala language, and we were the only people who were still using those anthems in that Friday night prayer meeting. Sometimes he would ask me to say a few words. There used to be fifty or sixty people attending then, when I started conducting the prayer meeting. We were having them in the church, and I would open it with the singing of a few Kwakwala hymns and then I might speak to the people or have someone else speak. I could speak our language fluently and teach my people the Bible in Kwakwala without any trouble. I was just the leader who directed it and I would approach some other person to teach oftentimes. At the end of the meeting I would say a prayer or ask the oldest person in the group to say a prayer. When we closed in prayer we would remember all the sick people, remember all the trouble that was going on in the world, ask God's guidance for all the people that were in authority over us, and all that kind of thing. Sometimes we would have visitors from the other villages and they would come when they knew about it. They were especially interested to listen to the Kwakwala anthems.

One of the things I liked the most was singing in the choir. When I was a very young boy George Luther used to teach me how to sing and he would be playing the organ, and that's why I joined the choir. We would practice every week and then sing on Sunday in the church. I remember one Sunday morning I was sitting in the choir seat and somebody came in the door during the service and came right up to me and told me quietly that Dave Matilpi had passed away. So I had to sneak through the back door and go down to the hospital. He had been sick in the hospital for quite a while. I felt very bad about it because he was a great loss to his village and to the whole Kwakiutl agency. He was a very respectable man in his time.

Just before Christmas I had finished enough of our new house to move in. Only the sitting room, the dining room, and the kitchen were finished, but we moved in anyway and we all slept in the dining room and the front room. Of course I was working every day to finish the stairway and the rooms upstairs. One day early in 1946 Mr. Todd came to me again while I was working on my house and said he wanted me to call a meeting of the boys who were close to me and had moved onto the Industrial Reserve. So I went around and told just the leading boys, like the Hanuse brothers and Simon Beans and some others, to come to my house. Most of those who came were ones who had moved over from Village Island. So we got together in my house and I told them about the word from Ottawa that they wanted us to amalgamate with one of the other bands. And none of them liked it. Not one of them liked it because after I had told them about it I explained to them my own way of thinking why I didn't like it. I had already explained to Mr. Todd but I told them, "This reserve was wide open for any person who wants to come here. Anyone would be welcome. But if we should come under the Nimpkish band then there would be a war among us. There are some people in the other villages that I would like to see come here and live with us because they are progressive Indians, but those Nimpkish people will not let them enter the reserve if we amalgamate with them." The result of that meeting was that we were all against it.

Of course Mr. Todd didn't like it very well either but he was forced by Ottawa to pass it on to us. He had even told me that there was one old gentleman in Victoria that was on our side. He told me, "That old gentleman doesn't want you to be a part of any band. He wants you to start a band of your own because he knows that you can make a better group of people the way you are living. He knows that you people understand more than the other people and that was why you made up your mind to come here, because this Industrial Reserve is altogether different from the other reserves. It was set aside by the missionary and the Indian Department from the early days for any progressive Indian to come and move here." I never did find out who that man was. But I told Mr. Todd again that if we could stay separate on that Industrial Reserve we would be the most outstanding village in the agency. But if we were going to have some people that were just going to hang onto our shirttails and that wouldn't really come along with us and progress, well, that was just going to be a nuisance to us. If we could have our own separate reserve we would have more courage to go ahead with all we wanted to do, like building a sawmill and a boat shop and having our own store. So I continued to stand up against the government and refuse to give in to what they wanted us to do.

During the next fishing season our boats did very well and I was top boat again for our company. I had started a little store where I just sold candy and fruit, but I wanted to get a bigger store going so after the fishing season was over I talked to Robby about it. I told him, "I think it would be a good thing if we opened a store together. The way I figure it our business is doing fine and we could supply our boats with groceries and things like that." That was my idea behind having that store. So old Chief Joe Harris of the Nimp-kish people had a little store that he wanted to sell, so we bought it in December of 1946 for $441 and called it "Sewid and Bell." We bought the building and the business, and of course we improved it. We had groceries and clothing, like work clothes, gloves, rain gear, and things like that. We used that store to supply our own crew with what they needed. We found it really hard for Robby and I to look after it because we would be out buying clams or fishing a lot of the time. My wife used to go and look after it and Robby's wife too, taking turns.

During the summers my wife and children continued to go up to the farm. They had a good time there but I had begun to feel that all that moving around wasn't too good a life. I decided to get rid of it because we had to leave it unattended for many months of the year and everybody who came by would just help themselves to tools and go there and damage the buildings and other things. I didn't like that but I couldn't do anything about it, so just before the fishing began in 1947 I sold it for $2000 to Oscar Soderman. He was a friend of mine who used to do a lot of logging around there.

Mr. Todd came to me one day and said, "Jimmy, I got another letter from Ottawa and they want you to go through with amalga-mating the Industrial Reserve with the Nimpkish people or some other band. I've been thinking about it and I'll tell you what I'm going to do. I promise you that if you will amalgamate with the Nimpkish people I will do all I can for you. I promise you with all my power as the Indian agent, I will improve this village. The first thing we will do is to build a new day school up here, and then we will build a road through this reserve. Then we will put in a water system for the reserve. If there is just a small group of people here we can't do it. We can't do it for the small group that are on the Nimpkish reserve, but if you should amalgamate then we could build a water system for you." It was absolutely necessary for us to get a water system because all we had was one water outlet and the water was so slow that it took a long time to fill up a bucket of water. "Well," I said, "I am going to talk to some of the boys. I'm not going to have any more meetings but I'm just going to talk to them one by one."

After talking with him I kind of made up my mind that if we could get those things to improve our way of life it might be worth amalgamating with the Nimpkish. That night I talked it over with close relations and told them, "If we amalgamate we are going to get a water system for nothing and it will be a good one. We will get a school and that's what I came here for. That will be a good thing for my children, not for me, but I'm only here to stand by them. It will be an advantage too to get a good road through here if we accept." After that I called my friend Hebber Webber in, who had moved down from Kingcome. I told him everything and that I was going to give in and accept what they wanted us to do. And I told Hebber to go up to Kingcome and talk it over with his mother and older brothers. So he took this little gas boat that I had and went up there for two or three days. When he came back he came right up to my house and said, "Jimmy, my mother and my brothers told me not to worry about them. They think we are all right here. They thing we did the best thing to move here and they told me to stay." We were all thinking that if they forced us to amalgamate and we didn't want to we could have moved back to our villages. So I told Mr. Todd that we were ready to go ahead with it and so he talked to the Nimpkish people and they were willing to ask us to amalgamate with them.

It took well over a year for my mind to be made up because they weren't going to force that on me. I still think sometimes that if I'd held out a little longer I could have had what I wanted. I still think that I shouldn't have given in but should have just brought the progressive people here. We could have had industries and all kinds of things to make this the most outstanding village. We had way more money than the Nimpkish people because we had lots of timber and when it was logged off we put all the money into a band fund rather than distributing it like the Nimpkish people did. I think that I could have really built that place up into a real industrious Indian village. I was thinking in the back of my mind that I would have liked to have had my own tribe there of progressive Indians from all over British Columbia. That was why I insisted, as the spokesman for the Industrial School Reserve, that when we amalgamated it would be on the condition that the Nimpkish band would be wide open for anybody to transfer into it.

So early in 1950 Mr. Todd called a special meeting of all the Nimpkish band and the people who were from the Industrial Reserve. We sat there with the young strong men that we had in our end and I told them again, "We will amalgamate with you on one condition. There is only one condition on which I will give in, and that is if this reserve is wide open to others who want to come and live here." Some of those Nimpkish people used to say that the reason I didn't want to amalgamate with them was because we thought they were no good and drank too much and things like that. I never did judge people for what they were on things like that. I told them, "I am going to amalgamate with you if you just open the doors for all the other people that want to come and join this band. If you won't do that then I won't have anything to do with it." Of course they all said yes and we amalgamated with them. The trouble was that it wasn't in writing and that was the worst part of it. I should have told them to sign an agreement with me to allow others to join that reserve. So Mr. Todd read a statement which officially transferred the title of the Industrial School Reserve property to the Nimpkish band. We had logged off the timber from that reserve and so had about $9000 in the bank, which was transferred into the Nimpkish band capital account. On top of that each of us brought our share of money from our original bands. I'll never forget that the capital account for the Nimpkish people at that time was only $3500, and after we transferred in it brought it up to $30,000. Joe Harris was still the hereditary chief then and he handled most of the affairs of the band with the help of the Indian agent. If there were any big decisions to be made they would call a meeting of the entire band to take a vote. So, although I had inherited positions in the Kwiksutainuk and Mamalilikulla tribes I was now legally a member of the Nimpkish band.

For some time Robby Bell and I had been talking about having a little sawmill where we could cut our own lumber for repairing our boats and building houses for our boys who were moving to Alert Bay. So about a month after we were amalgamated with the Nimpkish people Robby Bell, Simon Beans, and I each put up so much money and started a sawmill. I went down to Vancouver and looked around for equipment which we had delivered to us in the Bay. The first thing we did was to start putting in some pilings on the beach because we were going to put the sawmill right at the edge of the water where we could easily get the logs we floated down. We decided to put it up over on the back of the island behind Alert Bay. We didn't know it but that was quite a windy place there with no shelter, and the pilings we put up that day were all washed out. We were very thankful that it was blowing that day because otherwise we could have lost a lot of equipment if we had gotten the sawmill completed before a stormy day.

So we had to move our sawmill over to this side of the island and we put it in the corner of the bay down past St. Michael's Residential School. Robby and I had changed the engine on the "Adele M." a few months before that and so we used the old engine to drive the sawmill. We began work right away whenever we were in on weekends or when the Fisheries Department closed down the fishing. Some weeks they only allowed us to fish four days a week and they had shortened the whole fishing season so we had more time. After the fishing season was over we would work at our sawmill whenever we had a chance. At that time we were allowed to pick up the beach logs which had drifted ashore on the islands around this area. If we found a log that had been stamped by a logging company we would report it to the Forestry Department, but otherwise we were allowed to cut up the logs we found and pay the government so much a thousand for them. It was quite nice. Sometimes when the log we found had been stamped by a logging company they would let us buy it from them at so much for a thousand. We only used small stuff because we couldn't handle the really big logs.

While the most important thing was to cut lumber for our boats and houses, we also started selling some lumber commercially to the people that wanted it. We trained Simon to work on the carriage where the logs came in to the saw. Of course I was working at the head saw where I had to determine just how to cut the log into the size lumber we wanted. I was doing that because I liked to get the most out of the log and make the best cuts possible. Simon's boy was tail sawing and piling the lumber up and Bobby and Oswald used to come and help us after school. We cut a lot of lumber and then stored it away in the shed we had built so that it would dry out. We made a few dollars to pay for our expenses by selling lumber, but we used a lot of the lumber for our boats and saved money that way. If you sent your boat to a machine shop or boat shop in those days to have it repaired you had to pay a tremendous amount and you never got out of the hole. Even if you repaired your boat yourself you had to pay very high prices for the lumber. So we would just cut up yellow cedar and other kinds of lumber in any size we needed for repairing our boats. We were just helping one another out in repairing each other's boats. If Simon wanted to repair his boat I would go and help him and if I repaired my boat he would come and help me. We had an agreement that we were going to help one another and not charge for labor. That was how we were able to pay for our boats. We changed the cabin and the deck on the "Frank A. M." and did the same thing on some of the other boats.

At about that time Mr. John Nygaard, the Pentecostal minister, wanted to build a church in Alert Bay. He came to see Simon and me about cutting up his lumber for him if he brought us the logs from the beach. We told him that if he brought us the logs and paid the stump tax, which was about $7 per thousand, we would cut it up for him and divide up the lumber equally. That was our deal, just like any other sawmill, and if he wanted all the lumber then he could buy the other half from us. So we cut all his lumber and loaded it onto our truck and took it down to the place at the other end of the village where he wanted to build his church. We made shiplap, two by fours, and all kinds of different pieces like he had ordered and put them through the planer. We cut all the lumber that he needed for that building.

One night I got a phone call that there was some trouble starting in one of the houses on the reserve. Some non-Indians were supplying some of the young girls with liquor in one of the houses. So I phoned the Royal Canadian Mounted Police and told him it was very important that they come right away because we didn't want to have to call later when these people started to make a lot of trouble. I told him that they were just starting to pack that liquor in there and that I thought it was time for them to come and tell them to leave the Indian Reserve. Well, by the way he talked I could tell that he didn't want to come because he was busy. So the next day I found out that none of the RCMP had come the night before and there had been some trouble. So Chief Joe Harris and Stephen Cook came to me. Those two leading men of the village asked me if I would go and sign some kind of petition with them about the RCMP. They were going to write to the attorney general, so I agreed, and the three of us signed it and had it mailed in by Barney Williams who was a lawyer there.

A few weeks later I was walking through the village down at the other end and the head man of the RCMP called me in and asked me if I knew anything about the letter that had been written to the attorney general in Victoria. He showed me a copy of the letter and my signature was on it. "Sure," I said, "that's my signature. I signed it with the two old men." He asked me why we did it and I told him, "Well, I made a phone call to your office here and told them that there was a man supplying liquor to the Indian girls at one of the houses on our reserve. I thought it was a good idea if he would go there and tell them to leave before there was any trouble. There was trouble later that night and your man never did go down and do anything about it. So when the two old men came to me we signed that letter. It is your duty to patrol our end because we are under the federal government just like the RCMP. We expect to be protected. I'm going to make sure that you patrol our end because I'm going to write to the prime minister in Ottawa and to our members there." I figured that it was something for the House of Commons to argue about. I don't think we had the right to vote as citizens at that time and it would have been different if the provincial police had been there, but the RCMP were under the federal government the same as us. Anyway, after that they used to come back and forth in front of our house all the time patrolling our reserve.

By that time I had been living in Alert Bay for nearly five years and I was really busy with all the things I was doing. We had our fishing business and our store and sawmill. I had finished my new house and our kids were going regularly to school although the older ones had already had to drop out. One thing that was quite different was putting on potlatches. The law against that was still strong and Alert Bay was really bad for that kind of thing. Even when the mounted police weren't very interested in whether we did those potlatches or not, there were too many old churchgoers who were squashing it. If you saw them in church after you had been taking part in it they would say, "There is the old devil." That was the kind of people that we used to have there, but they knew they were wrong because you couldn't judge people on their appearance or on whether they took part in those potlatches. Once in awhile, if I wasn't too busy, I would go to one of the other villages for some potlatch that was being put on, but I didn't do anything myself or put on anything at Alert Bay. Sometimes something would go on at Alert Bay in a very quiet way, and without calling all the people together someone would go around to the homes and give some things away.

left to right: Emma, James Sewid's mother, Henry Bell, his uncle, and James Sewid, his
. The infant at the far left is Emma's youngest sister

James Sewid held by his grandmother Lucy Sewid, Alert Bay. His wife's mother's uncle Yakatan is on the left

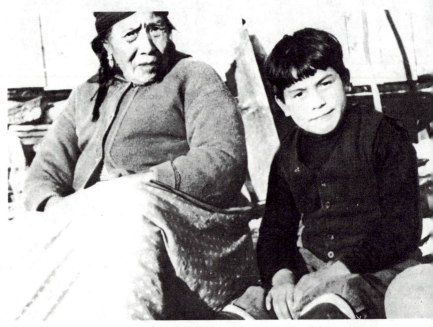

James Sewid (age 7) and his grandmother Lucy

The home of James Sewid's wife, Flora, ca. 1918

James Sewid's house, built in 1945, Alert Bay

James Sewid (center) in sports days parade, 1965, passes his house in Alert Bay. He wea
the vestments of the Anglican church and carries his Indian talking stick

Seine boat designed and owned by James Sewid

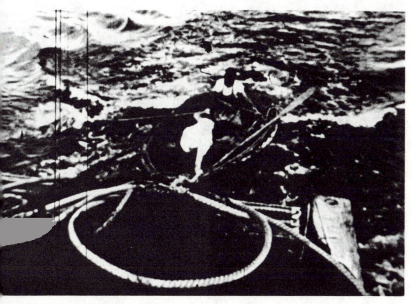

Members of the crew push off to set out the net

The net being set

James Sewid and crew restoring the net

sing the beam for the
mmunity house, 1965

e beams of the
mmunity house in place

Kwakwala Arts and Crafts dance group in the community house. *Left*, Flora Sewid; *third from left*, James Sewid

The *hamatsa* mask of James Sewid

6   A Very High Ranking Man

In those days the leading men in each of the Kwakiutl tribes were referred to as "chiefs." They were the ones who had inherited the high positions in the clans of that tribe like my grandfather, Aul Sewid, and Jim Bell. The man with the highest position was usually the spokesman for the tribe and looked upon as the chief of the village in which he lived. The government usually recognized this man as the chief of the village and the Indian agent would work with this man on any of the business the tribe had to do with the government. In a few cases, like at Village Island, the government had recognized another leading man of the village who wasn't the spokesman or the highest ranking person. They might do this because the highest ranking position was held by a woman or someone who was hard to deal with because he didn't know any English at all. For any important matters such as leasing of timber rights the Indian Department had started a more democratic way by having a general meeting of the tribe where the people voted. This worked pretty well, but it was often hard to get enough people out to those meetings to get a decision made since we had to have at least a quorum.

When I had been at the Native Brotherhood conventions I had heard that the government had made a new section of the Indian Act which allowed a tribe to have an elected council instead of an hereditary chief. Some of the other villages outside of the Kwakiutl agency had already gone over to that. So I started talking to Mr. Todd about this. I told him many times that I thought it was about time that we got into that new section of the Indian Act and had an elected council. Of course some of the people would not go along with me and they thought I was crazy to talk like that. I didn't want the elected council because I was prejudiced against any hereditary chief or anything like that. Old Joe Harris, who was the chief at that time, was a great leader in the church and his wife was my godmother. Mrs. Harris always used to refer to me as her nephew.

He was one of the first ones to move down and live on the land that had been the Industrial School Reserve. He was one of the first pupils to go to school under Rev. Hall.

The main reason I was for the elected council was that it would give the people a chance to elect who they thought could do the most work for the people. Also, rather than just one person they would have two or three working on the council along with the chief councillor. I thought it was more democratic that way. When there was just one chief running everything it was more like a dictator. Another problem was that in order to get some of the business done we had to have a general meeting with at least a quorum present of the voting members of the band. My people didn't care about meetings and sometimes there would be a meeting and only twenty or thirty would come when we needed fifty. It was also too hard for one man to try and do everything with just the help of the Indian agent. If there was a chief councillor and three or four men to work with him on the council it would be possible to get more things done for the people. Of course outside of the government for that particular village I was all for respecting the hereditary chief in that village. I thought it was a wonderful thing if we could respect the elders and the great men of the village. I was all for that. I always respected those people when I was a little boy and I thought it was good.

In 1950 Chief Joe Harris died and so I went to Mr. Todd again and told him that I thought we ought to have an elected council. So he wrote to Ottawa about it and one night he came to me and said, "Well, Jimmy, we've got word from Ottawa. Since the chief died they said they wanted us to have an election. This will be the first village to have an elected council." So I said, "That's fine. That's what I have been wanting for a long time." So Mr. Todd put up a notice on the band bulletin board for all voting members to attend a general meeting on October 28. There were about three hundred members to the band at that time but only about seventy who could vote.

So the day for the meeting came and we met in an old poolroom down near the waterfront. We had a general meeting first to discuss some of the business of the Nimpkish band and Mr. Todd was leading the meeting. We discussed a request by the British

Columbia Power Commission to have a right of way through the Industrial School Reserve and then voted to give them permission. The Hanuse boys had started a little logging company and we passed a motion for them to log off some of the timber from our reserve. Several applications were accepted for people to transfer into the Nimpkish band. Then Mr. Todd opened up the meeting for elections for chief councillor, after telling us that we were going to come under the new section of the Indian Act which allowed us to have an elected chief and council rather than the hereditary chief. He said we would be allowed one chief and three councillors because we were allowed to have one councillor for each one hundred members of the band. He told the people that the council could appoint various committees with one of the elected councillors as their chairman to make recommendations to the council on matters which affected the welfare of the people. The council when it was elected would assume the responsibility for the affairs of the Nimpkish band and would have authority to act on all matters after Ottawa had approved and confirmed their election.

First they had the nominations for chief and then before voting on the chief they nominated people for the councillor positions. Wilfred Hanuse, who was my countryman from Village Island, nominated me. I think that Dan Hanuse and I were the only ones nominated for chief who were not original members of the Nimpkish band. I was also nominated for one of the councillors along with almost twenty others. Well, we voted after that for chief and I was elected because I had the most votes. I'll never forget after they announced that I had won the election that Wilfred Hanuse shouted at me and said, "Give a speech!" I never used to give speeches in those kind of meetings but I got up anyway and said, "I will do my best." That was all I said, and then I sat down. Then they voted on the councillors and Dan Hanuse, George Alfred, and Herbert Cook were elected.

I didn't even know that I was going to be elected but after that meeting I went home and thought about it. I thought about how I had lived in the Nimpkish village with old Lucy and there was no doubt that there was somebody unknown that was always on my side. I couldn't begin to imagine what the original Nimpkish people would have thought if they could have known that I had become chief councillor of that village. And I asked God for His guidance in this new job as chairman of the council. I thought about my favorite text in the Bible. It was in the Old Testament where Solomon was left to be king by his father, King David. He thought to himself that he was too young and he wasn't capable enough to look after the many people that his father had left behind and so he asked God for wisdom. It was a wonderful thing that this young king asked for wisdom rather than wealth or a long life or to be strong. He said, "No, I'd rather have wisdom to understand my people and to try and make the best for them all the time that I will reign over them." That was my favorite text in the Bible and I always read it. I still do that today and I have been doing it ever since I was first elected, and I think that is the source of the great help that I know I have been blessed with. Many times I have pointed that text out to my children.

I felt badly about being elected because both my father-in-law and my uncle, who were original Nimpkish people, had been nominated but I was elected over them. I knew how they felt and I felt that I didn't want to hurt their feelings. I figured that one of them would get in anyway instead of me. I was really shocked because I didn't think I had a chance in the face of all those Nimpkish people. I don't know what happened but I had the most votes. There must have been quite a few of the young people there that were from the same village that I came from. I'm not sure how they felt but I knew that Ed Whanock used to treat me as his own son and look after me. I'm sure that he felt glad that the rest of them didn't get in but his son made it. That's the way I saw it, but I didn't know. I thought old Moses Alfred thought the same way. "My son is in and I think it's good."

Of course I began to hear that some of the rest of them were making remarks like, "Why should he run us? Why should he come and run our village? He is an outsider!" I don't think they felt good that I won the election and was to be the chief councillor and so they were making all kinds of remarks like that, but I just heard it from other people. They didn't dare to come and tell me. One thing I always said was that the people never came and said it in front of me. Later on I even challenged them in the meetings that if they had anything against me to say so. I felt that was the time to say it, but they never did say it in the meeting. I felt that was the only place where we could settle our disagreement. So they just continued to say that all during my term in office. "What business does he have to run us? He's an outsider!" I never paid any attention to them. They were so narrow-minded. I felt that if they were good enough and thought that the village should be run in a different way they could have come to me and spoken to me about it. Then we could just work together for the betterment of my people.

When I was first elected chief of that village I used to talk to the elders of the people. I would ask them what they felt we could do and then tell them what I would like to do. I knew that they never used to approve of all the things that I wanted to do but they could just tell me. I thought it was a good thing to treat them as advisers and as elders of the village. I wouldn't like to take anything on my own if I knew they were against it, especially because I was a newcomer to that village. And everything we did after that had to be passed by the council and we didn't want to hurt any of the people. I'd be the last man to try and do something to hurt my people. If I hurt them by doing something wrong then I was going to hurt myself because everything we did in that council was down on paper. Of course there were some people who were opposed to me but they didn't bother me a bit. I knew sooner or later that there was going to be quite a change and if I was strong in my stand then everything would be in the past and our village would progress.

Mr. Todd came to me after that election and promised he would help me with anything I needed. He used to tell me, "If you want anything, Jimmy, if you want any meeting, you can come any time, nighttime, daytime, my time is yours. Anything you want me to help you with I will do it." He was a wonderful Indian agent. I never saw any man like him. He really lived up to his promises to me and he really worked hard with me for my people.

Right after the election I was planning to go down to Vancouver to settle all my business with the company. I used to go down every year after the fishing was over to settle my business. Flora's parents and her aunt and husband were going down to go along with some other people. I talked to Flora about going and she said she didn't think it was right that we should all go down and leave her because she was getting ready to go into the hospital any time to have a baby. She was kind of mad because she felt everybody was going to leave her. Well, since everybody else was going to go I decided I should stay and go when they came back. A few days after they left I woke up one night and saw Flora getting everything ready so I asked her, "What's the matter? What's going on?" "Never mind," she said, "you go to sleep." But I kept asking her because I saw her fooling around and getting her things ready and I knew something was wrong. So I got up and told her we'd better get in the truck. I didn't have a car then but only an old British army truck. She said, "I don't want to go to the hospital." Well, I was worried then and told her to get ready quick. I was worried that I was going to have to experience a thing like that, having the baby born there at home. So I gathered up all the pillows I could find and put them in the back of that old truck. She kept saying, "Don't get panicky!" But I told her, "You better get in that truck quick because I don't want to keep you here." It was after midnight so she got into the back of that awful old truck and I started to drive her down to the hospital. She kept saying, "Slow down! Slow down! Take it easy!" I was just rushing down that old dirt road as fast as I could taking her to the hospital. I took her in and told the nurse to look after her and then let me know what was going on. I went back home and went to bed.

The next morning I got up early and grabbed the phone and asked the nurse, "How's my wife?" She said, "She is doing very well. She is very strong. You have two little girls." I said to her, "Will you repeat that again?" "You have two little girls. They're twins." Well, I couldn't believe it. I just hung up the phone and didn't know what to do. I phoned her sister Nora, who was home, and told her, "Flora's in the hospital and she has just had twins, twin girls." Well, Nora said, "Oh, I don't believe it." "Well," I said, "I didn't say it. That's what the nurse told me." So she phoned the hospital for herself and the nurse told her that they were twins. I waited until 9 and then phoned my daughter Dora in Vancouver. I told her that her mother was in the hospital and had just had twin girls and that they were both doing well. She wouldn't believe me and when she told her grandparents who she was staying with they wouldn't believe me either, so I just hung up. Nobody would believe me.

So I went to the hospital and saw Flora and asked her how the babies were. She said, "They are all doing well. You better phone Dora in Vancouver and tell her to get a twin buggy and get two alike of all the baby stuff." So I rushed home again and phoned Vancouver again and asked Dora to get us a twin buggy and then she really got panicky. She told me about it later. They all were beginning to believe it and everybody started rushing around. At first they thought I was just telling them a joke. They all went into a big store and got a twin buggy and everything else for the twins. I felt awfully proud to be the father of twins because that was the first time that that had happened in our area. I had heard about twins but had never seen twins that looked just alike. In the early days I used to hear the old people talking about some people who had had twins way before I was born but there hadn't been any born recently. I really felt good. I was a very proud man. I went down to the store and got a couple of boxes of Japanese oranges which had just come in at that time. I took them up to the hospital and told the nurses to pass them around to all the wards. Everybody in Alert Bay heard about it and was happy about it. They were born on November 22, 1950, and we named them Emma Georgia and Mabel Wilhelmina.

After the twins were born I went down to Vancouver and took care of my business with the company. Right after I returned, it was the first or second week of December, there was a big storm that came up. It was a very high tide and there must have been a fifty- or sixty-mile-an-hour gale blowing. The Royal Canadian Mounted Police phoned me and asked me if I could get a boat to go out to Green Island, which was in the channel between Alert Bay and Vancouver Island. They said there were some men on that little rocky island. Well, the tide and the waves were so big that the island was almost covered with water and I didn't think anything could hang onto those rocks because the waves were so strong. I told him I would go right down and get my boat.

When I came down to the wharf I saw Robby running around with the "Adele M." out in the bay so I called him in and told him I wanted to go out and see if there were any people on that island. So we went out and it was real rough. The waves were going over the bridge and we had a hard time getting out there. I was on the wheel and we went right into that little island and couldn't see any men or anything like men. So I went in and went to the police station after Robby dropped me off at the wharf near their office. I went in and told them that we had looked and looked but nobody was there. Well, he said, "It must have been a false alarm." So I just walked away and came back to my house.

As soon as I stepped inside, before I had taken my coat off, the phone rang and it was the police again. This time they told me the full story. They said that the person who had told them said they had seen the Hanuse boys' boat tip over near that island. The boat had a lot of boom chains on the back and the waves were so big that they just threw the boat over. I told him, "Why didn't you tell me that in the first place?" So I just hung up the phone and ran out after telling Flora to phone around and tell some of the other boys. I don't remember just what happened then because I was really upset. I was mad because now it was two or three hours after it must have happened. I met some fellows walking down the road and gave them orders to get their boats and tell everybody to get out there and help us look for the Hanuse brothers. The tide had changed by them and the wind was kind of dying down a little.

I went over to the boat taxi place and got hold of Stanley Hunt and we got the speedboat and raced right across to the sandbar near that island where those boys went down. We found their boat right away with the stern down and it looked like it was anchored by all those boom chains which they had on board. We put a line on the boat because it wasn't too far under water and pulled it across and pulled it up on the beach to see if there was anybody in it but there was nothing. It was getting quite late and dark so I just phoned everybody in their boats and told them to be ready as soon as it was daylight the next day and we would all go out again. The next day was a fine day so we got all the boats that were available and put young men ashore all along the beaches of all the islands around there. We had our phones on and were phoning back and forth between the boats but we couldn't find any of the bodies. The tide had been so strong that we couldn't find anything.

Oh, I felt very bad. I really felt bad because we didn't get their bodies to give them a decent burial. That was a big thing for three brothers at one time to drown, Alex, Wilfred, and Fred Hanuse.

Alex and I had been very good friends. We grew up together in that big house at Village Island and the whole family of Harry Hanuse were close relations of ours. When I moved to Alert Bay, Alex and all the Hanuse boys moved too. Alex and I used to do things together all the time and when he was married I was his best man. It almost drove you crazy to lose three brothers like that at one time. It had never happened to us before and I think the whole village felt the same way. It was terrible, and I especially felt bad because I felt that those boys had a lot of respect for me and we came from the same village and I knew that they always spoke very, very highly of me. I will never forget when Wilfred Hanuse nominated me for chief councillor and when I was elected he called on me to make a speech. I will never forget Wilfred for that because he was a very fine boy. And it was terrible because they all left behind little children to be raised by their mothers.

A few days before the end of December we held our first council meeting. We made a ruling that we were going to have a meeting once a month. I led the meeting and the three councillors and the Indian agent were there. There was so much business to be taken care of that we held another meeting a few days later in January of 1951. Herbert Cook, Dan Hanuse, George Alfred, and myself were four young men that were very young and very active. That was the best council I ever had because those men really worked. We really got things going fast with those three councillors. The first thing we did was to form several committees made up of members of the band with one of us four as chairman of each committee. Dan Hanuse took the building committee, which looked into the housing conditions and the inspection of such things as sewage and water supply. George Alfred took the recreation committee and we set about designating certain parts of the reserve for recreation purposes. I took the entertainment committee and Herbert Cook took the fire protection committee. This last committee was very important and we set aside money for putting in a fire hydrant and fire-fighting equipment. Mr. Todd had gotten us a new water system so we could use that for fighting fires.

One thing that came up right off was about paying for the water the people were using. I proposed to the council and it was passed that all members of the Nimpkish band who were connected to our water system on the reserve should pay $1 each month for water. Any outsiders who were living on the reserve and used our water were to be charged $2 each month. Well, a lot of the people didn't like it. They wanted to have their water free and be exempted from having to pay. But we were appointed to do what we thought was right for the Nimpkish people and as chairman of our council I was thinking of the future. I knew that village was going to grow because I just made that village wide open so that if anybody wanted to come there they could. I knew we were going to need more pipe and another well to supply the people in five or ten years.

The council voted to allow two different logging companies to log off some of the timber from our reserve. The money that came in from that sort of thing was always divided in half. If we got $2000 then $1000 would go to Ottawa to the capital account of the Nimpkish band and $1000 would be distributed to the members of the band. They divided it up among every member of the band; even if it was a one-week-old baby or an eighty-year-old man, it didn't make any difference. They all got equal shares. I didn't approve of this and I told them straight that we were a very poor people financially and that we didn't have enough money to do what we wanted for the village. We had to have money to build up the village and I explained that to the original Nimpkish people. They had been doing it for years and we had nothing to show for it in the village. Another thing was that there were some members of the band that had moved off the reserve into Vancouver or other places and although they received their share they weren't around to contribute anything to the village. So our council passed a motion that instead of returning the money to each individual it would go into a band fund that could be used for the business of the band. Of course I had a lot of opposition and there were a lot of people who didn't like it. They had been doing it the other way all those years and they couldn't see why we should change it. I did what my council thought was best, and even though it wasn't particularly good for me or my family, it was good for the village as a whole and everybody benefited from it. We saved enough money to fix up the council hall and get fire-fighting equipment and carry on other business. One thing we did right away was to hire a bulldozer to clear an area up behind the day school for a park and ball field. I felt that if we could pay for it all then it would be ours, but if the government paid for it then they were going to claim it. I wanted the Nimpkish people to pay for it because it was going to be ours and any time the children wanted to use it they could.

In every council meeting there were lots of small things that came up, like voting on people who wanted to transfer into our band and paying various bills that came in and things like that. One thing that come up during those first council meetings was about a hall on our reserve that belonged to Mrs. Drabble. Originally, old man Johnny Drabble had built that hall. He was a very active and progressive Indian who was a very close relation of mine through my grandfather, Chief Sewid. He was half-Kwiksutainuk and half-Nimpkish, and he used to refer to me as his grandson. He used to like everybody to have a good time. He would give a potlatch and call all his friends into this hall he had built and give away apples and candy. He had built this large hall for himself with his own money, and when anything went on in Alert Bay the people used to go and use the old man's hall. He had a little lean-to in the back where he lived with his wife. When I was a teenager running around in Alert Bay he would call me in and say, "Grandson, any time you want to have a dance you let me know and you can come and use my hall with your friends." He had a player piano with a wide ribbon on the reel and I used to go there with my friends and have a little dance. If there was a wedding going on they would often use that hall after the wedding.

Well, when the old man died, the old lady was living in that house alone and I used to go there and talk to her. She used to really feel good because I would go and talk to her and ask her how she was doing. She was having trouble because the house was a big building and hard to heat and it was falling down and getting rotten. Whenever people would come to visit Alert Bay they would just move into that hall and stay there for a few weeks at a time. The old lady told me that she didn't like everybody using that hall, so I talked it over with my council and the Indian agent that we should get rid of that house and get somebody to build a new house for her. So the council passed that motion and we tore down that hall and Dan Cranmer built a little house for her and she moved into it. We had a lot of opposition on it from some people who said that we were doing something that we shouldn't do. I just told them, "The old lady was the owner of the house and she was the one to say what she wanted. After old Johnny Drabble died she agreed that she wanted a little house to be built for her and that is why we did it." I don't remember anything else that happened but I know that we had quite a time.

In the early spring when the sockeye came into the Nimpkish River, which was part of our reserve, the council appointed me to be in charge of the drag seining for the people to get fish for food. We usually made a net and the people took turns going over to the river to get food fish for their own canning. We weren't allowed to drag seine just anywhere we wanted but only on our own reserves. When they caught a lot of fish it would be brought back and distributed to the people in the village. After a few years we gave that up because there weren't enough fish in that river to make it worthwhile.

For some years the white people in Alert Bay had formed a committee each year which tried to raise money to help support the hospital. This hospital week committee, as it was called, would meet during the spring and plan ways to raise money. That year I was asked to be on the committee. I was the only Indian on the committee and they elected me to be the chairman of that committee, which was the first time that an Indian had been the chairman. I called the committee together and we discussed different ideas for raising money. Mr. Cameron, a friend of mine who was the fisheries officer, used to watch me like an old watchdog to see if I did anything as the chairman that wasn't according to parliamentary procedures. He used to get after me and correct me if I did anything wrong, which was a wonderful experience for me. After we had met a few times I asked my committee to all come back to our next meeting with some definite suggestions of things that we could do.

Before we met again I thought a lot about what we could do, and it just came to me that it would be a good idea to bring the potlatch custom and the dancing out to the surface again and let the public see it because it had been outlawed and lost. I had the idea that we wouldn't go and do it the way they used to do it when they gave people articles to come and watch the dancing. The way I figured it was going to be the other way around, like the theaters, operas, or a good stage program which was put on and the people had to pay money to get in. I knew it was going to draw the outside people like from Beaver Cove, Sointula, and Port McNeil. When our committee met there were several ideas that people suggested we try. One thing we decided to do was to sell tickets for our May Queen like they had done in previous years. Tickets are sold in the name of different girls and the people buy tickets for those girls. The girl who has the most tickets becomes the May Queen and all the proceeds would go into the hospital week fund. My job was to try to raise money, as the chairman, and the more money we raised the better it would be for the hospital. So I said to my committee, "Why don't we put on an Indian dance?" One of them said, "Well, you would have to be the one to do that." So I said, "Fine, I'll do it if you will pass it in a motion in this committee." So they passed it.

The first thing I did was to go and talk to Bill Scow, who was one of the leading men of the people. All the old people were still alive then and we wrote a letter to all the chiefs of the different tribes to come together and bring their dance regalia with them when they came. So when they came I called a meeting for all the chiefs in the community hall. There were a lot of them, about ten or fifteen of the leading men of each village. I was in the chair and Bill Scow was beside me because he had the responsibility as a member of a subcommittee to write to all of the chiefs. It was quite a big meeting and I got up and said, "The reason I brought all you people here, and I hope you brought your masks and stuff, is because we would like to put on a big do. We would like to put on a big Indian dance. I feel that you chiefs all did your duty and gave big potlatches in your days but now that is gone. But you are still the rightful owners of all your masks and things. I think it is a worthy cause to bring you here and we can all support St. George's hospital because we all use it. It will be good for the whole district if we can make some money to contribute to the hospital."

I must have been facing a couple of hundred people in that hall and they were all the chiefs and prominent men. None of the non-Indians on my committee had come with me and I was facing all those people alone. I didn't know what I was going to be up against until one fellow got up and spoke: "Oh, now that we are all here you think you are going to use all our stuff just like that! It cost us money to show it because we always gave away lots of things when we performed with our masks and other regalia. We have all spent all kinds of money to show our stuff before in the Indian way and you aren't going to just bring us here and ask us to show it in this new way." After he sat down a lot of other chiefs got up, and there were many who were against putting on that dance. I was just sitting there with Bill Scow at a little table facing the people. I let them get up one by one and say what they wanted. I was just sitting there and thinking, really deep thinking, that if I just sat there and took what they were saying I might as well quit my job. I might as well give it back to them in very harsh words. And that was the time that the potlatch came back to me while I was sitting there thinking and listening to them. I had some masks and other regalia but I had never given a potlatch to show it. That was the time that I decided that I was going to bring it to the public because they made me mad, really mad. Everybody knew that I owned those things but it was only a matter of showing them and then it would be announced that I was still the rightful owner of it all.

Well, after all the chiefs that wanted to had spoken and all had said the same old thing I got up and spoke. "Thank you very much," I said (of course I was speaking our language). "Thank you very much. You have come on your own expense to Alert Bay as I stated when I first welcomed you. You have come for a good cause to support our hospital. I don't want you to forget this. I'm not a prophet but I'm going to tell you something. Every one of you are going to go into that hospital before you go to the Happy Hunting Grounds. The reason why I brought you here was because I know that the hospital is good for you. It is not just for the Nimp-kish people but for all the other people as well. I have been working for the hospital and raising money for the hospital and none of you have put one cent in there. This was the only time that you could have put something towards this hospital. Now, I have my boats ready and you can all go home. I'm going to take you back to where you came from and I'm going to pay for your expenses. You might as well get out of here. That is all I can say. I want you to go."

You could have heard a dime drop in there. It was real quiet for a minute, maybe five minutes. Everybody was just stopped. I was quite young too and I didn't want to get up again. I was sitting there thinking that if Jim Bell was alive that he could come in there and squash those people to pieces. He was that kind of man and he wouldn't want anybody to talk to me like that. Well, I knew I had some friends there somewhere. I had a lot of uncles and I would say that I was a lucky man. Spruce Martin was still alive and Mungo Martin was alive and Chief Tom Johnson and Ed Whanock were there. Billy Matilpi of the Matilpi people was there, and I think from the Scows at Gilford Island and with Toby Willey and his brothers from Kingcome I had about ten uncles. Henry Bell was there from Village Island as well as Tom Dawson. So Ed Whanock got up and I guess he knew that I was mad because I was really shouting at the top of my voice. "Well, Jimmy," he said, "put me on your list. I've got quite a few masks and I'm going to perform tomorrow night. I've got nothing to be ashamed of. I've been showing all my masks for many, many years and I've given away a lot of money and I will do it for nothing so that I can help this worthy cause of saving people." Oh, that was it! He really hit those chiefs when he said, "I've got nothing to be ashamed of." I just held my head down and was waiting. Billy Matilpi got up next. He was from the Matilpi people and related to me through my grandmother Lucy Sewid. "Jimmy," he said, "Put me on because I'm coming." Then there was Mungo Martin and Spruce Martin. Pretty soon all of them got up one by one and said, "Put me on," and they were just pleading!

The worst part of it was that some of them didn't bring their masks. They had to get a boat and get their masks and I had to pay money to hire speedboats for them to go and pick up their masks. It cost $15 or $20 to hire a speedboat, but that didn't stop me. The next day we all got together to practice and then all those people started fighting among themselves about who was going to be first and who was going to be next. The tribes of the Kwakiutl nation are all in order; the Fort Rupert Kwakiutl are first, then the Mama-lilikulla, then the Nimpkish, and so on, and everybody wanted to be in the right order. For instance, there were four or five people who wanted to put on a dance from the Kwakiutl people at Fort

Rupert and they wanted to be in order as well, so we had to be very careful. I whispered to Bill Scow, who was writing down what our program was going to be, to just go along with them, because we didn't want any more trouble in our family. I wanted to do this thing right because it was like a test case and was going to be the first one and it was going to be a big one. So we put everybody in order and they practiced all day. As they came in according to the rank of their tribe we gave each one so many minutes to do their dance and then we cut it off. There were some of the dancers that we didn't use because we only wanted to use the good ones.

That night the hall was really crowded with people from all over the area. As the chairman I got up and made a speech at the beginning of the evening. I said, "I want to welcome all you people from the white communities who have come tonight and I want to welcome all of my people who are going to put on this performance. In the early days when the Indian people used to put on this kind of dance, the chiefs used to call the people together to come and watch their dance and they paid them to come and watch. Tonight we are going to reverse it. You people that are here tonight have paid to come in to watch this wonderful performance that is going to be put on for you tonight by my people. I'm sure you are going to enjoy it and it is for a good cause." So then each dancer began coming out, and it was announced what dance he was doing and we tried to interpret it all to the white people as the dances were performed. We must have had a five-hour do there that night and I think it was one of the biggest dances because all the big chiefs were there, the prominent and noble men of all the villages. I brought out some of my masks that belonged to me and showed them for the first time that night. And that was the time that I made up my mind that I was going to learn my songs and make some masks, and if I wanted to put anything on I could just grab my sack and go to it. I had taken part in the small potlatches at Village Island and some other places but I hadn't given anything since moving to Alert Bay. And I lived to see all those people that were making those harsh words and remarks to me in that meeting go into the hospital before they died.

My mother was not too well at that time so I would go and visit her. I really felt that my mother had a rough life. She had a lot of respect for me. I knew this because she used to talk to other people about me, even white people, and they used to tell me that she had a lot of respect for me. One time my stepbrother, Gordon Matilpi, got into some trouble. He was a heavy drinker and was in court all the time, and since he was under age my mother used to have to go there. I went there one time when she had gone to juvenile court with Gordon, and before the court started the policeman was talking to her. Bill Scow was interpreting for my mother and he asked her, "I hear that you are Jimmy Sewid's mother. Is that right?" Bill told him that it was true, and the policeman asked Bill, "Why is this boy here so different from Jimmy?" Well, Bill told him that he didn't know and that he should ask my mother. So he asked my mother, "Why is Gordon different from your son Jimmy?" I'll never forget the way she answered that fellow. She said, "I didn't raise my son Jimmy; his grandparents raised him. Maybe that is why he is different from his younger brother." So I thought that was very nice of my mother and I really respected her for that because maybe some other woman would have just said, "I did this for him and I did that for him." She had a rough life because she married my father and he didn't live very long, and then Johnny Clark died a few years after she married him. I think my mother was just a teenager when my father died. I think she did the best she could raising me because she wasn't old and experienced like my grandmother Lucy.

She had been having trouble with a rupture because she was a real big heavy woman. I told her that I thought she had been suffering too long with it and she should go and get it fixed up. So she went into the hospital in Alert Bay and they operated on her. She was recovering very well for four or five days when I got word to go to the hospital immediately. A man was waiting for me in front of the hospital and took me right in, and the doctor told me that she was dying right then and that there was no chance. I don't know what happened but she was in a very bad pain and about a half hour after I got there she died. I really felt bad. I felt that I had lost the only thing I ever really had in my life. I had never seen my father and now my mother who had had such a rough life was gone too.

Robby and I were still operating our store but we weren't making any money on it because the people owed us a lot of money. We were able to provide our crews with supplies but otherwise we just about broke even. The kids used to come into our store from the big residential school and get $2 or $3 worth of candy and fruit and then say, "I haven't got the money now; I'll pay as soon as I get it." The older people used to do that too and some would come in and say, "Well, can I have $10?" They owed us a lot of money and sometimes we just wrote it off, which wasn't very nice for the business. I guess we were too softhearted, which wasn't good if you are going to be in business. Then the A. B. C. Packing Company moved their store at Knight's Inlet cannery to Alert Bay so I thought there was no sense in carrying on any longer. We sold the building to a friend in order to pay for some of the equipment that we had bought. I didn't think it was right to close up and still owe money on some of the things we had bought for the store, so I moved the ice cream freezer and some of the other stuff into my basement. Then we got a young girl to sell fruit, candy, ice cream, and pop to the kids after school. After St. Michael's school let out in the afternoon they would just come pounding on our door. I carried that on for a couple of years after that but it wasn't the best so I let it go and closed down everything.

We were still operating the sawmill over in the corner of the bay and doing very well for our boats as well as selling a little lumber. We needed a new planer and I noticed an ad in the paper that there was one for sale in Campbell River. There was no ferry from Alert Bay to Campbell River at that time and it was necessary to go all the way to Vancouver and then over to Nanaimo and take a bus up to Campbell River. So when I went down to look at it I stopped in and saw Norman Corker, the manager of our fishing company. I just stopped in to say hello to him and the people in the office there. While I was there Norman called me into his office to talk to me. "Jimmy," he said, "we want you to fish on our new boat that we are going to build. The 'Frank A. M.' is getting too small for you now and we want you to use the new one. You have been catching too many fish for that small boat and you have been the high boat every year for a long time now. You need a bigger boat so you can pack more fish." "Well," I said, "I can't do that. I can't go and make money for you. I want to use my own boat. I have my own boat and

I'm doing all right; why should I fish for you?" So he told me to think about it on my way up to Campbell River and then stop in on my way back and we could talk it over. He said they were only going to build it if I used it.

So I went on my way and didn't think anything about it because my mind was made up. On my way back I stopped in again and Norman said, "Well, Jimmy, did you think about what I told you?" I said, "No, I can't do it." "Well," he said, "why don't you build this boat yourself? We will finance you like we did with the other boats that you have." Of course I argued with him. "I have too many boats now. Two is enough." He said, "No, you can't stop now. You should go ahead and build this one. We are going to have it built in Sointula and you can go there and plan the boat yourself just the way you want it and supervise the building of it." So I asked him to give me time to think about it.

So finally I decided to go ahead with it. I went over to Sointula and talked to Mr. Anderson, who was a friend of mine. He was the man that Norman had said was going to build the boat. He told me that they were going to build a boat 14 feet wide and 52 feet long because that was what the company wanted. "Well," I said "if the company is going to let me buy the boat I want it 15 feet wide and nothing less. And I want to draw the plan myself and I'm going to let you look at it. I want a shallow bottom, not a deep one." So he showed me the plan that he was going to use and listened to what I wanted and told me that it couldn't be done. He argued with me for a couple of days. "Jimmy, it can't be done. It will be ugly and it has never been done to build a boat that wide at that length." So finally I said to him, "This is going to be my boat. I'll tell you what I'll do. You phone me tonight and if you don't make up your mind tonight to build it like I want it I'll have it built in Vancouver." So he called me that night and told me they would build it like I wanted, and they started building it after that. And I kept going over to check on how it was coming and all the things they did on that boat were planned by me. I remember that I wanted a stream-lined stack on it and was trying to make a sketch of just how I wanted it. I was lying in bed thinking about it and making some sketches and my wife was fixing her hair. She put a kerchief around her head and when she put this kerchief around her head it was kind of slanting and so I drew a picture of it. Then it came to my mind that that was just the shape I wanted for the stack, and when I took it over to Sointula they thought it was a wonderful plan. So I told Flora that I had planned the stack just the same as her! A lot of the plan for that boat I took from the "Frank A. M." but made it longer and higher and bigger. I continued to go over every other day or so to see how they were building it and to supervise it until it was done.

The boat was to be completed around May and so I was discussing with my family and Robby what we were going to name the new boat. It came to my mind that we should call it the "Twin Sisters" and name it after the twin girls who had just been born. Of course it was necessary to write to Ottawa and get it cleared so that it would be the only boat with that name. We sent in three names, the "Twin Sisters," "Native Queen," and "Nimpkish Queen," in that order, for their approval. It was time for the boat to be launched in Sointula and we still hadn't heard from Ottawa. So I got a lot of my relatives and friends and went over for the launching. I asked my friend Mr. Davies, who was the minister at that time, to come along and say a few words when it was launched. My wife christened the boat and named it with all three names since we still didn't have any word from Ottawa. We knew that one of the names would be all right. She broke a bottle of champagne on the front of of the boat, which I thought was a waste, and then we had sandwiches and coffee served to everyone. We had quite a big do there and everybody was happy and all my relations were there.

I really enjoyed fishing on the "Twin Sisters" that year and I was really catching a lot of fish. I had had some trouble with a pain in my side off and on for a few years. It just felt like a needle sticking in me, but it would usually go right away after a little while. One day that summer my wife was cooking on the boat and she fixed some boiled beef that had a lot of fat on it. I used to like to eat fat stuff and I took a cup of the soup water from that beef that was real fat and drank it. Boy, that was dynamite. About three or four hours after we had eaten the pain in my stomach was just like somebody had stuck a knife in there. I walked around on the deck of the boat and lay down while we were waiting our turn to make a set. There were three or four boats ahead of us, so I would lay down for a few minutes and then when I couldn't stand it I would get up and walk around again. My wife asked me, "What's wrong?" I told her not to talk to me because I used to get mad and I didn't want to see anybody. I just liked to stay by myself and bear the pain. Finally I said to Oswald, who was on the boat with me, "Take me into the hospital because I'm sick." So we started out for Alert Bay, which was about half an hour away, and all the way there I just walked up and down on the deck. We pulled up to the wharf near the hospital and that thing just felt like it was going to break, and then suddenly it stopped and I didn't feel any pain. I was going to ask the boys to get a wheelchair and take me up to the hospital, but instead I just told them to get back out and try to catch some fish and then come back that evening. I told my wife she had better go home and that I didn't want her to come up to the hospital with me because I always liked to face my own troubles. I didn't want her to come with me and I didn't want her to worry.

So I went down to the hospital to see Dr. Pickup. I told him that I felt ashamed of myself to come here, but that I had a very sharp pain that had lasted about an hour but as soon as I landed on shore it had disappeared. He told me to go home and come back the next day or to come back right away if the pain came back. The fishing was over for the week so I went back the next day and they examined me. They tested my blood and gave me all kinds of other tests and then Dr. Pickup said, "I'll tell you what to do. You go home and buy yourself a big chunk of bacon and fry some eggs and eat them." That was the sort of thing that used to make me sick, so I went home and started cooking that food. Flora asked me what I was doing so I told her, "I'm going to cook myself a big feed and try to kill myself!" She was wondering what I was doing. So I ate that meal and waited a while but couldn't feel any pain. After that he X-rayed me but couldn't find out anything wrong, so he decided to send me down to Vancouver to see a doctor down there. We had a ten-day tie-up on the fishing so I flew down and had a lot of X rays and tests at the hospital for four or five days. The doctor found out that I had some stones in my gall bladder but since I didn't have any pain he said to go back to fishing. He told me what to eat and that if I felt any more pain I should come right down. He said, "You're getting older now and it's not like when you were a teenager. You had better cut down on the amount you eat." So after that I didn't feel the pain any more and went back to fishing. We had a very good reason and I was top boat that first year on the "Twin Sisters."

I was still working hard for the church as rector's warden and singing in the choir and leading the Kwakwala prayer meeting. The church committee used to meet every month and we discussed the finances and the problems of fixing up the buildings. It was always my biggest argument in our committee meetings that we needed to bring more people into our church. I thought that was more important than anything else. Sometimes we were up against financial problems and not able to pay our bills, and I felt that if we had more people coming to the church we were naturally going to get more money put into the plate.

It was about that time that some of the older leaders in the church died. Just before she died Mrs. Cook used to call me to her house and talk to me. She encouraged me to carry on what she saw I was trying to do for her people. She was very strong for the Native Brotherhood and she used to say, "Jimmy, some of the results you may not see, but your children or your grandchildren will. It takes time." I often think of her because she used to prophesy what was going to come in the future. She was a great help to me. When she died I was out in the "Twin Sisters" fishing, and I went in because I felt awfully hurt. I had lost a great friend. I felt the same thing when Mrs. Harris and George Luther died. I knew that I was left with a great responsibility carrying on all they had told me to do. And it came to my mind that I wasn't going to run away from that or make excuses. I knew that although they were already gone they had looked up to what they had seen in me and what they expected me to do. The same thing with my grandmother Lucy. She used to say to me to stand up in front of my people and to teach the gospel to them and I will not let her down even if she is gone. It is a wonderful thing to live up to.

I really enjoyed singing in the choir for the church and in a glee club that started in Alert Bay about that time. I joined the glee club because I liked singing. Jim Robinson, the barber for Alert Bay, was the director of the glee club, and there were both Indians and non-Indians in it. Max Whanock was a good bass and he and I joined it together. We used to have a practice once a week and then we put on some concerts in the community hall for the people of Alert Bay. Jim Robinson moved away and after that the glee club didn't last very long. I really enjoyed being a member of it.

At Christmas time that year I went around from house to house to collect about fifty cents from those people that I thought could give something so we could put on a little Christmas party for the children. We had done this for several years and I used to go around with George Luther before he died. I always had a nice party for my own children and always put up a nice Christmas dinner for my family, but as chief councillor of the village I didn't feel it was right that some of the poorer children didn't have anything. I thought it was right to buy something for the people who were poor and couldn't afford to buy anything and I thought they appreciated it. Since we had stopped returning the shares from the timber sales to the people we were able to use some of that money for part of the expense of the Christmas party.

For about a month before Christmas about fifteen or twenty of the young people would get together and practice, and then just before Christmas we would go from house to house singing carols. We carried a little organ and a lantern and went clear through to the other end of Alert Bay. We would start at 7 o'clock and it was usually 2 o'clock in the morning before we finished. Some of the stores like Doug Chong's and others would give us a box of apples or something to eat. It was snowing that Christmas and some of them asked us in for a cup of coffee. Some of the homes felt it was nice when we sang outside their houses and they would call us in to sing some more. Mr. Todd called us in and he told me, "Jimmy, if you didn't come by and sing for me and my wife it wouldn't be Christmas." Then he gave us as much food as we could handle, candy and cake and other things. There were always a lot of little children who came along with us and they really liked that. Mr. Todd would just pass out candy to all of them. He was a wonderful man and I thought very highly of him. And while we were singing some of the people like Mr. Todd would give us a couple of dollars which we added to the money for the party. Then we bought some little toys and fruit and things and had a little party in our hall for everybody in the whole village.

In February of the next year we had a council meeting with a lot of the Nimpkish people present. Right off at the start of that meeting one of them got up and started questioning the right of the council to spend the money that was going into the band fund. A lot of people had been talking about that and they didn't like it that the money from the sale of our timber wasn't being distributed to all the members. So I told them, "We had elections and we are just like a municipality; we are the governing body of this village. We have the full power to spend the money the way we feel is right. And remember, we don't just govern ourselves as a council but we are governed by the Indian Act. We have to check with the Indian agent about whether the Indian Act gives us the power to do what we want to do. We use that money to buy things for the good of the people as a whole and not just for a few people." Well, even after that there were some of them that didn't understand and didn't like what we were doing.

I felt it was fine for them to question us any time they wanted to. I liked it and I knew that they liked to know what was going on. I thought that the council meetings should be wide open at any time. If we were going to have a meeting I thought it should be published and tell that we were going to meet on a certain date, and then the people could go sit down and listen if they wanted to. We did that sometimes and I liked to have it at least once or twice a year, like at the beginning of the season. Mr. Todd thought that was fine but there was an Indian agent later on that didn't approve of it and thought it wasn't necessary.

Well, anyway, at that same meeting a little later on, one of the leading men of the original Nimpkish people got up. He said that only the original Nimpkish band members should be allowed to vote for new members to join the band. He said that the council had been allowing people to transfer into the band for the past year and he didn't think there was any place to put all the people who were going to come if we kept it up. Those people were really criticizing me and they thought I was a fool to talk about keeping the reserve wide open for anybody who wanted to transwer in. So I got up and I was really arguing with them. I said, "When I moved here to Alert Bay I moved onto the Industrial School Reserve. It was set aside by the first missionaries and the Indian agent for the people that had been to school, were married in the church, would have nothing to do with the potlatch, and would live a good clean life. It was after I was building my house there that Mr. Todd came to me and said that Ottawa wanted us to amalgamate with some other band. I objected and told him that I wasn't going to amalgamate with anybody. I told him finally when he promised us a water system and a new road that we would be willing, but we weren't going to go to anybody to amalgamate—they had to come to us. And when you Nimpkish people decided you wanted to amalgamate I said we would on one condition—that was that this reserve would be wide open for anybody to come in and you all agreed on it."

Then I went on: "We have five hundred acres of land in our end that used to be the Industrial School Reserve and that is plenty of room for lots of people to come here to live. When we first amalgamated, you people only had $3000 in your capital account and we had over $9000 plus all the shares from our original bands. When we amalgamated it brought up the capital account to over $30,000! I object to allowing only the original Nimpkish people to vote on new members to the band. That isn't fair. If we amalgamated with you we have just as much right as you. That's the way I see it according to the laws of the white man and what they call democracy. I will not accept it any other way. If you don't want to allow everyone to have the right to vote on new people coming to this reserve then you can just tell us and I will resign!"

As soon as I said that the other members of my council all threatened to resign also. Then a lot of people got up and discussed the whole problem. I remember some of my boys like Robby Bell got up and spoke against what they wanted to do. Then Mr. Todd got up and talked a while and reminded everyone of the decision that had been made at the time we amalgamated. Finally after over an hour of debate George Alfred and Dan Hanuse made a motion that there be a vote of confidence for the members of the council and the work they had been doing in accepting new members into our band. That motion was carried unanimously and so we continued to be in office. That was the reason why I was so unpopular, because they didn't want any outsiders to come in and they still felt that I was an outsider trying to run them.

It wasn't very long after that that we had the Native Brother-

hood convention at Alert Bay. I had been going every year to
different places like Prince Rupert, Terrace, Hazelton, and Campbell River. I was in charge of getting everything ready for the
people who were coming to Alert Bay and I had a lot of help from
the old people. They were very active in those days in entertaining
the people who came from outside of our village and I had all the
help I wanted and everybody was cooperating. I appointed a number
of committees to look after the things that needed to be done. We
had an entertainment committee which looked after the entertainment that was put on every night at the banquets or at the meetings.
There was a banquet committee which planned for the evening
meals which were eaten down in the hall together. There was a
visitors' committee which was responsible for meeting the people
on the wharf when they came in and telling them where they were
going to stay and welcome them to our village. We had a housing
committee which went around and asked the people how many they
could each take in their house. Some of them would say they could
take a couple, or two single girls, or whatever they had room for.
We provided beds for some of the families so they could put up
some of the visitors. Usually at the other conventions when they
would have a banquet the Native Brotherhood would pay for it
out of their funds, but not when they came to Alert Bay. We raised
the money to try to do it on our own.

So the people started arriving and the visitors' committee showed
them to the houses where they were going to stay. We got a truck
which took bread and bacon and eggs around to all the houses where
visitors were staying and gave them enough to provide them with
breakfast. We didn't expect our own people to have to pay for the
visitors' breakfasts because that would have been too hard on some
of them. Everything went very well. There were meetings during
the day and at lunch time everybody would eat in the hall. I felt
that nobody was suffering from having to provide for their visitors
and everybody was enjoying the convention.

For the banquets in the evening we had different people who
volunteered to put them on. Some of the leading men of the village
came to me and would say, "I want to put the dinner on on a certain
day." Then there was a committee to look after all the dishes and
things like that. One family would be assigned to each table in the

hall, and they would bring their own forks and knives and dishes and bring them down in a basket and set up the table. There were a couple of girls acting as waitresses at each table and they were just running back and forth to the kitchen to get more food when anybody wanted it. As soon as the dinner part of the banquet was over, the person in charge of her table would gather up the table-cloth and put it with all the dishes in the basket, and then we hired a truck to drive them all home. They took them home and washed them up and got ready for the next day when they did it again. It worked out very smoothly that way and nobody was having to do too much work.

All day long the convention would sit in the hall and carry on their business. A lot of government men from the provincial and federal government attended. Right after the meal the chairman of the banquet committee would come in with a little note and give it to whoever was the chairman of the banquet that night and announce there would be a break for about a half an hour. When they all returned we would have different people get up and give a speech. Sometimes we had two or three government men talk to us and sometimes it would be the visitors from different Indian villages from all over British Columbia. And we were able to talk to the government about the old age pensions, the fish prices, the liquor rights for the Indians, and the land question. I kept bringing up the problem of our Indian schools and told them that we felt the schools should be integrated with the white ones where this was possible. And finally after a week or more the convention ended and it was very successful.

After that it was time to go out fishing again. My manager had come to me a year or so before that and told me that we were going to need some more skippers, so I used to train some of our young boys to be skippers. I watched among my crew for those boys who were really good workers, and then if they were willing to be a skipper I would recommend them to our company and they would be given a boat. Some of my crew were the lazy type that didn't care. They would just go down and sleep and didn't care to come up on the deck or up on the bridge to help me look for fish. I couldn't make a captain out of those kind of people. I watched them carefully and could see the way they moved around the boat whether they were ready or not. I would try to hang onto the good ones as long as I could but it was very difficult because my boss wanted men that I could recommend.

Mike Lazich was still working with me and he was a big help and very reliable. On weekends he would live on the "Twin Sisters" and watch out for all of my boats. At that time his wife died and poor Mike was really going to pieces and drinking quite heavy. I talked to him many times and told him that he had to cut that out. I went down to Vancouver and he was just shaking and he said, "Oh, I can't help it. I've got a bunch of little kids and I don't know what I'm going to do." The youngest one was only about six or seven years old. So I told him straight, "I know that it is going to be very difficult to live with your young children, but I want to tell you right now that your job with me will always be there. You can depend on me. If you want to you can come up and see me any time you feel like it. You can always work for me." He seemed to get over it and came back up to fish with me for the remainder of the season. Mike always used to bring a bottle with him on the boat and I didn't mind because he knew how to drink. Sometimes he would bring a case of beer and when it was hot he would take out a bottle a day and drink it. One time we were fishing over near the mainland and it was real hot, about 85 degrees. We just took off most of our clothes when we were fishing and the water wasn't so good, and when we took a break he would put the beer in the ice and give me one. It was really nice and quenched your thirst.

One time that summer we were fishing over around the mouth of the Nimpkish River. I was just drifting around waiting for the tide to go down because that brings the fish down from the mouth of the river and you could usually catch a lot. I was sitting up top with some of the members of my crew talking and I didn't realize that we were being carried right over close to the sandbar that was there. So one of my crew noticed that the water was getting shallow, so real quick I kicked the engine ahead and then tried to back up but we were stuck on that sandbar and the tide was still going down. The boat just keeled right over on its side. My boss was over at Alert Bay and he used to always look through his glasses at the boats he could see, and when he saw us he came over in his little boat and wanted to know what happened. I told him that it was an accident because we didn't know that we were drifting along. There was another seine boat nearby that tried to pull me out but it was too late. So we just stayed there until late afternoon when the tide came up again and floated us off that sandbar. We lost half a day and I didn't feel so good because all those years I'd fished around the mouth of that river and I knew it very well. I knew all the sandbars. I felt bad because we had lost time and everybody else was fishing except us and there was quite a few fish coming down.

That fall I went in to Mr. Todd and asked him when we were going to have the next election for chief councillor and the council. He said to me, "There aren't going to be any more elections for chief councillor. When the band came under the Indian Act related to elected chiefs, you came under the section of the act which made you the chief for an indefinite period of time." "Well," I said, "I don't want it that way. I want my people to come under the other section of the Indian Act where we can have elections every two years. I think it is better to be under that and then if anybody wants a change they can change who is the chief and on the council. How can we change it to the other part of the Indian Act?" So he told me that we could write to Ottawa and then the band would have to vote on it. It had been my understanding all along that we were going to have elections every two years. Mr. Todd wrote to Ottawa and we held an open meeting then to decide about the elections. Before that meeting was held Mr. Todd left our agency and I was very sorry to see him leave.

When that meeting time came Mr. Dickie talked to us about coming under Section 73 of the Indian Act. Everybody was informed that if we decided upon it we would have elections every two years and the chief councillor would be elected by a majority vote of all those who had the right to vote in the band. When he finished I made a motion that we come under that section and it passed. The elections weren't held until January of 1953. Another thing that came up at that meeting was whether the band should set aside money for building and improving houses. A lot of the houses on the reserve were in very bad condition. The Indian Department had set aside some money for building houses, but they would only give half and the band had to give the other half. Since most of the people couldn't afford much we voted to set aside

$10,000 in a fund. There were a lot of people then who would go to the Indian Office and get a few hundred dollars or maybe a thousand from that fund and the government would match it so they could build a house. They were supposed to pay back the money they got from the band fund but we never got much of it back. I didn't know too much about all that because the government never did help me build my houses. I used my own money whenever I built my own house and bought my own lumber.

On December 20 of that year my two oldest girls, Dora and Louisa, prepared a big dinner at our house to celebrate our twenty-fifth anniversary. It was quite a surprise to both Flora and I and afterwards there was a special service and a lot of the people from the village came to visit. Stephen Cook made a little speech and congratulated us and wished us a lot more happy years together. Some of the people brought gifts for us, some silver trays and other silver stuff. Those kids just cooked it up themselves and I was quite surprised.

Early in January we had our election meeting. Mr. Dickie was sort of filling in until they got a new Indian agent, and Mr. McGregor had come up from the Indian Office in Vancouver and he spoke to that meeting. When the time came for nominations I got up and told them that I would not allow my name to be nominated. I refused to take any office because I was fed up. I had had a very difficult time and I'd really had it. It was like going through hell some of those times with all the opposition that I had. It was a thankless job for which I never got any pay. Most of my time had been spent working for the people and I hardly had much time for my own family. Many times I spent my own money on things that were needed or when I traveled for the business of the band. They never gave me any traveling expenses. I had tried to do my best with the little education that I had. I found out later that it wasn't the right thing to not accept any office that night. After I said that in the meeting I sat down and was just silent. I was the spokesman for the boys who had come from that new reserve and they all just sat quietly and didn't say anything. Dan Cranmer was elected chief councillor and the three on his council were George Alfred, Billy Cook, and Herbert Cook.

I continued to work for my people in many ways even though I wasn't the chief councillor. I was an experienced man and the people used to come to me for many things. People would call me up when they had some problem or needed help and they still do that now. I had a number of people call me up, like when their baby had died and they didn't have enough money so they asked me if they could bury their child in our graveyard. So I just called up the undertaker and told him to get a little casket and take care of the child and charge it to me. I would just loan the money to those parents but I didn't expect that they would pay me back. I have helped people a lot of times when they needed money and often I would never get payed back, but I liked to help my people.

Mr. Findlay came about that time as the new Indian agent. I used to go sit in on the council meetings when they were open. They continued to carry on the business of the band, like paying bills and accepting new members into the band and things like that. One thing that came up was some trouble with the Pentecostals who were holding meetings on the reserve. The council finally wouldn't allow the white Pentecostal minister to come on the reserve to hold meetings. When the Pentecostals came and started to hold meetings they were really bad. What I mean is that they used to have services in different homes every night and it was just like somebody died in there. They would be yelling and jumping around and shouting. I used to hear it when I walked by one of those houses but I never paid any attention to it.

So it wasn't long until the teacher went to the chief councillor and told him that a lot of the kids were sleeping on their desks during school. He said that he had tried to wake them up and asked them what was the matter and they would say, "Oh, no, I'm not sick but I didn't get to sleep 'til 3 o'clock this morning because my mom and I went to that big do last night." So they wrote a letter not to have those meetings on the Indian reserve any longer but to have them off the reserve. There was a real big stink about it and even the non-Indians got in on it. Some of them came to me to talk about it and I told them, "Don't talk to me about it; I'm not the chief councillor now." I guess they were upset about the way they had kicked them off the reserve without giving them any warning or anything.

When the Pentecostals first came they attracted many of our people because they liked something new. It wasn't too good because an Indian village is just like a family. I felt that the Anglican church was there for us, and we were all baptized and confirmed there and married there and when we die we are going to be buried there. They have done very well for us. When the Pentecostals came into Alert Bay and to the other villages also, a couple members of the family would start going, maybe a wife and son. So the father would try to talk to his wife and son and say to them, "Now, don't overdo it. You were out until 4 o'clock this morning. Where were you?" He might think something different was going on. I had to take a trip up to Kingcome one time because the Pentecostals had gone up there and that whole village was divided. The fathers and the sons were divided, the mothers and fathers, they were not on good terms, and the way I saw it it was not a good thing.

There was one of their leaders who was a very strong Pentecostal and every Friday night he would put on a service at the same time we were having the Kwakwala prayer meeting. They drew a whole crowd after them and we had just the organist and a handful of people. I was conducting it and we were singing the hymns in our language, but I didn't mind because the way I felt they were going to come to us later anyway. If they were going to be married they would come to the church and when they were going to be buried they would have to come to the church. So this fellow came to see me at my house and said, "I wanted to come and see you because I feel we shouldn't be divided. We should worship together. I feel awfully bad, I feel guilty because I think that I have done wrong. I don't know what to do so I thought I would come and see you because you are the leader of the church here and you have been the chief councillor."

So I said to him, "What do you want me to do? Do you want me to come and join your service? Do you want to come back to our church? Don't expect me to come because I'm not a Pentecostal. I'm a true Anglican and I would like to die in the church. Don't try to blame us for being bad boys because we aren't. We only have a few coming to our Kwakwala prayer service, but thank God for that because the good book says that 'if one or two are gathered together in My name I will be in the midst.' I wouldn't say that you are wrong but it seems to me that you feel that you are wrong. I know that if you are dividing people that is wrong and it is not what God wants. God wants us to be one because to be together is one of the best things in the world no matter what you are doing. If we are together and work together on many things we are going to be strong, especially in a place like Alert Bay and especially in an Indian village. If you were in a big city that would be different. Some of these people go to a different church every night just because they want to see what is going on. They don't go there to worship God. We have been having this Kwakwala prayer service every Friday night since Mr. Hall came years ago and taught our people Christianity. Why don't you go and have your services some other night like Wednesday or Tuesday. Then some of our good people might like to come to our service. That is what I think is right and I'm glad you came. I had thought about going to you but I didn't think it was right and I'm glad you came. I don't think we should carry on this way because it is dividing the people. Whenever you go like to Kingcome or some other Indian village you are dividing the people. They all have their church and this is really dividing them."

He listened to me very attentively because he was a very good friend of mine. It wasn't very long after that when he went to another village in a gill-netter and there was a big storm and the boat tipped over. Two of them survived that and we went there and looked for the bodies and found two others. There were little kids on the boat and I figured that they were trying to save them when they were drowned.

During the fishing season when the people have a few dollars in their pockets we used to have more trouble with drinking and that sort of thing. There had been quite a bit of trouble that summer and some of the people were kind of upset at the way the Royal Canadian Mounted Police treated the Indians when they were drunk. I suppose that they tried to protect us in a way. If an Indian was drunk they just threw him in jail and they still do that. I suppose that is what they call protecting us so that they won't get into further trouble. That was the only protection that we had from the police. Drinking is a weakness of my people. There was no other trouble from the Indians as far as I could see. I think about 90 percent of our people have been thrown in jail for being drunk. I don't know if they treat the white people differently, but it would always be in the paper that there was about twenty or thirty Indians who were thrown in jail for being drunk and only one or two white men. So anyway the council brought it up about the way the RCMP were waiting at the door of the beer parlor for the Indians to come out. They wouldn't let them go directly home but if he looked a little drunk they would take him and throw him in jail. At that time we were allowed to go into the beer parlor but we couldn't buy any liquor of our own to take home. They also discussed some of the Indians who didn't try to get along with the RCMP. Then they wrote a letter to the Indian superintendent in Vancouver about that problem.

I think that liquor is the root of all the trouble and the weakness of the Indian. As far as I see it there is no such thing as a criminal Indian. If it wasn't for their drinking the Indian people would be wealthy people. They are a praying people. I wouldn't say they are better than anybody else, but they just take everything easy and they don't care whether they are going to have anything tomorrow as long as they get by. That is the thinking of an Indian. We haven't been around the white man and his way of life for very long to learn it. A white man puts away maybe $20 a month for maybe five years and then he will have enough to take a trip, which I think is a wonderful idea. Some of our people have hardly ever been away from Alert Bay. They get their money at the end of the fishing season and just go to the beer parlor and spend all their money. That is their life. Some of those Indians would go into the beer parlor when it opened and sit there until midnight when they were kicked out. It was just like in the old days when people would rather go to the potlatch than to their job. When the potlatch system was going in full swing I used to feel that it was better to go out herring fishing or on some other job rather than to go to the potlatch. Now it is between the beer parlor and working on a job. Some of those people have jobs but they just say, "Oh, I don't want to work now. I'll stay here in the beer parlor and get a job anyway some other time." I found that I couldn't talk to those fellows who were under the influence of liquor.

There were quite a few Indians who tried to get in on the same kind of business I have in owning my own boats. Then when they put something down on a boat they have trouble paying it off. They just think about themselves and drinking. When they are in port they just go ahead and drink and drink. It is out of this world the way they drink so that I just can't describe it. I can't understand why they do that. I have tried everything I know, even talking to doctors about it. One doctor told me that there wasn't anything you could do to help them but it was up to them to help themselves. In the early days people used to be more careful because they were afraid of what other people would think. If they went and got a bottle from a bootlegger and held a big party in their house and the people started getting drunk and shouting, they would just tell everybody to keep their voices down because of the neighbors. They were afraid of what they would think. But that had begun to change and the people would have parties and start singing and yelling and I would have to go over and tell them to get out of there. I didn't see any harm in having a few drinks, but if they were going to have a big party that went on all night it wouldn't be any good for them and for the children that were living in that house. That was the time that those people just lost control of themselves and they would start fighting and lose their wives and everything.

I would take a drink myself but I can't ever remember getting drunk. I guess I must be missing something or I'm a fool or something. I remember when I was a teenager and used to go to Vancouver and they would have a drinking party, and when they started getting drunk and fighting I would just take off and say, "That's enough boys, see you tomorrow." A lot of times people would ask me to go to a party with them and I would go over to their house and have a little drink, like if it was their daughter's wedding or something. I didn't want them to feel bad so I never refused, and I felt that if I could go there and they could see the way I handle my drinking it might be a little influence on those who drink too much

and just go haywire. I knew that they couldn't quit drinking altogether. I didn't feel it was right that the Indian wasn't allowed
legally to buy his own liquor because you can't tell anybody in this
world to just quit it. I remember when I used to go to Vancouver
and one of the big shots at the cannery would invite me up to his
house for dinner. Before dinner he would be having a little drink
and they never gave me a drink. He would give me a soft drink and
say, "That's all I can give you Jimmy." He was a respectable man
and that was before the law was passed to allow Indians to have
it legally. I used to just laugh because I didn't mind but I did feel
it was too bad that an Indian could not sit down and have a drink
with his friends. In the United States when everything was dry
there was all kinds of bootlegging and fighting and murders. That
was the danger of it. I was beginning to feel that it was necessary
to teach our people how to use the liquor because we learned about
liquor from the white man. There was no drinking among the
Indians in the early days but after the white man came they started
to use it. We didn't know the first thing about how to drink, and
I think it was just like a propane cook stove to an Indian. If you
gave one of those to an old Indian who had never seen it before he
would hurt himself. He would fool around with the valves and
that thing might explode and hurt him. If somebody was kind
enough to go there and teach that Indian how to use it then he
could learn to use it properly. I began to feel that something should
be done to teach our people about drinking in the right way.

I tried to make it very plain to my children when they became
teenagers about what can happen to the man that drinks. I used to
tell them, "You can be a very good man who is successful in your
business and you can lose your job overnight. If you are going to
mix drinking with working and you don't attend to business you
can lose your job. I have seen some real good captains who were real
highliners lose their jobs over drinking. If a person likes his drink
he should take it the way it is supposed to be taken. It shouldn't be
abused or it can ruin your life." I couldn't see any harm in having
a little drink together at Christmas time or on special days. Of
course there were some Indians who would never drink at all. I
guess they felt the way I did in going through too much in their
younger days with some of the older people getting drunk at the

canneries. Some of them wouldn't touch it at all even when they were offered a drink in someone's home.

While some of those Royal Canadian Mounted Police were just there to protect the law and arrest the Indian any chance they had, there were a lot of good ones too. I had some good friends there who would stop and talk to me on the street or whenever I went into the police station. I felt it was important to respect the RCMP and it was also good for them to go among the young people and talk to them. Some of them used to come and play soccer with the boys and be real friendly with our Indian people. I thought that was the way it should be. Every RCMP that I saw was just the same to me and I would go and talk to them. Some of the young boys don't like the RCMP and they just talk cheeky to them. A lot of times I have told them, "That is not the right attitude because the RCMP are just human beings the same as anybody else. They are here to protect us and if you fellows get into any kind of trouble they are going to step in. Nobody will call them unless you are in trouble. If you don't get into any kind of trouble then we don't need them. If there is trouble we surely need them because they are here to protect us."

Just before the fishing season I took the "Twin Sisters" down to Vancouver and had one of the new power blocks installed. The year before that I had gone down with a lot of the other skippers to see this new thing that they were demonstrating. There were about three or four seine boats that were loaded with skippers and boat owners that went out inside Vancouver Harbor, and we watched one of the seine boats make a set and then pull the net in with the new power block. The power block was driven by a rope and it worked all right until the rope broke. It broke three or four times while they were demonstrating it. I was sitting beside a fellow I knew who made winches and hydraulic equipment for boats and he whispered to me, "Don't touch this thing because it is new. I think I can put a hydraulic on it and make it work good. Don't touch it, leave it alone." What he meant was for me not to buy one until they improved it. Some of the boys in Alert Bay bought one that first year they were out but I just continued on in the old style, pulling by hand. That second year when I had mine installed it was driven by hydraulic power and we never had any trouble with it.

Late that summer I talked to Robby Bell and Simon Beans about extending our partnership in the sawmill to a boat shop. They thought it would be good so I applied to the council for permission to build a boat repair shop down on the beach near St. Michael's Residential School. The council asked me to give them a written application for the boat shop and a sketch of how it was going to be built. After I did that they gave me the permission, so I got some lumber from a friend of mine who had an old floathouse he didn't want any longer. We cut it up to the right sizes and built the boat shop. I bought some more equipment like a band saw and other power tools and we used that shop to repair the cabins on some of the boats. We even built some small skiffs in that shop but we never built anything larger than that. I was hoping to interest some of the younger boys in working there because I thought it would be a nice little job for some of them if they would stay at it.

I was becoming more active in the work of the Native Brotherhood and late that year they made me the associate editor of the newspaper published by the Brotherhood called *The Native Voice*. The first article I ever wrote was in December 1953, and this is what it was:

OPEN LETTER TO BRITISH COLUMBIA NATIVES
by Chief James Sewid, Coast Editor, *The Native Voice*

This is an open letter by me to the Natives of British Columbia. "The Native Voice" is the official "Voice" of the Native Brotherhood of British Columbia, a voice now heard all through British Columbia, the United States and Canada and in fact all over the World. It has been heard for eight years. It has told the story of our race and our fight against discrimination and the fight for better education, better conditions and equality for all our people.

Without this "Voice" our problems would never have been heard. It has carried on and kept alive the voices of our great leaders who have passed on.

Alfred Adams, our late President, traveled from one end of British Columbia to another bringing hope and courage and unity to our people when they were in danger of dying out.

The late Mrs. Constance Cook, the late Chief Calder of the

Naas, and many other great founders of the Native Brotherhood of British Columbia, for years worked for the advancement of our people and have given them so much; all this the "Voice" has publicized. This "Voice" is the official Voice of the Native Brotherhood of British Columbia. If we lose it, no one will know of the work we do and no one will hear of the problems of our people. It is thus our duty to support our "Voice." There are 31,000 Indians in British Columbia. If we could get even one-half of these to subscribe to "The Native Voice," it would grow bigger and stronger, in our fight for justice.

I am asking you this Christmas season to stand behind the "Voice" and the Native Brotherhood so that we can carry on and fight for your needs; only through unity and work will we gain our objective.

Right after the first of the year I had a real surprise one morning in church. I was singing in the choir that morning as I usually did, and after Mr. Hayhurst finished preaching he announced that there was to be some special awards given out that Sunday and he asked Mr. Findlay to come forward and conduct the ceremony. So he came up and called Bill Scow and me to the altar and announced that he had been asked by the minister of citizenship and immigration to present Coronation medals and certificates to both of us. Bill Scow was president of the Native Brotherhood of British Columbia and Mr. Findlay said a few words about his work for that group and for the Indian people and then pinned the medal on him. After that he turned to me and said, "By command of her gracious Majesty Queen Elizabeth, I have been asked to present to you this medal to be worn in commemoration of Her Majesty's Coronation last June. You have been chosen as an outstanding example among your people. Not only by your own industry and service to your people but by your private and family life and church life, have you shown yourself to be a leader of men. It is in recognition of this that I am also empowered by Her Majesty to pin this medal on you." Then he pinned the medal on me and gave both of us a certificate which said, "By command of Her Majesty, the Queen, the accompanying medal is forwarded to be worn in commemoration of Her Majesty's

Coronation, Second of June, 1953." I was really surprised because nobody had told me anything about it, that it was going to happen.

The work of the church was very important to me. I didn't always live up to what I was supposed to, and one time one of my children was very sick. I guess I was kind of failing in the church work because there were times when I just drifted away from it for a while. I wasn't paying much attention to what I was supposed to be doing. So one of the children got very sick and was so near death that we were all scared and just didn't know what to do. I asked the doctor if I could go in and see her, so I went into the room and I said to myself, "I don't know what is happening but this kid's going to be taken away from me. I must have failed in what I'm doing. Maybe this is going to shake me now." So I kneeled down beside this little kid and asked God to forgive me if I had done something wrong, because I felt that maybe He needed me and I had failed in doing my work for my people. Then I said, "If you should spare this child I will go out again and do my work again and really go back to what I had been doing." I knew that I had failed somewhere. So I went out of that room and stayed around for a little while and then came back to ask the nurse how she was doing. She said, "Oh, she is doing fine. Her temperature went down just about an hour ago and everything has turned for the better." And I knew what had happened because I had actually experienced that, and from there on everything seemed to influence me to carry on what I have been living up to. Sometimes a man who is too busy with other things can neglect the greatest work of all, helping along in the work of the church.

I remembered the old people that I used to see as a little boy, praying to God in whatever they did. When I visited the old people and all my relatives we would sing hymns in Chinook and Kwakwala. When the olachen fish first came in the springtime there would be a group of twenty or thirty people sitting around eating because they always invited everyone in to have dinner with us. After they finished eating I used to listen to the old people say thank you to God for giving them that nice food. In anything they used to do they would pray to God, like when they used to go out in the canoes they would look up and say, "Look down on us while we go on our journey." I was brought up in a Christian home and I really tried to live up to it. I really believed in prayer and always had. I have been through many jobs and many of them were very dangerous. I used to go up in the spar tree and sometimes I would be up one hundred feet. I have seen a lot of accidents while working in the logging camps. So I always said my prayers while I was doing my work and I have always felt that somebody was helping me. I really believed that whether I was fishing or logging or whatever I was doing somebody was helping me. I guess that is what you call faith and I have great faith in prayer. I often pray to God in the name of our Lord Jesus Christ because I believe He was actually God according to the teaching of my religion. That's the teaching I had when I was a little boy and with what little knowledge and schooling I have I can't change it.

I have been asked many times what I think will happen to me after I die. A lot of times I have seen very respectful men who have died among our people. Many times, even if he was from another village, the people would invite me there and we usually held a memorial service in his house. I would be called on to say a few words and sometimes I have found it very hard to find the words to say for him, especially if it had been a pretty rough man who had drowned or been killed in an accident. I don't know whether I'm right or wrong but the way I usually explained it to the people was like this: "We have a really rough time in this world. We're all going through a very rough life. According to the Bible, when our Savior Jesus was here He went through a rough life and in the end He was crucified. Nobody liked Him and everybody was against Him, including the ministers in those days. In the end they crucified Him and He was nailed to the cross but that was not the end. Maybe they can do that to you and do something to harm you. Maybe you have had a rough life but thank goodness we have another life we can live in another world. Maybe this man that has died was going through a very rough and tough life while he was with us in this world. Maybe that is why he has been taken away from this world to get away from this hard rough life." I didn't say that to try to satisfy the people but that was my belief.

Another teaching that I learned from the older people was that people died and go into another world, and then they can die in that world and go into another world. I think they got that belief

from some of the little stories and legends and that was their belief
because I heard them talking like that. I think they used to say that
a person died three or four times and then came back to this world;
regeneration I think it is called. My wife's mother used to say that
my daughter Louisa was really one of the old people from Gilford
Island who was killed during the massacre there, because Louisa
had a little mark under her eye just like that lady. I believed that
because I had actually seen other people that the old people said
used to be here many years before and died and then came back.
They had a special mark on their body or something else by which
they could recognize them. I have sometimes wondered if I was
somebody many many years ago. I know that many times when I
have traveled to some new place for the first time I have had the
strange feeling that I have been there before. Even though I know
that I have only been there once I had the funny feeling that I have
been there before. Sometimes I have thought that it might just be
my mind or something because I have been traveling. But I do
know this, that if I try to do the best I can in this world I am certainly going to be looked after when I go from this world. I have
talked to many people who have called me in when they were on
their deathbed. I have seen a man coming down and standing beside
them telling them he wanted them to go into the next world, and
it happened when I was fully awake. There was a girl who told me
that somebody was taking care of her and had asked her to get
ready to go the next day and that was when she died. This is my
belief.

Another thing I have thought very seriously about is the worst
sin that a person can commit. I have talked to many ministers about
what they think and they answered me that according to the good
book God can forgive you. There are all kinds of sins that a person
can commit, such as telling a lie, doing something wrong to one's
friends, or saying something to hurt a friend. But I think that the
worst is when a man leaves his wife for some other woman. Maybe
that other woman will have a husband and they will fall in love or
whatever it is called and get married. The wife of that man will be
hurt very much and if they have children they will be hurt also. And
the other party will hurt her husband and her children. Everybody

will be involved and say, "What kind of a man is he?" I think that
if a young man runs around with some woman and then feels sorry
and tries to break away from that there is no doubt that our God
will forgive him. If a man goes out and gets drunk and spends his
money and doesn't come home to his wife and children he will be
hurting his family and himself as well. If he comes to himself and
goes to his wife and asks her to forgive him I think God will
forgive him. If a person steals or says anything wrong to his fellow-
man he can be forgiven if he asks God and the people he has
done harm to. If a person feels guilty and asks God to forgive him
then he will be forgiven. But if a man leaves his wife and family as
I have seen some do and lives with another woman who also had a
husband and family then he has a lot to do to make up for it. He
has done wrong to both families and to all of his friends. I think
that is one of the worst sins that I have seen. I've seen people do
that and then go and join some other church where they can get
married and they think they are all right. Once one of them said
right in front of me that he had a better church than ours. I don't
think so. They may talk big but they forget that they have stolen
somebody else's wife.

In February of the following year it was time for the Nimpkish
band to have elections again. We had a general meeting and before
the nominations I got up and told the people what I thought the
new council should be looking after. I told them they should try to
get the street lights fixed on the road and also to arrange for transportation for the kids who were going to be going to the provincial
school in Alert Bay in the fall. Most of all I said that we needed to
have 100 percent cooperation by the people in meeting the obligations we had for projects for the improvements of the band. Dan
Cranmer, George Alfred, and Herbert Cook were nominated for
chief councillor and George Alfred was elected. Then they had
nominations for the councillors and I was elected along with William Cook, Simon Beans, and Robby Bell. I got up after that election
and talked to the people about the problem of juvenile delinquency
which I thought we should do something about. I wanted to work
under George because he didn't have much experience and I felt
that he needed me. Whenever there was a public meeting he would

come and talk to me about it and often I would go there and speak for him. He made many contributions in helping my people and I was able to give him a few pointers.

Ever since I had first put on the Indian dance for the hospital week the people had been asking for it each year. I was chairman of that committee for three years and we put a dance on each time, and then after that someone else was on and they put on a dance a couple of times but it wasn't as good as the first ones. I was thinking that we should do something else and so even though I wasn't on the committee that year I made a suggestion to them. I thought it would be a good idea to have a salmon barbecue like the people used to do it in the old days and charge everybody for coming and eating and all the money could go to the hospital fund. That year they decided to do that and so I went out on my seine boat and caught fish myself. One day I went out and my net got tangled up in the wheel and I drifted onto a snag and I ripped my net all to pieces. I decided that was a little too much because that cost me money but it didn't cost anybody else money, and so the next year we bought the fish. So we put the barbecue on up in the field and a lot of people came and we really made good money off that for the hospital.

I think it was that same year that the Native Brotherhood convention was held up in the Queen Charlotte Islands. Ever since the Kwakiutl had gone into the Native Brotherhood some of our people had been going to the conventions held every year at different places in British Columbia. The different tribes of British Columbia had been divided up and each area had a vice-president who was elected at these yearly conventions. They had asked me a few times to be the vice-president for the Kwakiutl agency but I didn't think it was right for me to take it then. I didn't pay too much attention to going to those conventions then because I didn't have time. I would have to be away for a week or ten days and I didn't think I should because I had been busy with my boats, the store, building my house, and working for the church. That year I decided to go to the convention way up at a place called Masset in the Queen Charlotte Islands. There were quite a few from the Kwakiutl agency who went with me and they had quite a big gathering there at that time. They had meetings every day to talk about the problems of the native people, such as getting better education, the liquor question, the land question, and the fish prices. Every year they would dissolve all the offices from the past year and have an election. When they held the nominations for the new officers someone from up north who knew me nominated me to be the vice-president for the Kwakiutl agency. So I decided then to accept the nomination and I was elected.

I was glad to be elected because I always liked to work for my people and I felt they should be represented. It was a big area that I represented and the grievances of my people must be heard truly. I felt that was the only way we could get what we wanted and present the problems to the different villages because I had to carry all the load of the tribes of the Kwakiutl nation. Shortly after the convention all the officers were called into Vancouver and we had a meeting in the Native Brotherhood office there. We talked about all the business that had been passed at the convention and went to the different departments of the government and talked to them about what we wanted them to do for the people. We talked to the people in the Department of Education and I thought that education was one of the most important problems at that time. When we first moved to Alert Bay the older kids went to school there, but they had to stop when they were fifteen or sixteen and several of my children had already reached that age. In those days when they were fifteen or sixteen they would just tell the Indians: "That's that. You go now. You're finished." That was the ruling of the white man over the Indian. No matter how hard you tried to keep them in school, when they reached that age they just told the Indians to go home. Not only that, but all the Indian children had to go to an Indian day school in Alert Bay that was separate from the school for the white children in the other end of the village. The teachers there were often unqualified to teach. They used to just send old missionaries to the village to try and do the best they could. The effect of that wasn't always too good for the children in school. We asked the Education Department and the Indian Department to get rid of the day school system. Also I felt that if there was a white settlement nearby then the Indian children should be transported there by bus to go to that school which was better qualified.

The Native Brotherhood had been fighting for integrated schools for a long time and that fall they decided to integrate the school at Alert Bay. They had just finished building a new high school there with the help of the Indian Department and these students who had reached grade seven were to start going to that school. My daughter Daisy was among the first ones to be sent up there. She came home crying a few days after school started and said she didn't want to go back to that school. I asked her, "Why don't you want to go back to school?" "Well," she said, "the kids make fun of the way I dress and the way I talk." So I told her, "You dry up those tears and go back up there. Don't come and tell me those things. I want you to stay there." So she went back and pretty soon she started bringing non-Indian kids to our house. She even brought some home for supper and it was proven that integration could work. She was my first child to get a better education and go through those higher grades of school. I hadn't been able to help any of my children very much with their schoolwork because I didn't know very much. I felt bad when they didn't do very well in school and I used to give them prizes or money if they got good marks. I used to give Daisy so much for every A that she got and she really did well in her schoolwork.

It wasn't long after that that the National Film Board of Canada sent some men to Alert Bay to talk to me about being in a film they were making on the Indian people. They had taken pictures of other Indians in Canada doing all sorts of work like nursing, logging, high rigging, building skyscapers, and farming. They wanted somebody from the coast Indians to be in the film and they asked me if I would be willing. I told them that as far as I could see I wasn't the only one fishing on the coast among my people. There were all kinds of fishermen up and down the coast in the same type of work and I felt they should be in the film also. Of course they said they had talked to some people in the government and they had wanted me to be a part of that film. Then they explained to me that it would be good for the younger people to see how I started my business. Well, that was very important to me because all these years I had been trying to talk to the younger people to get in on some business like I had done. I started very small and really struggled with just one boat. So I decided to go ahead with it and they sent some men to Alert Bay to start taking pictures.

The first thing they wanted to show was how I started my business. So they took a picture of me talking to the bank manager who loaned me the money to pay down on the "Frank A. M." The man who cosigned with me wasn't there at that time. I wasn't only acting but I was actually doing my fishing while they took pictures. I went out on the "Twin Sisters" and they told me just to go ahead and fish in the normal way. So I made a set and caught a few fish and they took pictures of me at the wheel and working on the deck and calling my other boat and things like that. After they finished taking pictures of the fishing they had me go up to the school and meet Alvin and Daisy who were up there, and they showed how the Indian kids were going to school with the white kids. Alvin was playing baseball and Daisy was just coming out of school and then we walked away together. I didn't feel anything special being in that movie. I felt it was important to be a part of it since the members of the Canadian government wanted me to do it. I suppose they wanted it for a record of what the Indian people were doing. They called it *No Longer Vanishing* because I understand that some people thought the Indian people were going to disappear. They thought it would be good to show in schools all over Canada so that the white people could see what the Indians did and also the Indians from different parts of Canada could see what the other Indians did. When I saw the film after it was done I felt it was good to show how our way of life on the coast was altogether different from my friends back east. I'm sure the Indians back there really liked to see how the coast Indians were doing. I felt good because I really put something into what I did, especially for the youngsters who could see what I had done with my fishing operation. I didn't say anything on the film. One man did all the talking to explain what was going on.

Robby and I had been doing very well on our boats and only the "Twin Sisters" wasn't completely paid off. Robby was skipper on the "Adele M." and I was skipper on the "Twin Sisters." We leased the "Frank A. M." to the company and they put one of the boys on it as skipper, so it was making money for us too. Bobby and Oswald had been fishing with me for a long time and were getting ready to become skippers. So that year our manager decided to put Bobby on the "Frank A. M." as skipper. Robby and I talked it over and decided that since our children were growing up and becoming skippers there might be some bad feelings among them over which one got to use the "Frank A. M." We decided that it would be better to split our partnership up since we both had been doing well and that would keep any trouble from coming up over who got to use the "Frank A. M." So we talked it over with our manager, Mr. Corker, and he worked it out for us. I bought the "Frank A. M." and the "Twin Sisters" and Robby bought the "Adele M." We had been doing pretty well in our sawmill business but about that time the government passed a law that we couldn't pick up beach logs any more. They hired some salvage people to go around and pick up all the logs, and if we wanted any we had to buy them from the government or the logging company they belonged to. I thought it was absolutely not fair to us but there was nothing we could do about it, so we stopped running that sawmill except when we needed a little lumber to repair our boats. We still have it but the equipment is getting rusted and we hardly ever use it any more.

8 People Will Do Anything for Him Because He Is So Respected

In March 1957 we had another election and I was elected chief councillor. My councillors were Herbert Cook, Robby Bell, Simon Beans, and William Cook. There were a lot of small problems that came up for me to deal with. One thing we had a lot of trouble with was trespassers on our reserve. The Nimpkish reserve was one of the hardest ones because we are right next to the white end of Alert Bay. We were half-Indian and half-white and we could walk back and forth between the villages. It was still against the law to bring any beer or liquor onto the Indian reserves. Although I didn't like the law it was our duty to abide by it and enforce it. We didn't have the rights that the other citizens of the province had, so there were non-Indians who were bootlegging liquor and bringing it onto the reserve. A lot of times if the mounted police were not around I would just go and tell them to get off our reserve. I know some of the people didn't like it and they figured that I was butting into their business. I felt it didn't matter, but what mattered the most was that we enforced the law. If we didn't do our duty and there was trouble then we couldn't expect help in other situations.

Another problem was that when the white man first came to this area the Indians owned all the area that is now Alert Bay. There was an Indian cemetery there which was right in the middle of the white end of the village after the Indian Department made this end into the Nimpkish reserve, so that part of our reserve was that cemetery in the other end. The property right from the waterfront clear to the back of the cemetery actually is part of our reserve. So the leaders of Alert Bay came to me one day and said they would like us to move the fence which runs along the road at the front of the cemetery back six feet. I checked with Dan Cranmer who had been chief councillor before and he told me that they had already moved it back once before so that they could make the road wider. I told those men from Alert Bay that we couldn't do it because that would cover some of the graves that were there. So we decided to build a cement wall to replace the fence which wasn't in the best condition. The white end of Alert Bay, which had been incorporated, had a gravel pit so I went and asked if we could buy some gravel from their pit. They refused to let us buy any gravel at all. Well, I was really stuck and it made me mad. I went to Norman Corker and he let me borrow a scow that the company had and we went over to another part of our reserve across the channel. We had some gravel on the beach there and at the right tide we brought the scow in on the beach. We had to use a horse shovel and a horse to scoop the gravel into the big shovel and then dump it into the scow. I hired ten or fifteen boys and they all had shovels to help. We worked hard and fast with all the shovels and got it loaded with gravel before the tide came in again.

Then we brought the scow across and beached it right at the cemetery and started to build the wall. The people at that end wouldn't even give us any water so we had to cart it all the way from our reserve. We were working on the road in front of the cemetery and many times while we were working some cars and trucks came and tried to go along the road. I just stood there and put up my hand to stop them. I told them that that was an Indian reserve and if we wanted we could put a fence up right there across the road. If they wanted to wait until we could clear the road in a few minutes they could or they could go around on the other road. Not too long after that they were putting in a pipe along the road right in front of the cement wall that we had built. While they were doing it they damaged that wall and it was all caved in in one place. I went over there and I really gave it to them. I told them, "You are trespassing on the Indian reserve. You could have put your pipe around the other way." So they had to get surveyors and survey it all and fix it up.

When I had been chief councillor before, we had passed a rule that every person living on the Nimpkish reserve would pay for their water. There were a lot of people who never paid their bill and we just couldn't get them to do it. I finally wrote a letter to Ottawa to see if we could take those people to court. I volunteered as the chief councillor of the village to go to court against them to try to get them to pay. Before that I had talked to them and sent them bills and done everything I could to try to get them to pay their bills. When a person signed up for water and we connected their house to the water line they agreed to pay for the water. If they were in the city we could have just cut off their water and then they would learn to pay their bills, but we weren't allowed to do that. My council asked me just to wait and see what happened but it never did any good.

We had another problem about the garbage that people had to get rid of. Our own people used to just dump their garbage on the road. There were some kids that came around to the houses and we would give them fifty cents to dump our garbage. They would collect garbage from the houses and then dump it off the wharf, which was no good because all the cans and things just washed back up on the beach. I talked to the people about their garbage being on the beach and they all told me that they hadn't dumped it there but it was the kids that picked it up. So I told them not to give it to the kids any more. About that time the leaders at the other end of Alert Bay came to me and asked if they could use a big pit on the back of our reserve to dump garbage in and then they would cover it up with a bulldozer every once in a while. I told them that we didn't want that because there were a lot of rats up there. So then they asked if they could drive through and dump it in the bay at the back of our reserve. So I talked to my council and we thought this might help solve some of our own problems of garbage so we decided to let them try it. We decided to see how it was going to work because behind the island there were some very big swells and tides and we thought it would carry the garbage out. They tried it for about one month and all the beaches were terrible. So we stopped them again and told them it couldn't be done. Then they tried to get us to do some other things and finally I told them, "Just leave us alone. We don't want any more to do with it. If you want to dump garbage, then dump it on your end. Get an incinerator or something. Make a proper job of it and then we can get people to pay." So sometime after that they got an incinerator and our people paid to have their garbage burned up there along with that from the other end.

Another problem that came up was about our teenagers running around at night. The people at the other end of Alert Bay were having the same trouble and they decided that they wanted to have a curfew at ten o'clock each night. I talked it over with my council and we thought it was a good idea, so I checked with the Indian agent about it and he said he would write to Ottawa and see if we could do that. So we got a letter from Ottawa which told us that we weren't allowed to have a curfew. That was why I didn't like for Ottawa to handle our business. Why should they come and interfere with what we wanted in bettering the conditions here in Alert Bay? That was my personal opinion. They didn't know anything about it. They got a report and just read what it said on that paper, but what do they know from that about the livelihood of the people here? We wanted that curfew and we asked for it many times but they always turned us down. For some reason we just couldn't have it. I don't know what the Indian agent wrote, whether it wasn't good enough or strong enough or whether he didn't put any teeth in that letter so we could get what we wanted. So anyway, the people in the other end of Alert Bay went ahead and passed the rule that all the young people had to be home by ten o'clock for their end, but we didn't have it in our end. When they blew that siren then all the white kids would just come down to our end. I told them, "You are foolish. I don't think we should just pass a curfew in that end. I think it is time we did something about our end also." But it never worked out and they had to give it up because we couldn't get a curfew in our end and it couldn't work. The law was sometimes funny and the Indian Department wouldn't go for anything like having a curfew for the whole of Alert Bay because they were different people and we were supposed to be different. They were whites and we were Indians. They cooperated and we couldn't cooperate. That was the most difficult village there was on the coast because it was half-white and half-Indian.

One of the biggest problems for the Indians was that they weren't equal to the other citizens of Canada, and that is still true today. I remember that during the war they started to tax us. The Indian agent told all the Indian people that they were just going to tax us during the war and afterwards we would be exempt from the tax. We didn't think too much of it because we thought it was a good idea to help along in the war. The thing I didn't like personally at that time was that we weren't recognized as citizens of the country of Canada and the province of British Columbia. We weren't allowed to vote for the federal or the provincial government. After the war was over they just kept on taxing us which we didn't agree with because we had no representation in the government. What I wanted most was to be given the vote so we would have someone to represent the Indian people in the government. Finally in 1949 we were allowed to vote in the provincial elections but we still were not full citizens of Canada and we were excluded from the beer parlors until 1951. We didn't feel it was right to pay the sales tax and the gasoline tax because the province didn't do anything for our dirt roads and none of that money ever came back to us. We had a dirt road on the reserve that ran right in front of my house and we would ask the provincial government to blacktop it for us. Everybody was using it, such as store trucks and gas trucks and taxis, but every time there was any fixing to be done on the road we had to do it on our own and use our own money. The municipality of Alert Bay paid their taxes but it came back to them and they repaired their roads and things like that. Even today we are far apart yet in being equal with the citizens of the country.

I have had a lot of associations with white people ever since I was a little boy. When I traveled I mixed with the white people and had friends among them all over. I never hesitated to go among the white people because I felt that it didn't matter what race one was. I have friends who are Chinese and Japanese too. It is awful hard for me to explain the difference between the white man and the Indian. I know for a fact that the white man has more education than the Indian, at least the people my age. The white man is better at managing money and things like that because the Indian doesn't know how to manage money or how to budget his money, and I think it is because they have never learned that. I have never wished that I was a white man because I believe in God and try to be a Christian person and it was my Maker Who made me like I am. I didn't choose to be an Indian and I wouldn't say that He made a mistake in making me an Indian. It wasn't my choice to choose my mother and father. I have to take it because the Maker made me like I am, an Indian, and I'm glad I am an Indian.

That fall the Native Brotherhood had their convention up at Bella Coola. I went up with some of the other people from the Nimpkish band and we had a very good convention. One day while

I was there I was sitting around talking with a group of the Bella Coola people, and I was telling them about the time many years before when they had come down to Gilford Island and massacred the people there where my grandfather lived. Then I told them about the time my grandfather had come up there with James Douglas on a big ship and the chief had let him marry his daughter so he could get all their masks and songs so he wouldn't attack their village. One of the men told his wife that night what I had been telling them and the next morning his wife came to me and said, "My mother wants to see you." So that afternoon I went to their house and sat down in the front room. The old lady came in through the back door and as soon as I saw her I stood up and greeted her. She was very very old and she came to me and just put both of her hands to my hands and held them a little while and then she turned around and walked out again. She didn't say anything but just walked out again with a little cane which she was carrying. The whole family was sitting around and this old lady's daughter said to me, "She remembered your grandfather, Aul Sewid, when he came and married her older sister. She was just a little girl then and she remembered very well when your grandfather came ashore here. That was what she told me." That seemed to me to be evidence of the story that I had heard about my grandfather. I was awfully disappointed that I wasn't able to learn any more about it.

Although some of the people still felt that I was an outsider in that Nimpkish band I didn't have nearly as much trouble as I had had during my first time as chief councillor. About that time one old Nimpkish man who really hadn't approved of what I had done, especially in making that village wide open for anybody to move there who wanted to, called me in. He was very very sick and he had turned to be a very religious man when he got old. He said to me, "I've been watching you and I think you mean well. I've been watching you and you are a valuable man to this place and I think you should carry on. I'm old and nearly finished but you are still young and I think you are doing a fine job for the people." As a man who practiced religion I had a very soft spot in my heart for those people who spoke against me. I felt sorry for them and when I walked out of that room I had tears in my eyes for them. I said to myself, "Thank God that I made him understand before we parted

with him." I thought he was a real man to ask me to come in and
see him. Just a few weeks after that he died. And I thought of all
my obligations and then the other people who might become chief
councillor, some of them were drunks and roughnecks. What would
they do if they took my place? That was what I thought about.

It wasn't long after that that the government held a workshop for
the leaders of the Indian villages from the West Coast. The chiefs
and councillors from all over the different agencies gathered at
Nanaimo. There were men there from the Indian Department and
from the provincial government and from the University of British
Columbia to discuss the Indian problems. We had large meetings
and then we had smaller meetings of about forty people to discuss
the various problems. The whole question of the chief councillor
came up in one of those meetings and I got up and talked to them
about it. I told them, "I don't like that name 'chief,' because it is a
cheap word. If you move into a village that you don't belong to and
people see that you are a very active and promising man and that
you are going to be a leader of the people, then they elect you as
the chief councillor. And right away the man who is the hereditary
chief of that village will envy you because he feels that you have his
name and position. I don't know the way you white people use this
chief business, like chief engineer and chief councillor, but I think
it should be changed. I always like to be called the chairman of my
council and I always refer to myself as the chairman of my council.
That is better because that's what I am. I'm not a big shot or anything like that. I'm just the man who sits in the chair and listens
to my council when we come together. It isn't nice because a lot of
people envy you and think you are a big shot who is higher than
them. It has got to be changed because the thinking of an Indian
is different from the white man." Well, after that there was quite
a discussion over what I said and quite a few of the people sided
with me.

I also talked to them at that meeting about amalgamating the
smaller villages with the larger ones. I had been talking to the
Indian agents and the Indian superintendent about that for many
years. I told them, "I've been fighting the government for many
years now, talking to them about amalgamating the smaller villages
into some progressive villages that are near towns and hospitals.

When those people move in from the isolated villages we could know right away which men would be good as members of the council. The people shouldn't just say that he is a newcomer and he can't be on the council or the chief because the chief is supposed to be the greatest man in the village. I think it is wrong for the Indian Department to waste money by building schools and wharfs and light plants in those isolated villages. The people in those villages are just fed up because there is nothing in those villages for them to stay for. There is no life in those villages and in a few years they are all going to be empty. I suppose some of the older people that don't have any education and who have been there all of their lives are happy there, but not the younger people. I don't think it is right just to have people transfer into the bigger villages one at a time, but we should get together and amalgamate those bands because I know for sure that the Indians are happier if they are together." We had a very good meeting there and I think it helped the government to understand our problems.

The municipality of Alert Bay decided to celebrate the centennial of that town in 1958 because it had been one hundred years since the white man had settled there. The town of Alert Bay had been named after a steamship, the H.M.S. "Alert," which first came there in 1858. The people at the other end set up a committee to decide what they would do for the centennial and the council of the Nimpkish band asked me to go ahead and be the chairman of our committee. I was on the other committee also. Our committee decided that we would try to fix up the cemetery for our centennial project since it was all in forest and overgrown with weeds. The totem poles that were on many of the graves were all just about ready to fall and some of them were already on the ground. While the cemetery belonged to the Nimpkish reserve many people from the other tribes of the Kwakiutl had been buried there. Because of this we didn't feel that it was fair for the Nimpkish people to spend all the money on their own. There was only one totem pole there that belonged to the Nimpkish and it was very important that we didn't touch those other totem poles. They weren't ours and we thought it would be a good idea if the people from the other villages would go ahead themselves and fix them up and paint them.

So I went around to all the other villages and held a meeting in each village to tell them of the project and explain to them why I wanted them to contribute some money. If they couldn't afford to donate some money toward that project we expected them to send some of their young people over to help us clean it up. We got some help from the Indian Department and many of the other tribes contributed money. After the first of the year we started working there. We had two people from each of the other villages on the committee and we planned out everything that we wanted to do. They all thought it was only right that I should be the chairman because I was the chief councillor of that village and the cemetery was on our reserve. A lot of people were working there every day on that project. Nobody except for a few of the painters were getting any pay at all. Everything was free labor, especially myself; I didn't get anything out of it.

I found that was a hard job to carry out. I usually didn't find anything hard to do. I was used to negotiating with people and I never found it hard to settle things by talking. I had approached my friends in the government many times and they just opened the doors for me and I went in and talked to them and told them their mistakes that they had done to my people. When I was there fixing up that cemetery and when we built that wall I rolled up my sleeves and really worked because I wasn't afraid of work. I could do anything, which was a blessed gift to me. I could make anything with my hands out of wood or with cement. When there was a project to be done I would be there to supervise it in the way I thought it would be best according to the plan decided on by the people. But the hardest thing I found was that I put myself into that project so deep that I got tired and cranky sometimes. The people still wanted to bother me and tell me that I shouldn't be doing it the way I was doing it. I just told them, "I called a meeting before we started and you should have been there to tell us when we planned it. Once that plan was decided on that is the way it is going to be."

Some days I had about fifty people there working and sometimes more. Some of the villages sent over fifteen or twenty young men to come and help us. The men who were painting the totem poles were also teaching some of the younger men to paint them at the same time. The women who were there would bring us cake and coffee in the morning and afternoon for a coffee break. Everybody was very cooperative in working together on that project. The municipality of Alert Bay decided to build a small library and museum right next to the cemetery. The provincial government gave so much money for each person both Indian and white and we just put it all into that library. I was taking quite an interest in that project also, because I thought it was necessary to have a place for the masks and Indian stuff. Most of the people were just putting all their things in their basement and people were breaking it. I put my big raven mask and the mask I wore when I was a hamatsa in there after it was finished.

One of my boys was skipper on the "Frank A. M." and I was still using the "Twin Sisters" that year. The manager of the company, Mr. Corker, was still coming to me for new skippers. He knew according to the books and tallys that I had been a high boat, not only for one year but I had been right up top as a good fisherman for many years. I think I had been the high boat every year since I was first up there for almost sixteen years. Even during the last year or two when I hadn't been the very top boat I was right up among the highliners. It was rather unusual for a skipper to be right up to the highliners all the time he had been a skipper, but that was what I had done. A lot of skippers that I knew who were real good hardworking men would be up and down, up and down. They would be up near the highliners one year and then drop right down to the bottom. I had seen a lot of good men do that and my boss asked me to talk to them and see if I could give them some help. Sometimes I found out that they were drinking too heavy or not really attending to their fishing, especially when we had short weeks. Sometimes the Fisheries Department would only allow us to go out two or three days in a week and we had to work awfully hard to get many fish in that short period of time.

I had trained quite a few of the men who were highliners in the company that I was working for. They would work under me for four or five years and they were treated very rough. When I thought they were ready, because I was the judge, I would tell my manager. Sometimes he would come to me and say, "We need a man, Jimmy, to be skipper next year." I would just tell him, "Well, you can have this man on my crew. He is ready." I had trained quite a few boys for our company and I felt that it was a big responsibility. My manager knew that those who had been on my crew for a number of years would be ready because they had been working under one who understands and was strict with the rules about the way he expected his men to be, the way he set and caught fish. It was a big responsibility not only to make a good name for myself and my company and my family and the families of those crew members, but I felt that if I did well then everybody working along with me did well. It was those people who didn't care and just didn't think about what was going to happen that day or the next, those were the ones that would never make a good captain.

One Sunday that summer we were going down through Johnstone Strait and we stopped at a place called Robinson Bite where there was a big bay. There was a boundary right there which the Fishery Department had set up and we could only fish on one side of that boundary. The fish were all going around just inside the boundary and there were about thirty or forty boats running back and forth there trying to find a position where they could make a set. It was about 4:30 or 5 and we couldn't start fishing until right at 6. There was a boat from the Fisheries Department there checking to see that no one broke the law. So I took the "Twin Sisters" way over in the corner of that bay and just stopped there. There was no other boat there because there weren't any fish jumping there. All the other boats were over on the other side of the bay. So we just lay around there and then the tide changed and I could see the fish moving towards us. That was the only position where we could let our nets go and nobody else could let go because we held that position before anybody was there. And right about two minutes to six all the other boats moved over towards us. The fisheries officer was there running back and forth and talking over his radio telephone to tell us when we could let go. So I told my crew to let out the net, and we made a very narrow set because we didn't have enough room to make a big set as the other boats were all around us. We started pursing up the net and I could tell that we were drifting near the boundary line and I was kind of worried that we would go across it. As soon as we had pursed the net up we could tell we had a big catch and we pushed away from the drifting tide and out into the middle of the strait. We pulled in the net and started to brail the fish and it was really a very nice load. When we

finally counted them there were 5200 sockeye in that one set and
that was the biggest catch I had ever experienced in one set. I knew
that the tide would change and when it changed the fish would
come with the tide over to where we were. Some of the other
boats got a few fish but not many. We were very lucky that evening.

Mike Lazich still came up every summer to work with me. He
had sent some money to a woman in Yugoslavia that he had known
and she came over and they were married and he was really happy.
He was the only one who had been fishing with me steady since
the wartime because the others had become skippers or I had had
to kick them off. I really depended on him, especially on those long
weekends. I could be sure that he would be watching the boat and
if there was anything we needed he would come and see me. I told
him if there was anything we needed he should come and tell me
and he was really good that way. If I had had two or three of his
kind I would have had an easier time. On Saturday afternoon we
would go over together, just me and him all those years, and we
would change the oil, fuel up, get water and groceries and other
things we needed. If he hadn't been around I would be all alone.
Every skipper liked a person like that who offered his services but
most of the fellows never did that. A lot of people called him
"Mike Sewid." He liked to go over to the beer parlor and just sit
there with those people and he knew everybody among our people.
Sometimes after his wife died he would get drunk because he was
quite a lonely man and I'd find him sleeping on the table, so I
would just go in and help him up. I'd say, "Come on Mike, get into
bed." He would say, "I'm sorry, Jimmy." So I usually said to him,
"That's fine, Mike, just go and sleep it off." Mike always called me
"boss." "What are you going to do, boss? What time are we going
to leave, boss?" I never did like to be called "boss," just like I never
did like to be called "chief." I didn't like to be called anything
above any other person.

Sometimes when I went to visit Mike in Vancouver in his home
I would see him giving his little kids a little wine to drink. They
say that they used to do that in the old country. They didn't care
that he was just a little kid. At first I though that was very very
wrong to see them drinking that wine, but I thought to myself
later that that was education. I thought it was wrong to hide that

stuff and then the kid grows up and suddenly he sees it and starts to crave it. He likes to find out if he drinks more than his parents what it would do to him. I began to feel that they should teach the Indian children how to drink. Many times I used to see some of the boys when they got a bottle of rum or something; they just took the bottle and opened it and drank it down. They didn't know how to take it. First thing you know they were drunk and then they didn't know what they were doing and they were going to take some more and just keep shoving it down their throats. I thought maybe they should be taught in school. They had been arguing about teaching the kids sex and things like that in the school and I thought they should have a class for the teenagers on drinking. They could pour something in a glass and show them how much they were supposed to give a person and then mix it with Seven-Up or ginger ale. Then they could just take it like people normally do.

In the fall I decided to call a special meeting of the tribes in the Kwakiutl agency at Turnour Island. I had been elected vice-president for the Alert Bay district of the Native Brotherhood each year since I first took that office, and I began to feel that it would be helpful if we could get together in our district. When I went to the conventions along with several other delegates we would usually report on everything that went on when we returned. The problem was that it took us a long time to go around to all the little villages and it was too much work for me to do as district vice-president when I had so many other things to do. I was spending a lot of my time traveling in my own boat and I didn't get any pay for it and I felt it was too much. I didn't have much time even for my own family. Then too, I liked to wait until I got a report from the Native Brotherhood office which had the minutes of the meetings and we didn't usually get that for three or four months after the convention. So I felt that if we could get the leaders of all the villages together once or twice a year we could help the smaller villages and we would be able to know their problems. I knew for a fact that it was much harder to get help in the smaller villages. If they wrote a letter and sent it into the agency office or the regional office in Vancouver they would have a hard time getting what they wanted. I felt we could work together because we wanted the same things for the smaller villages as we did for the larger ones. We could help them and they could help us.

I talked to the Indian agent and told him that I was planning to have a meeting of the leading men from all over the Kwakiutl agency. I didn't ask him to come because I didn't feel he should come to the meeting as the Indian agent. I felt like the Indian people should get together by themselves and if the Indian agent was there sitting down a lot of the people would be afraid to come out with what they wanted to say. I felt that it would be best if all the people could come out with what they wanted to say and then I could put it in writing and hand it to the agent after the meeting was over. When I told him he said, "I think it will be all right, but don't come to me for any expenses." I said, "I'm not going to go to anybody for any expenses. I'm going to go with my own boats and take my people over there with my own boats. I'm going to see to it that everything is paid for as far as the expenses of the delegates of the other tribes."

I talked to some of the leading men of the villages, and I knew that the Turnour Island people were very strong and they were very helpful to all that I was doing. They were more or less sympathetic to all the work that I was doing, so I asked the leading men there if we could have the first meeting of the intertribal council in their village. They said that would be fine and they would be ready for us when we came. I wrote to the other villages and they all sent some of their leaders, and when we got there we elected one man to be the chairman of the meeting. It worked out very fine for everyone. We discussed the plans the government had to limit the licenses of the people who fish and the medical plans that the people in those isolated villages didn't have too much chance to know about. They might listen to some of those things on the radio but very few of them understood what it was all about. I liked to tell all those other villages what was going to happen to all the Indian people so that we could help them and they weren't going to be left behind. We just sort of dragged them along with us.

In March 1959 it was time again to vote for the chief councillor and councillors of the Nimpkish band. Every meeting during the past years we had been accepting new members into the band from the other bands of the Kwakiutl agency. We had grown from about three hundred members when I was first elected chief councillor until we had over five hundred members and we were authorized to elect five council members to assist the chief councillor. At that time I was elected again to be the chief councillor and William Cook, Herbert Cook, George Cook, George Alfred, and Robby Bell were elected to be the councillors. Herbert Cook was a very active man and had been on my council the first time I was elected. He was also the secretary of the Native Brotherhood and I used to travel with him to the conventions. He was a good man and we worked together on a lot of things. When we returned from the Native Brotherhood conventions he was like my right-hand man. Every time we came home from a convention the people in Alert Bay would be ready for us with a fire up in our hall and coffee and sandwiches ready. They would notify all the people that their delegates were coming home that night and they wanted everybody to gather at the council hall. That little hall used to be just filled right up with the people, especially the old people who are gone now. They really cared about what was going on because we went to those conventions for them and not just for ourselves. We would come into the hall and give our reports and I would be speaking in our language and Herbert Cook would be speaking the English language. I used to just tell him to carry on where I left off. He was a very very good worker and a real big help to me.

Right after I was elected I got a phone call asking me if I could get some of our Indian people to come down to Nanaimo in July when Queen Elizabeth came to that city and put on an Indian dance. So I got the people together at Alert Bay and had a meeting with them and told them what was going to happen. So they agreed it would be good if we could go down and we started having rehearsals every so often. There were young people and old people there practicing their dancing, and I told them that if they didn't have any regalia they weren't going to go down. We were going to provide transportation for them but we weren't going to have them go down to Nanaimo as white men. We practiced our songs and dances and got everything ready and when July came we went down to meet the Queen.

At Nanaimo they had set up an Indian village in a big field and there were people there from a lot of the other tribes. Some of them were making sweaters and Mungo Martin was carving on a totem pole. There were over three thousand people gathered there to see the ceremony. Queen Elizabeth and Prince Philip first went up on a platform where they met the dignitaries of the city and Dr. Kelly and some others. Flora was up there with them dressed in her regalia to represent the Indian people to the Queen. Then the Queen came down from the platform and moved toward the exhibitions that had been set up in the Indian village. The Salish people did some dancing and then she came over to our group. I was standing in front of the dancers in my regalia and mask and Queen Elizabeth and Prince Philip came over to where I was standing and I said to the Queen: "Your Majesty: We welcome you and his Royal Highness to Vancouver Island and on behalf of the Indian people we bestow upon you the name, Arohmuthl, which means 'Respected by all, Mother of all People.'" I had a rattle in my hand and as soon as I had bestowed that name on the Queen I started to shake the rattle and the singers started singing and that whole group of Indian dancers started to dance for her while she walked along in front of them. We must have had about sixty dancers there with all their regalia on. We did part of the cedar bark dance which was used during the hamatsa ceremony and then we did the feather dance which was for peace.

The next couple of years were busy ones with the work of my council, the church, the Native Brotherhood, and all of the other things I was doing. In July of 1960, the government finally gave us the right to vote in the federal elections. In that sense we were full citizens but we still didn't have the right to bring liquor into our homes on the reserve and there were many other ways that we were not equal. I found that it was more and more difficult to get the people to help in things that needed to be done. I would go right there and do the work myself many times. We fixed up our council hall and I worked on that. Every year we went over in our boats to do some food fishing for the people and often I was in charge of that. There were houses to inspect and fire-fighting equipment to keep in good condition and many, many other things that needed to be done for our village each year. I felt it would be different if I had an office and got paid so much each day. Then I could go to the office each day just like any businessman and I could take a vacation with my family. I thought it was a big responsibility to be the chief councillor, and many times I had to neglect my family and fixing up the house and things like that because I was working for my people.

I thought it was very important that a chief should be trying to live a good life and trying to cooperate with the good things of life. I've seen some chiefs of other villages who just did everything wrong and went and took part with their people in big parties where things got real wild and they just broke windows and things like that. Sometimes I had meetings with them and they just didn't know what they were talking about. Those kind of chiefs tried to talk to their people and nobody would listen to them and nobody would believe them because of the kind of person they were. If a person was going to be a loose man he wasn't going to mean anything to the good people among his tribe. I didn't like that and felt that they should just put some better man in that position and change the ways of the people. I had many close associates, hundreds of them all over, and I had to be very careful because I found everybody was different. People were not all the same and I found that if I was with one man and went into the next room to talk to another one, he would be altogether different. People are human as far as I am concerned and I haven't met anybody that I dislike. I always felt it was up to the way I treated people and that was how I was going to be treated. Sometimes people would tell me that a certain person was no good but that there was no such person as a perfect man on this earth. I felt that we had to try to do something to show how we felt and to help that person who might have done something wrong. I was going to try to help him because that is the way I believed and I have tried to do that all my life no matter whether it was an older person or a younger person. I have made a lot of mistakes and I can admit that. I had made a lot of mistakes in my everyday talk with people, but I liked to know about my mistakes because I didn't like to stick with them. I liked to go and talk to the man that I had wronged and tell him that I shouldn't have done it.

A lot of times people would come to me for advice. They had something they wanted to do and they used to come to me and ask me what I thought they should do. For instance, a person would be thinking about marrying a certain girl and come and ask me what I thought. Sometimes I would come out with something and sometimes not because it was awful hard to predict what would happen. Sometimes older people have come to me and ask me whether they should get married again and they wondered whether it would interfere with their children or their everyday life. It was awfully hard to judge. I never liked to judge other people and I never did that. What I thought of them was that they were people the same as me.

Early in 1961 Mr. Rodgers, who was our minister, talked to me about taking a more active part in the work of the church. I had been leading the Kwakwala prayer meeting for many years, singing in the choir, preaching in the church, and carrying out my job as rector's warden. He wanted me to become a lay reader in the Anglican church, which would give me the authority to baptize a child if he was dying and no minister was around, conduct funerals, and take part in the service every Sunday morning. So I agreed to become a lay reader in Christ Church and on March 16, 1961, they held a special service where I was licensed to be a lay reader. Archbishop Harold Sexton sent me a certificate which said:

> HAROLD, by Divine Permission, Archbishop of British Columbia, to our well beloved and approved in Christ, James Sewid..
>
> Greeting: We do by these presents grant to you our license to exercise the office of Reader in the Parish of Christ Church, Alert Bay, within our Diocese and jurisdiction, on the nomination of the Reverend C. B. Rodgers, Incumbent of the said parish; and we do authorize you to perform the duties of a Lay Reader, under the guidance and direction of the Incumbent of the parish, and in accordance with Cannon XXI of the Cannons of the Diocese of British Columbia.
>
> March 16, 1961   HAROLD—Columbia Diocese

After that I began to take part in the services, reading the lessons and singing the responses. I had quite a lot of responsibility in the church. Earlier our services used to be half in English and half in Kwakwala but at that time they were nearly all in English. When the minister was away, I gave the sermons on Sunday morning.

Since I was helping the minister with the service, I stopped singing in the choir.

I had seen many ministers at Christ Church because they were always changing around every year or two, although some of them stayed for five years or more. Some of the ministers we had were very good men who really went out to the people, while some of the others just stayed in the church and rang the bell and expected the people to come to them. Some of the ministers who came wanted to change the ways of the people and the way they worshiped in the church. For instance, we used to always have a special service on Sunday afternoon for baptizing children. Sometimes there were ten or fifteen children all there together with their parents and families and godparents, and it made a real nice service. We felt that it should be a service of its own and not just something that was done during the regular church service. Some of the ministers wanted to change it and have the baptism service in the morning or the evening service. I didn't think that it was very nice to change it. I felt that when we had a lot of babies there and the regular service was long anyway that it wasn't very good to try to put both services together. Sometimes we had the same problem with some of the ministers wanting to change the funeral services and not allow the people to buy an expensive casket and send lots of flowers. I felt that if a person was gone from this world and we were going to pay him our last respects, then it was up to the family to decide what kind of a funeral they wanted. It really meant a lot to our people to do a lot of things for a person who died, especially for a very noble and respected person like a chief's son or daughter. They used to put a lot of expensive jewels and other things with the person who had died, especially when it was someone who had come from a very well-known family. I always compared our custom to the Egyptians who used to do that to the very noble people, and I thought we just sort of liked to carry on the custom of our people from the early days. That was what some of the ministers in our church wanted to change. I felt it was wrong for a person who came and stayed among us for a couple of years to want to change those kind of things. It would be all right to change it if he was going to stay with us for life. When that person would leave then we would go back to what we had wanted. I have been so close to the Christ Church of Alert Bay and that was the way I saw it.

A lot of the older people were very helpful to me in my work for the church but there was one thing that I didn't like. They couldn't do anything when I was away. Whenever I was gone they wouldn't have the Kwakwala prayer meeting because there was no one there to lead it. They always waited for me to do the leading in the things we did in the church work. About that time we started the St. Andrew's Brotherhood which is a men's group connected with the Anglican church. I was elected chairman of our group, which was made up of the minister and about five or six men. We would meet every couple of weeks and discuss the problems of helping people. Our work was to try to approach people to bring them to church and help those that were not doing anything to help themselves. We would go to those people who were having trouble, such as not getting along in their married life, and counsel them. I was especially concerned with the young people who just went haywire and became uncontrollable. At our meetings I would hear reports from the other men after we had said the Lord's Prayer and the Creed and prayers. Then we would talk over problems and appoint the men to go visit anyone who was having trouble. It was very important to me and I liked it because we were able to talk to people and it was someone else visiting them besides the minister.

Shortly after I became a lay reader, I was elected again to be the chief councillor of the Nimpkish band. We elected five councillors and they were Alfred Hunt, George Cook, Herbert Cook, George Alfred, and Robby Bell. It wasn't very long after that election that my uncle, Chief Tom Dawson of the Kingcome people, came to Alert Bay and invited me to attend a big do that he was going to put on, and he wanted me to bring some of the people up in my boat. So I went up with some of the people and he put on this big do that lasted for several days. On the final day after there had been many Indian dances and many things given away, he was giving away his personal belongings, doing what I think is called "making a will." He was sitting on a box up in front of all the people, and he called me up to where he was sitting after he was through telling what was going to belong to each of his own children.

When I went up he talked to me so that everyone could hear.

"Jimmy," he said, "I am very proud of you and that is why I wanted you to come forward here today. I have been very proud of you and your work for our people. I have always thought that you have inherited what you have been doing through your mother's side and your father's side, especially Chief Odzistales of the Mamalilikulla people. He was a good leader of his people. Your grandfather, Chief Aul Sewid, was also a big man in his time during the potlatch days and a strong leader. He was well liked by the first governor of British Columbia, James Douglas, and he used to interpret for him and help him in many ways. That is why I think you are like you are today. It has been just natural for you to work through the Native Brotherhood in your own way for our people. I would like you to accept this gift, this little token from me, this talking stick. It was made especially for you by Benny Dick of Kingcome and I have paid him for doing this for you. This talking stick represents your crests on your mother's side and your father's side. I want you to take this talking stick and use it whenever you think you can.

"The first crest at the bottom is Tsunuqua who was a giantess This is the crest of the Temltemlels clan from your mother's side. Temltemlels was the first man of that clan and he had the supernatural power to turn into the Tsunuqua. The second crest is Tselkamai which means 'owner of the cedar bark dances.' He was also a great man with many supernatural powers. The next one is the double-headed serpent Sisiutl, and I have put it on this talking stick because it represents the strength of the Kwakiutl people. The next one is the Cedar Man. In the early days when the people heard the flood was coming, he went inside of a big hollow cedar log and after the flood he came out. The next one is Yakatnalas which means 'The Whale' and comes to you from your father's side. The next one is Qolus and that is the same as Odzistales which means 'he is so big that he can hardly move around.' You have that name through your grandfather, Aul Sewid."

So I took the talking stick from him and said, "I thank you from the bottom of my heart because this will give me more strength in what I am doing. I will treasure this wonderful gift especially because I know that some people like yourself have been quietly standing by me in all that I have been trying to do for our people."

It was awfully hard to talk when I answered him and I had tears in my eyes as I thought of my grandparents and my father and mother who had passed away many years before. When I returned to Alert Bay after that do, I was really touched by that wonderful gift and I started to think about putting on a do myself.

The next year I talked it over with my wife and my in-laws about calling the people to Alert Bay for a do when they came for the sports day in the spring. The reason I wanted to do it was because when Chief Tom Dawson had given me that talking stick it made me feel that I should do something to show the people that I could do it on my own. Of course, in previous years when I was young, I was involved in many potlatches with the help of my grandparents and with the help of my uncle, Toby Willey. I had used my own money and belongings in a potlatch after my wedding, but I hadn't done any for over twenty years. I wanted to do it to announce that I had received that beautiful present from my uncle. I talked it over with my in-laws because the purpose of that night was going to be to announce and give my grandchildren names that were associated with the particular dances. The custom was that everything was to come to me from my wife's family and then I could pass it on to my children and grandchildren. Many of my relatives had given names to my older grandchildren, but that was to be the first time for some of the others and all the names that had been given to my children and grandchildren would be announced again. So I sent Simon Beans around in his boat because he was a very close relation of mine to invite the villages to come to Alert Bay. He went around to Village Island, Gilford Island, Turnour Island, New Vancouver, Fort Rupert, and Kingcome and invited all the people to come.

I asked my uncle, Chief Tom Dawson, to be the master of ceremonies, to announce the different names and dances. We met in the council hall at about 8 o'clock, and the first thing was some of the people of my wife's family got up and gave a speech and announced that the articles and some names for that do were coming from my wife's side of the family. Even though I was the one who gathered all the stuff together, it was the custom that it was supposed to come from them that night even though I had given it to them. After that Tom Dawson started announcing the dances, the singers who I had hired that day started singing, and different ones of my relatives there started coming out and dancing. I went out first and danced the hamatsa dance, and Herbert Martin was dancing right along with me as well as two or three hamatsas who were my relations from other villages. They usually did that just to show their appreciation of what I was doing there that night.

Then Tom Dawson announced the names that had been given to my children before and then they danced. Most of my children had danced before, like at Simon Beans' potlatch, but some of my grandchildren had never danced. Bobby's oldest boy danced the kind of dance that Aul Sewid had gotten for the first time among the Kwakiutl. Bobby was wearing the chilcat blanket that night because we had received that right from Odzistales of the Mama-lilikulla. The dancing went on until nearly eleven o'clock, and they only stopped when it was announced that someone was going to dance and they told the name that he was going to receive.

My wife had gathered up some things like towels and small household articles and I took some money out of the bank to give out to the people. After the dancing was over, Tom Dawson announced that there was going to be a little intermission and Henry Bell and Simon Beans went around for me and gave out some money. My wife had given the articles to her family and they were passing the things out. I had taken about five or six hundred dollars out of the bank and I just gave that money to Henry Bell who gave it out along with Simon Beans. They gave out about ten dollars apiece to some of the chiefs and some of the younger men got two dollars and the women got a dollar each. Everybody got something but I considered them all just small presents, just tokens. While they were giving out the money and articles we served everybody coffee and sandwiches and cake. There were over two hundred people there including some of my non-Indian friends.

After we had given everything away, Chief Tom Dawson got up and gave all the other chiefs a chance to say what they wanted. Many of my uncles got up, like Mungo Martin and Henry Bell and Sandy Willey, and made speeches. They all thanked me for putting on that do and said they were all happy to see me do that thing that night. Then they each gave a wonderful speech about the history of my family, especially on my father's side about Chief Aul Sewid. They didn't have to tell it but they just liked to bring it out when they made their speech. All of the chiefs of the other villages already knew all about it anyway and they didn't have to be told, but they just wanted to say that. They thanked me for the wonderful hospitality that I had given them when they came to visit the village where I was chief councillor. Just before it was all over I got up and made the last speech. "I want you all to know," I said, "that this is not a big do as far as I'm concerned. It is not like the ones in the past, the real big potlatches. The reason I put on this do was to announce to you all that I have received this talking stick from my uncle, Chief Tom Dawson. I want to announce in public that he had it specially made for me. I want to thank you all for coming and to say that I'm not going to boast about what I have done tonight. It was just a small token and I just wanted to do it. I felt like doing it and I didn't have to trouble anybody or anyone else by borrowing from them to do this. I can do it on my own of my own free will. I want to make sure that nobody can think that I was just doing it because I felt like I had to pay for my name or anything like that. It is the duty of a descendant chief to do these things and I felt that it was my duty to go ahead and do it. Thank you all for coming."

It was nearly midnight when it was over and the people all went to the homes where they were staying. They all stayed around for a few days because the sports days were going on right after that in our village.

A lot of people were transferring into the Nimpkish band each year from the more isolated villages, so that when I was elected again in 1963 to be the chief councillor we had over six hundred members. We elected six councillors since we had the authority to elect one councillor for every one hundred members in the band. After they were elected, I assigned each council member certain duties. Herbert Cook was to look after the tax dues; George Alfred took the responsibility for our water system, which included the water pump, water tank, pipes, and fire hoses. Robby Bell was to take care of the cemetery to keep it in good order, as well as the garbage, housing, and sewage problems. Arthur Alfred took over the responsibility for the council hall and the recreation activities of the band. Arthur Dick was appointed to be fire chief and look after some of

the fire-fighting equipment as well as the job of being sure that all
dogs on the reserve had licenses. My oldest daughter, Dora Cook,
was elected to be a member of the council that year, and she was
appointed to look after the problems of health and the people who
were on relief. I thought it was a good idea for my children to take
the responsibility for leadership. I knew though that it would be
a hard job to be a leader because I had been a leader of many things
and I never got one cent for what I had been doing all those years.
Dora did very well and was very responsible in her work on the
council. She was the first woman to ever be elected to the council
in our village.

Dora's husband, Billy, had been on the council before and we
appointed him that year to act as the secretary to the council. He
had had a bad accident sometime before that but was able to act as
the secretary, and he did a very good job. I was out fishing when
he had his accident but I could hear the people in Alert Bay talking
about it on the radio phone and trying to get a plane to take him
down to Vancouver. When I came in and landed I went right to the
hospital, where he was. He was in the emergency ward and I
talked to Dr. Pickup who said, "I can't do anything for him. We
are going to charter a plane to take him down to the hospital in
Vancouver." Billy had been out fishing on his boat and they were
pursing up with the winch when his clothing or something got
caught up in the purse line and it pulled him into the winch and
really threw him around. His crew were all shocked and stood there
looking, and he was able to get to the switch and turn the winch
off himself or otherwise he would have been killed. I went down to
the airplane float with him when they flew him down to Vancouver.
He was on a stretcher and I talked with him but he didn't feel any
pain or anything. He has had to be in a wheelchair ever since, but
he fixed up his boat so he could still be the skipper even while he
was in his wheelchair. Dora would go out fishing with him and help
him.

For a number of years I had heard about the Masons and especially all the work that the Shriners were doing to help other
people. They had hospitals all over the states that were to help
crippled children, and I felt that I should belong to that kind of a
group because I had always been donating a few dollars to some

of those kind of charity works. So about that time I approached some of my friends about how I could become a Mason. I wanted to know how to go about it because I understand that they were a group that were helping people that needed help. So I went through the ceremony to become a member of the Discovery Lodge in Campbell River.

That winter I went up to Kingcome and Simon Beans put on his last potlatch up there. He had invited all the people from the other villages to go and we gathered in an old community house that was still standing up there. They built a fire in the middle and all the people were sitting around the sides of the house. Henry Bell was going to be the master of ceremonies for Simon Beans, but he was unable to come so he asked me if I would do it. I was also dancing the hamatsa that night. When everybody was gathered there I got up and told everybody that I was receiving the money and the articles from Simon's wife's people which would be distributed that night. That was the Indian way of doing it, even though Simon was the one that had gathered up all the money and articles. Then I told the people that I was very proud of Simon and our grandfather, since in the Indian way I called him my grandfather also. I told them, "Simon is living up to the name of his grandfather every year. His grandfather was one of the great men of Village Island where we grew up together. It is no doubt that he is walking in his footsteps." I just pushed him up a little like that. Then the dancing began and I was announcing which names were to be given to his grandchildren when the different people were dancing. When I danced the hamatsa that night there were about a half a dozen hamatsas dancing who were related to Simon. We didn't wear any masks but we all had cedar bark rings around our necks. After the dancing was over I went around with some others who were helping me and passed out about five or six hundred dollars to all the people that were there while Simon's wife's people were giving away some articles that she had gathered up. We all had sandwiches and coffee and cake and everybody had a good time.

In March 1964 we had the Native Brotherhood convention in Vancouver. Guy Williams was elected president again and I was reelected one of the vice-presidents. At that meeting one of the most important things that we discussed was the problem of

Japanese and Russian fishermen catching fish along the coast. Many of the Japanese boats were catching salmon out in the North Pacific and we felt that this was reducing the number of salmon which returned to their spawning grounds. The Fisheries Department was concerned with conserving the salmon, but they usually only restricted fishing around the mouths of the streams where the fish spawned and that hit the native fishermen the hardest. Fishermen from France and the United States were also fishing right close to our shores and we felt that it would be best to establish a twelve-mile limit along the coast that would be only for the Canadian fishermen. Since there was a discussion going on in the House of Commons about the problem, it was decided at that convention to send Guy Williams back to Ottawa to talk to the government people and make known what the native people wanted. I was appointed to go along with Guy and talk to those leaders about our problems.

I was really looking forward to going because I had never been east before. We went to Ottawa in May and when we got there we went around and talked to many of the leaders in government. We met at the caucuses of the different parties of Parliament and told them that we felt it would be best to have a twelve-mile limit. Then we met different members of Parliament and submitted briefs on the problem to them so that they could talk about it in the House. Another thing we talked to them about at that time was the law they were going to pass that all skippers of fishing boats had to be certified as captains. I was kind of worried because the Indian skippers like myself didn't have enough education to pass those exams. I didn't feel that it was necessary for the Indians because the Indian people knew the coast. We really knew those waters because we were born fishermen. They were also talking about limiting the number of fishing licenses that they were going to give out, and we talked to them about letting the Indian people have the same number of licenses and not cutting them down.

In our spare time we went and visited different leaders. I went in and saw the minister of Indian affairs and told him that we would like to see some money available to start some Indians in their own businesses, such as building boats, canneries, or some other kind of industry. I told him that what was happening was that the Indians were going to the Indian agent for relief, and it would be better to employ them if they had some little industries up along the coast. He was very sympathetic with what we were asking for and we had a very nice visit with him. I went to see Tom Barnett who was a personal friend of mine and the one who was representing my area. He was very kind and told me that any time I wanted to rest I could just come into his office and lay down on the nice couch that he had there. I saw Senator Gladstone too, who was an Indian from Alberta. He was the first Indian that ever became a senator. I had met him before and he was very nice to us because after all he was one of us and he was very pleased that we were there. He gave us all the information we wanted and said we could use his office any time we wanted to just walk in there. We talked to the minister of education, health, and welfare about keeping the Indian TB hospital open in Prince Rupert because they were talking about closing it down.

A number of times I went and sat in the House of Commons and listened while they were debating. I was really impressed with how they conducted that debate in the House of Commons. It was very, very educational and it was the very thing I had wanted to see. One day I was standing by the door when the people all gathered around and everybody was running back and forth. I didn't know what it was all about but I was standing by the great big entrance to that building when the secretary-general of the United Nations, U Thant, walked in. He was a very fine gentleman and stopped right where I was when he was passing by and said "How do you do" to me. I got a pass from one of my friends in the government and went in and heard him give a very interesting speech. It was the very next day that the prime minister of India, Mr. Nehru, died, and the ambassador from India in Ottawa came before the House of Commons and said a few words and then members of the Canadian government got up and said a few words. It was quite a thing to see.

While I was there I had a picture taken of me standing all by myself in the entrance of the Parliament Building. I felt very honored to be selected to represent my people there to the government, and I thought about those two old gentlemen, Alfred Adams and Eber Clifton, who had called me aside many years before in Alert Bay to talk about the work of the Native Brotherhood. I remembered that they had told me that someday I would go to Ottawa to represent my people to the government and it had come true. Those old gentlemen were both dead when it finally happened.

Guy Williams wanted to go on to Montreal after we were done with our business in Ottawa, so I thought I would go along with him. When we got there I told Guy that I had an old friend there, so we looked up his name in the phone book and called him up. His name was Tony Plane and he used to run the engine for me on my fishing boat. He came right over to where we were because he was very pleased to see me. We went for a drive around the city and looked over the big Indian reserve that was there. Then we went and talked to the man who was in charge of the 1967 centennial and looked over the place on a big island in the St. Lawrence River where they were going to put all the buildings for that exposition. He pointed out where they were going to put up an Indian village. I told that gentleman, "I think it would be a wise thing for the centennial committee and the government if they want a big show from the Indians to get some people from all the different groups to plan it. You could have some carvers working and some people making baskets and the other things from the different provinces right across Canada. You could bring so many Indians from each province to take part in this big do and maybe we could put on some Indian dances. We could sing the songs in our own language and it would be very interesting." He was very much impressed with what I said. I knew there were some white people learning our dances but he said, "If we put on some Indian dances and ceremonies there will be no substitute for the Indian people themselves putting that on."

Then Tony took us all over the city. I had never been to a night-club but we went around to many clubs and just looked around in each one for a while. We went for most of the night and Tony was very happy that I was there because he hadn't seen me for a long time. He asked me to stay and work for him because he had a great big machine shop. I told him, "I can't take a job working for you because I don't know what I would do if I came to work." "Well," he said, "it doesn't make any difference. I'll give you an office and you can just sit there and I'll buy a house for you." I think he felt good because I had given him a job fishing with me and he had earned enough money to go to Montreal and start up his own business. He had done very well and had thirty or thirty-five men working for him. I really was interested in seeing the Indian people back there because I liked to see what progress they had made, because the Indians back there had met the white man four or five hundred years ago and we had only met the white man a hundred years ago. I wanted to see how much progress they had made in such a long time but I was disappointed. They had a very nice village there but it wasn't the way I liked to see it. I don't think they got along with the white people there. I talked to one girl and I said to her, "I suppose you all work here in Montreal and you must have a good job for yourself." She said to me, "Oh, no. We don't associate with the French people. We just don't like them. They fought against the British and we had made a treaty with the British to be on their side. We would like to keep it that way." It was awful hard for me to ask her questions. I don't imagine that they get any help from the federal government because they are all treaty people. Some of them signed a treaty and sold their land for something like a plug of tobacco each year. I really felt like a stranger back in Montreal, and I wasn't sure why. I always felt at home wherever I went, whether it was a place like Seattle or Village Island. I have some friends in Ottawa and I felt safe with my friends there. Maybe it was because they spoke a different language in Montreal.

When I got back from Ottawa my wife told me that Alvin, my youngest son, was going to get married. I didn't like it very much because the wedding was going to be in Saskatchewan. I knew Alvin was engaged to this girl from the Cree Indians and I wanted to do something for him when he got married, the same as I had done for my other children. They were all married in the church and I used to give them good receptions and big dos. It would cost us a lot of money to go back to where he was going to be married, and it would be kind of hard on her family if they got married in Alert Bay. So I decided that when Alvin returned from Saskatchewan, I would put on an Indian do. It wasn't the same as the receptions that I had put on for the other children when they got married. But when he came back it was just about time for the sports days in Alert Bay, so I invited all the people to come to the do the first night they arrived in our village. There were about two hundred people from all over the agency who gathered in the council hall that night.

I had received another chest with some dances in it from Moses Alfred. I had already used the earlier one he gave me with the hamatsa dance in it for Bobby. This second one had a different dance in it, the feather dance, which was for one of the other societies. I thought I was going to give the names and dances to my second oldest son that night but he didn't want to go. My oldest son already held the hamatsa cedar bark dance and according to the Indian way I couldn't mix them. So Alvin danced the feather dance that night. At the start of the evening my wife's people got up and made some speeches and announced that they were giving me that chest with the feather dances and the names for my grandchildren and all the money and things to give away. Of course I had gathered some money and my wife had gathered some articles to give away, but it was the Indian custom to receive it in public from my wife's people. Then the singers started to sing and the dancers began to come out and dance. We had been in such a hurry to get ready for that that we couldn't do it in the proper way, with all the dancers going out and coming in with their masks of the different animals. I did use the chilcat blanket because that was in my family and lots of button blankets and the headgear that went with the feather dance. All my relatives danced that night because when they felt happy they always liked to dance and perform for the people to show that they were part of my family and related to my grandfather. I had one of my uncles, Chief Tom Umpkeep, acting as master of ceremonies and he was announcing the names and the dances. Then he passed out money to all the people that were there. He gave ten dollars each to the leading chiefs from each of the villages and maybe two dollars to the young men and one dollar to the women. Then we gave away quite a lot of apples, oranges, and candy, and popcorn for the children. My wife gave away some articles but I didn't pay too much attention to what she gave away because that was her own doings. It cost me nearly two thousand dollars that night.

After they had given away all the articles and money I got up and made a speech. I said, "Thank you for coming tonight. The reason why I did this tonight was because I felt so happy that Alvin was married. I always liked to do a little bit for my children because that was what my family did for me when I was married, so I feel that I should do it for my children. This is the last of my boys. I always like to treat my children alike and I have done something for each of them when they were married, but Alvin wasn't married in Alert Bay and that is the reason why I have done this. I like to do this not only for my children but for my stepbrothers and stepsister. I have stood for the expenses of each of their weddings and it usually cost me between a thousand and fifteen hundred dollars. Usually we just put on a reception and a dance in the white man's way for the others but tonight I wanted to give this Indian do. I want to announce that I am doing this for Alvin because he has married this girl from the Cree people. I am happy that he has married into the Cree people, but according to the Kwakiutl custom I am not allowed to use their dances and regalia. I want to thank you all again for coming." After that everybody went home.

In the fall I went down to Vancouver and had an X ray and the doctor told me that I still had those gallstones. They hadn't bothered me too much except that I had had a lot of gas in my stomach. So he asked me, "Do you want to take them out?" "It's up to you," I said. "If you want to take them out, I'll go through with it." So it was decided and a few weeks later I went into the hospital in Vancouver. I never felt afraid. I'd seen a lot of people go through the same kind of thing. I wasn't worried at all. It was going to be and if I didn't make it that was the way it was going to be. Of course, I knew that everybody at home was more worried than me. The doctor came in and explained to me that they were going to poke something in my arm and I would be asleep before they operated. I knew that the day was coming, so the night before they were to operate on me I went into a very nice little chapel that was there in the hospital. I kneeled down and just gave myself to our Maker and said, "What is going to happen is entirely up to You."

The next morning the doctor came and gave me a shot in the arm and then they took me on the elevator to the operating room. I didn't even know what was going on and I didn't feel any pain. The next thing I remember was that one of the nurses was tapping me and telling me I had better wake up. She told me I should try to stay awake for a while. The next morning they got me up and had me walk around a little They had a big bottle there and were feeding me through my arm. A few days later I was feeling better and just lying in bed thinking about my grandchildren when I got a letter from Harold, my oldest grandchild and Bobby's oldest boy. It was just a short letter that he had written asking me how I was getting along and when I was going to come home. All of Bobby's kids signed that letter and I was really glad to get it because I was really downhearted that day. I didn't know whether I was going to pull through that operation or not. The next day I felt better so I got busy and wrote a letter to Harold and told him that I was getting along fine. I wrote, "I am in the hands of some real good doctors and I only wish that you carry on what you are doing in school and work hard and maybe someday you can be a doctor. You would be a great help to a lot of people who are suffering like myself." Later their mother told me that when he received that letter, he made up his mind that he was going to be a doctor. When I was a little boy I never thought about what I was going to be when I grew up. In the Indian's mind, I don't think they know what they want to be when they are young. That is a new thing. The Indian people didn't used to plan what they were going to be when they grew up. When a job opened up a person would just go there and work at it. They didn't used to think about being a doctor, a lawyer, an anthropologist, a captain, or anything like that. My oldest grandson was only about nine years old and he was doing very well in school. When he got that letter from me in the hospital, he showed it to all his friends and to his teacher. I've been thinking that it would be a good thing if I could put some money away to help my grandchildren go on to some higher education.

9 You Are Proud of What You Have Done in Potlatching

In the last few years it seemed like there was an increasing number of juvenile court cases in Alert Bay. It wasn't all from there because the magistrate in Alert Bay handled the cases from many of the other villages and towns in that area of British Columbia. I had been thinking a lot about how we could help our young people for a long time. I had tried to get a curfew for the whole island but that hadn't worked out. I had worked for integration of the school which we finally got. I think Alert Bay was a difficult place because it was half-white and half-Indian and also during the summer there were lots of outsiders staying there. Our reserve had grown to over seven hundred members and the town of Alert Bay had grown to about the same number of people.

A few years before that I had been talking to an Indian friend of mine from Sechelt which is on the coast north of Vancouver. This man was named Clarence Joe and he was on the village council at Sechelt. He told me that they had had a lot of trouble with juveniles there also and that Magistrate Johnson of Sechelt had formed a committee to help those kids who got into trouble. Clarence Joe told me that Magistrate Johnson was quite a help to the Indian people and was all out to help them along as much as possible. I talked to him several times about our problem and he wrote me a letter but I didn't think too much about it then. Well, in about 1963 or 1964, there were eighty-five children in one year that were in court for getting into trouble and had to be sent away to a correctional school. When that happened I began to think seriously about what we could do, and no doubt the attorney general didn't feel too good about it because we were just a small place. One time he came to Alert Bay and the Indian agent told me about it but I was out at the time. He called a meeting with the local magistrate and the policemen and they talked it over, but that was the end of it and we didn't hear any more about it.

Then the attorney general approached Magistrate Johnson in Sechelt and asked him if he could help us get a committee started in Alert Bay to help deal with the juveniles. So Magistrate Johnson wrote me a letter personally and asked if it would be possible for him to come up and have a meeting. He said he was going to bring my very good friend Clarence Joe with him. We expected him on a certain day, so I called a meeting with both Indian people and the white people in the other end. I asked the local magistrate, the principal of the Indian school, and some of the other people who I thought were interested to come. My council was there and the principal of the high school and Rev. Burroughs and some others. We had a meeting in our council hall and we more or less just listened to what Magistrate Johnson had to say and Clarence Joe. We were sitting there taking notes and asking questions. They showed us a book that had information to guide their committee. He said that their committee was to stand in between the court and the juveniles because when they sent them away to correctional school it didn't always help, but the kids just got into trouble when they got out of there. He said that his committee had the authority to go into the court and present what they thought should happen to those kids who got into trouble. Well, we had a lot of arguments with the white people because some of them said that they thought it was our problem and that they shouldn't take part in it. So I got up right away and said, "In my mind that isn't too good because after all our children are everybody's problem. If we try to do something for them in our own Indian reserve they just go to that end of town and hang around the café and stay out all hours of the night. When you people try to do something for your children in your end, they just come down to our end because you have a curfew in your end but we don't. If you try to do anything about your children, they are just going to move into our end, and it isn't only our children but the white children as well. I think that we must get together and have a curfew for the whole island and try to enforce the law for the whole island and just forget the line between us. We must get together and we must work together, your council and my council." Well, we didn't come to any decision at that time and Magistrate Johnson and Clarence Joe went back to Sechelt.

Some of the white people were very much more concerned with

the problem than I was because they were working close to the children at school. I talked to Mr. Tinney, the principal of the high school, and some others and we thought that something ought to be done very quickly so we called a meeting. I invited my council and the magistrate and some of the policemen and the leading men from the white end of the village. I reminded them about Magistrate Johnson's visit and said I felt we needed to start a committee to deal with the juveniles. So our magistrate said he thought it would be a good idea to have this committee. Then we got into a big argument and they said that Magistrate Johnson had only suggested that we have the committee for the Indian people. Someone said that it couldn't work for both ends because they had a village commission in their end with their own bylaws and we had our band council and we were under the Indian Act and had our own ways of operating. Finally I got mad because I knew that they were just thinking, "You have bad kids in your end and we have the good kids in our end!" So I told them, "It must work out because after all we are the people of this island and we must mind the laws of the country. They are the children of this island and we can help them. We can form a committee from the island and we can work together and we can stand between the child and the law before they take them to court. We can take the child and try to do something to help the child!" So we finally came to a decision and they gave in, but they asked me to be the chairman. I said that I wouldn't but I had to do it because they had given in to have that committee. So I said, "I will be the chairman from our end but there must be a cochairman from your end." We formed a committee by electing five from our end and five from their end. We called it the Cormorant Island Youth Guidance Committee and Dave Lawson and I were the cochairmen with the following members: Dora Cook, Ethel Alfred, Joan Burroughs, Jenny Dong, Henry Beans, Robby Bell, Art Tinney, and Rick Morrow.

So we wrote to the attorney general and told him we had formed that committee and we got letters which gave us the authority to go into court and stand between the court and the children. We began to have meetings every other week and discuss the problems of the kids who were getting into trouble. When the police picked up a boy who had done something wrong, they would call me right up and ask me to come down to the police station. I would go there right away or someone like Mr. Tinney or Mr. Burroughs and talk to that boy. We had people outside of our committee who were helping us and we could call someone up and say, "There is a boy that is in trouble tonight and I wonder if he could come and stay with you." So they would just take him in because sometimes his family would be having trouble or his parents would be drunk and the kids were running around. Sometimes we brought a problem child to our meeting and his parents would sit in there and we told them what we wanted done. Lots of the people criticized us because they thought the Youth Guidance Committee was going to boss their kids around. During the first month there were a lot of kids who dropped out of school because they were in trouble. When those boys went to court they were charged with what they had done wrong and then the parents would be questioned. Then the magistrate would ask the Youth Guidance Committee for its recommendation because we are the only outsiders who had the authority to go into the court at all times. We usually recommended that the boys get a suspended sentence so we could get them back in school because we felt it was best to try to keep them out of the delinquent boys' home. Oh, I had all kinds of criticism at first but I think the parents are beginning to understand now. I think that in the first year we reduced crime among our juveniles almost 70 percent. We established a special receiving home right next door to the Royal Canadian Mounted Police Station, and Ethel Alfred, one of the Hanuse girls, lived there and had kids stay with her who were having problems at home.

We had to be very honest with people because we were dealing with something that none of us knew anything about. It was very hard work and the most difficult committee that I have ever belonged to. We dealt with everything, even with the parents and how they behaved and how they ought to behave. We had to look into those families that were having trouble and find out what was wrong with the home. I had to go as the chairman often to this house and that house and talk with the parents. There was no thanks for our work and everybody was criticizing us. Mrs. Tinney was our secretary and she would just write all the letters and I would go and sign them. Most of our work was among the Indians but there was some among the white people too. We didn't have any treasurer because we didn't want to have any money. We knew that if we had the money, the people might come to us and say, "I'm in trouble, I'm in jail, will you pay my fines?" That was why we didn't want to have any money. We could ask the village commission or the Board of Trade or my village council for money if we needed anything. There was no problem raising money to send people to special meetings in Vancouver or something like that. Of course, most of what we did was confidential and our meetings were confidential and can't be discussed. I liked the work on the Youth Guidance Committee even though it was hard, and I had a hard time finding people who were suitable to work on there with me.

When I first moved into Alert Bay there were only about one hundred and thirty in the Indian village and by 1965 there were over seven hundred. So when the elections came up again we had to elect seven councillors. I was nominated to be the chief councillor by Jack Ambers and it was seconded by Henry Speck. The election was to be held about two weeks after we had the nominations and I didn't think I was going to be elected because I ran against a very strong man in that village. I had thought about declining the nomination because I had been a chief councillor for five terms and that was too long. I wanted to see someone who had some experience take over, but, on the other hand, sometimes I thought it wasn't time yet because it took me all those years to build up what we had. I enjoyed doing it for the people and I liked to work for my people because I was part of that village. I might as well state that I had experience also because I made a lot of dealings with the government and with the incorporated area of Alert Bay. Well, we had the election and I was elected and my council members were Robby Bell, Dora Cook, Billy Cook, Sam Hunt, George Alfred, Arthur Alfred, and Arthur Dick. Our village had grown because so many outsiders had moved in from the isolated villages, and the people from the outside villages were more for me and that was why I was stuck for the job.

I talked to my council about having the Alcoholics Anonymous come to Alert Bay and start something for those people who were such heavy drinkers. Some of those people had been asking us to help them to try and get away from their drinking. They wanted help and they admitted that they wanted it, and I was glad for that because the doctor had told me that you couldn't help them unless they came to you and wanted to help themselves. I also tried to get some films on drinking and have them shown in the high school and in the day school. I still thought that the most important thing was to teach the kids about it. That was my only answer to the drinking problem because everything had been brought to us from an unknown world across the sea. We didn't expect any of these things in the first place. Today we are learning more and more things all the time. I think it took the white man a thousand years to get what he has today. We only met the white man a little over one hundred years ago. I can't imagine what the Indians are going to be like in fifty or one hundred years. It will be quite a big change and I think now we are in an age when we are really balancing. The more we mix with the white people the more change will come. My great belief is to be integrated.

That year we ran out of water so we talked on our council about drilling another well. The village was getting bigger and bigger and we had to prepare for the future. I was also pushing for a new sewer system in my council. Anyway the man came and started drilling our well, and in 1966 it was finished and it really gave out a lot of clean water. The Corporation of Alert Bay was having all kinds of trouble with its water, which came from a pipe over on the mainland that runs under the water. They say when you were in the bathtub you came out dirtier than when you got in because the water was so dirty. We came to an agreement with them about supplying them water from our well. I felt that if we could work together with them and with my council we would have a nice little island. We could do things that we would like to do for the island as a whole. I thought we should never mind the Indian and never mind the white man but we should just consider them equal. I didn't know how they felt but that was how I felt because unity is the best thing in life. If you are united you will be very strong, but you divide and there is going to be a lot of trouble. During the last few years we had quite a good relationship between my council and the commission in Alert Bay. Furthermore, I was the first Indian to join the Board of Trade and they always respected me and asked me any questions about what we were doing on our end. I would tell them, especially what I would like for us to do together. These were some of the reasons I felt I should stay on as chief councillor. I always thought it would be a wise thing for a retired chief councillor in any village to be asked to sit in with the council and to act as the adviser.

In my lifetime I have seen many changes in our way of life. Nearly all the respectable old chiefs had died and many of the ways of my people were dying out also. While I had learned many of the ways of my people when I was a little boy, my own children didn't learn as much. Some of them used to ask me about the old ways and I would tell them that there was some good and some bad in our old ways. I liked to see that the young people go ahead in the modern life that we are leading today. I didn't feel it was right to try to hold anybody back from going along with the progress of the world. At the same time I thought there were many things from the early days that should be preserved. There was no doubt that the world was changing and the Indian people were changing also and it couldn't be helped. Maybe in a few years when the old people have all died off such things as our language will be forgotten, and I felt it was important to do something to preserve the language. I thought that maybe the Indian Department could put aside a little money so that they could pay somebody to go and teach the people to speak the native language and do such things as carving and making baskets like they did in the earlier days.

I thought it was very important that our food should be preserved. My wife and I had built a little smokehouse in back of our house and we were about the only people that were smoking fish anymore. We really liked smoked fish and a lot of our friends came to us to smoke fish for them. Some species of salmon we smoked for only twenty-four hours and then we would put it in cans or in the deep freeze. Sometimes we would smoke them for about eight or ten days, what we called a hard smoke, and then put it away until we were ready to eat it. Then we would take it out and slice it like bacon and maybe soak it, but we didn't have to cook it. Sometimes we would barbecue it on the open fire and then leave it in the smokehouse overnight. There were many different ways to smoke fish and we just lived on our smokehouse. Our whole family liked that kind of fish and some of the other people who didn't care enough to smoke their own still came to us and asked for smoked fish.

Another very important food was the olachen oil. Just before I put on that do after Alvin got married, Simon Beans and my wife's aunt went up to Knight's Inlet to make olachen oil. When they came back, they had quite a bit made, especially for me. They asked me to go and give it out to some of the people in Alert Bay, so I gave it out and everybody had one or two gallons. It used to be quite an honor to receive olachen oil at a feast in the old days because that was a very precious food to all the Indians. I liked to use it with any kind of fish or clams or seaweed that I ate. We used to go out sometime in May to the islands and gather seaweed from the rocks. According to the old Indian people it was really good when it had only grown five or six inches long. It was quite dark and flat and we just pulled it off the rocks at low tide and laid it on some screens made of cedar wood to dry it out. Sometimes we would roast it in the oven and then just smash it up so that it was just like tobacco. Sometimes we would eat it plain or boil it mixed with fish eggs or mix it with clams or dip it in olachen oil.

We had lots of ways of cooking fish and I felt that we ought to be able to do something to preserve some of our ways of cooking. The Chinese and Japanese all had different ways of preparing food and we should be able to continue using our ways also. We could cook halibut or salmon in many more ways than the white people even knew about. We could cook clams in many different ways too. We took them whole out of the shell and dipped them in flour and then fried them, or we barbecued them and then smoked them. I used to live on fish that had been barbecued or boiled in oil and it would be different for every meal.

Another very important thing about the Indian way of life that I thought should be preserved was respect. The Indian people used to be great on respect and I think we modern Indians are lacking in that today. Respect was and it still is the most important thing in my life. If you respect a person, even if you haven't ever seen him before, you will be friends. I respect my friends and speak very highly of them and that is very important to the children. You can see the makings of a man or woman when you see them show respect to those people in authority. I remember how old Lucy used to teach me that the first step in Christianity was to respect and obey the older people. The way I see it today the most important thing is to respect your elders. I began to feel that we were losing that along with many of the other things of our old way.

Like any other nation, I would like to preserve the arts and crafts of the Indian people because I think they are beautiful. Those old people who really knew how to sing and dance and carve were dying off and I felt that something should be done to preserve those good things from the old way. When I first moved to Alert Bay, Simon Beans and I used to talk together about building an Indian community house. We talked to the older people of that village about it because we wanted to show the kind of house that we lived in when we were little boys at Village Island. In those days there was nothing but Indian community houses there. All we did was just talk about it. Some of the people thought it was too hard, and some of them thought it couldn't be done because building a community house wasn't like building a modern home. It was very easy to build a modern home because you could look at the plans and then order all the lumber and things cut to the right size. The people who we used to talk to about it all died and just Simon Beans and I talked of it together. When Henry Speck moved to Alert Bay we talked of it some more and began to feel that it was time that we did something to carry out our ideas. I felt it would be good to build one of those big houses and try to do something to preserve the arts and crafts of our people.

Finally in 1963 I had brought it up to my council and told them my idea. I told them that it would be a good place for the tourists to go and look around when they visited our village. It would be nice for the people who could do a little carving to have a place and for the women who had been making rugs and baskets with Indian designs on them because they could sell them to the people who came. We could have a workshop in the back and provide tools for those who didn't have any, and the people could go there to work and it would be a little income for them. I told them that it would belong to the Nimpkish people but that we could form an organization and anybody who wanted to belong to it from the different villages could. It should be open to all the Kwakiutl people from the other villages. So Robby Bell made a motion that we set aside some land up near the ball field to build a community house. The council passed that motion and appointed me to be in charge of getting the building started. Right away I formed a building committee of Henry Speck, Simon Beans and his wife, Charlie George, Max Whanock, Arthur Dick, Billy McDougal, my daughter Dora, and my wife Flora. Then I went and talked to the Indian agent and explained to him what I wanted to do. Mr. Roach was the agent at the time and he encouraged me to go ahead with building that community house. I asked him if we could get a few dollars from the winter works program which provided jobs for some of our people. We got permission to use some of that money so we were ready to start to work.

Before we did anything more I made my plans. I made a little office for myself down in the basement of my house and started making all the plans for the building. It had always been my hobby to build things like houses and I had built quite a few but they were all modern homes. I had no idea how to build this community house because I had never seen it done before. I made the plans according to the early ones that I had used to live in when I was a little boy. We had to have four big house posts for the frame and I got the building committee together to decide what we should carve on those totem poles. We decided to use the most outstanding crests from several of the different tribes rather than just the Nimpkish crests. The front house posts were to have the Grizzly Bear crest at the bottom and the Qolus, which was a large supernatural bird, at the top. Both of the poles were to be just alike. The back house posts were to have the Tsunuqua or wild creature of the woods at the bottom and the Thunderbird at the top. The small cross beams were to have the Sisiutl or double-headed serpent carved on them. Most of the houses that I had seen in the early days had just put a plain log there without any carving on it but we decided to put the Sisiutl on it. I was to be responsible for the architecture and engineering, Henry Speck was responsible for advising us on the artistic part of it, and Charlie George was to direct the carving of the house posts and cross beams.

After we had decided on the designs of the house posts I decided to build a little model that would be just exactly like the frame structure of the building. I had one of the boys carve four little totem poles and, using the scale of one-half inch per foot, I built that little model. The house was to be seventy feet long and fifty feet wide. When the cross beams which were to be carved with the double-headed serpent were put in place they would be seventeen feet high and support two huge seventy-foot long logs running the length of the house. I wanted to have those big logs three feet in diameter. I decided it would cost too much money to make our own shakes so we just ordered rough lumber from the mill for the sides and the roof. Simon Beans was going through Johnstone Strait one day and came across a big long log that still had the roots on it, and he towed it back to Alert Bay. He came to me after he had towed that log in and said, "Jimmy, I think we should go ahead with that house whether we get any help from the other people or not. I think we should go ahead and do it on our own. Another thing, Jimmy, I'm worrying about you—that nothing happens to you." That was just before I was to go down for my operation in Vancouver and I had told him about it. "I'm worried about you," he said, "but anyway, let's go down and roll that big log up so that it won't float away because I'm going to go up to Knight's Inlet to do some hunting. I'll be back before you leave to go to Vancouver to the hospital." So we rolled that log up and cut it into four big sections and later we carved them for the four house posts. Then Simon Beans left on his boat to go hunting.

A few days after that I was sitting in my house with Flora and her aunt and we had just finished eating lunch. Simon's wife came in to visit us and while we were sitting there the telephone rang and it was someone asking for Mrs. Beans. She got the news that Simon had died while up on his hunting trip and they were on their way to Alert Bay with his body. The other boys had been off hunting and Simon was on his boat when he saw a deer on the shore. He had rowed to the shore in a little skiff and climbed up the side of a cliff to shoot that deer when he had had a heart attack and fallen down that cliff. I don't know how to describe it but it was really a shock to me. Simon was my right-hand man and he was the man that had worked with me to build all that we have today, not only in Alert Bay but also when I was living at Village Island. He was part of everything that I had been doing over the years, such as building the light plant, the wharf, the sawmill, the boat shop, and helping me build my house. He was part of my life and the man who stood by me in everything and he knew that what I was doing was the right thing. He wasn't going to hesitate to back me up.

I remember that Simon was a very quiet and a very nice man. He used to help me in my work for the people and also in my everyday life. He came and helped me when I would have to get wood for our house, fixing up our home and fixing up our boats. I remember the time that he came to me and asked for advice about buying a boat. He said he had made good money during the fishing season and he asked me how to go about trying to get a boat. Of course I encouraged him and told him that there was no doubt in my mind that he would get a boat in the company he was working for because he was well up and a good fisherman and a very good man. I knew the heads of the B. C. Packing Company that he was working for and they spoke very highly of him, and that was how I knew that he really made a name for himself and that was why I didn't have any doubt that he was going to get a boat. I told him that I would go down to Vancouver with him, and so we went into the B. C. Packing Company office and talked to the people that were concerned with selling boats. He named the boat that he wanted and then I spoke for him. He spoke English but he wanted my knowledge as a man that had been through that kind of thing before. I told them how the company that I was working for had financed my boat and asked how much Simon would have to put down and then if they would back him up for the rest. That was what they did and he did very well fishing on his boat. We did many things together working for the good of both of our families. I felt very bad that he didn't live long enough to see that community house completed because he was one of the main persons behind that house.

Shortly after we had decided to go ahead with the building I asked a friend of mine, Harry McQuillin, if he could try to get a couple of big logs for us that were seventy feet long. He had a logging camp over on the mainland. When he had located two good logs he came into Alert Bay and left a message for me to go and pick them up. I was away at the time and when I returned the person who had gotten the message forgot to tell me about it until two months had gone by. As soon as I heard about it I went over on the hospital boat to pick them up. I went up to the office of the logging camp and asked for Harry McQuillin. The person at the office told me that he had sold the camp and was no longer around. "Well," I said, "I guess there is no sense in trying to get those logs now because I don't know the person who owns the camp." I talked it over with the fellow on the hospital boat and he said he would talk to the foreman of a logging camp that was on a lake up in the Nimpkish Valley. I received a letter from him about three or four months later and he said that he had our logs if we could come over and get them. So I went over and towed them into Alert Bay.

While the boys were working on the carving of the house posts, I hired some men to put a twelve-inch concrete footing all around the house. I did this so we could then fill it in and have a level dirt floor. They also put in big blocks of cement for each of the house posts to stand on. They did a very good job putting in the cement because I was there supervising what they did. I was paying the carvers and the other men who were working and we began to run low on money, so I went around and got donations from the Board of Trade in Alert Bay and some individuals who were very interested in it and thought it would be good for the whole island. We also got some money that the government had set aside to help those communities that were working on projects for the British Columbia centennial year.

In the back of my mind one of the main reasons for building that community house was to have a place where we could try to preserve the art of my people. I knew that it was going to be lost if we didn't try to pick it up and it wasn't just because the people were losing interest. The main reason that our customs, dances, and art were dying out was that they had been forbidden by the law against our will. In fact, many of our people had been put in prison for refusing to give up their way of life. Old Herbert Martin had gone to jail for that and it was people like him that were responsible for preserving many of the old customs. After we had started with the carving and building I called a general meeting of the Nimpkish band and told the people that we thought it would be wise to form an organization of some kind to revive the arts and crafts and work in the community house when it was completed.

We decided on the name "Kwakwala Arts and Crafts Organization." In order to get the people to belong to it and take an interest in it we printed up membership cards and charged each member a dollar a year to join it. I told them when the building committee was finished with the house we were going to dissolve that committee and call a meeting of all the members of the Kwakwala Arts and Crafts Organization to appoint the directors.

Then I sent this letter to all the other villages in the Kwakiutl agency:

> Box 245
> Alert Bay, B.C.
> February 11, 1964

TO CHIEFS AND COUNCILLORS OF
THE KWAWKEWLTH NATION

Dear Chief and Councillors:

This is to inform you that an Organization has been formed at Alert Bay for *all Kwawkewlth Natives*. The name of the group is the Kwakwala Arts and Crafts Organization. The aim of this group is to revive the Arts and Crafts as well as the dances of our people.

To be a member of this organization you must be of Native Indian *Descent*. A fee of $1.00 to be forwarded to Mrs. Dora Cook, Alert Bay, B.C.

A Community House is, at present, being constructed at Alert Bay. When completed it will be used as a workshop for those who cannot afford the required tools, etc. and of course it shall also be used for the performance of our Native Dances. The members who are unable to work at Alert Bay are requested to forward the articles they wish sold to the Organization and they will be sold for them. This Organization is also formed to stop exploitation of those who have tried to sell their articles to dealers themselves and have not received the full value of their work.

It is very important that we back this organization for it is for your benefit. There is a great demand for our Arts all over the world. Letters have been coming in from numerous people requesting different articles when they heard about our organization. If we do not take a firm stand now, we shall lose our dances, carvings, etc. to the non-Indians as well as to the other Nations. These people know the great demand and value of our Arts for they have already begun to learn and produce them. These are ours and our people should be the people to benefit from them. Let us not lose our Arts like we did our lands, for if we do we shall regret it.

As you know unemployment is getting worse each year. Let us help one another and start an industry of Arts and Crafts for our people.

Your support would be greatly appreciated. We would request that you read or pass the information in this letter to your people. Any comments would be welcome.

Yours truly,

James Sewid

Early in 1965 the house posts were finished and I had moved the big seventy-foot logs up to the place where the house was being built. Some of the boys used adzes to make them perfectly round with little grooves on them. The rafters also had to be roughed out by hand because they represented kelp. The doctor told me I wasn't supposed to be doing any of the heavy work because it was only a few months after my operation. I was supervising everything and working there about twelve or fourteen hours a day trying to finish it before the fishing season began. St. Michael's School had a tractor that they let me use whenever we needed it, and I used it to move the house posts from my boat shop on the beach up to the community house site. Then we built a large A-frame and by using a block and tackle we were able to set the posts upright on the cement blocks. Then we poured more cement around the base of each pole so they would be real strong. We made grooves on the head of each of the poles and they had to be exactly right so that the cross beams could just rest in those grooves. We put the cross beams on after the cement was set.

The hardest part of building that big house was to raise the big seventy-foot logs which were to support the roof. Each of those logs weighed over five tons. The problem was how to get them up on top of the carved cross beams which were seventeen feet tall. I

phoned all around to the logging camps to the people that I knew
and they were all quite willing to help me but they all said, "Jimmy,
we just haven't got that kind of equipment." They said if I set up
a big A-frame they were willing to give me cables, hand winches,
donkeys, and things like that if I wanted them. I had four or five
different ideas about how we might lift those logs up but none of
them worked. I went to Vancouver and tried to get any heavy
equipment that was going by Alert Bay, such as a crane on a big
scow, that could call in there for a couple of days and put those
things up. There was a big forklift truck from the government
wharf and I talked to them about it and they figured they could
lift those logs. I told them I didn't think they could do it but they
said they were going to try. They came and hooked onto the end of
the log and couldn't even budge one end because they were so heavy.

One day it came to my mind that when I used to live in that big
community house at Village Island my grandfather had explained
to me how they had raised those big logs. When I was in that house
I could see those big timbers on top of the house and I used to talk
to my grandfather about how they got them there. He had explained
to me that they moved them up inch by inch by seesawing them
back and forth. So right away I phoned my friend at Telegraph
Cove and asked him if he had any timbers that were about eight
inches by eight inches and eight feet long. He said he had a lot of
railroad ties and he could give us all we wanted. Well, I changed
my clothes because the boys were still working up at the house
and I told them, "Take the 'Twin Sisters' and go over to Telegraph
Cove and pick up some timbers." I explained my idea to them and
then I figured out how many we were going to need to raise those
big logs. I measured the exact height that each log needed to be
raised.

The big logs were lying on the ground right outside of each
front and back house post at exactly the right position that we
wanted them. When the boys returned with the eight-foot timbers
we got a little hydraulic jack and began jacking up one end of the
log enough to get one of the timbers under it. Then we jacked up
the other end and put another timber under it. We fastened two
guy lines onto the big log so that it wouldn't roll off the timbers
we were putting under it. As the logs went up they just rubbed

against the totem poles because the guy lines were holding them. I was standing right nearby watching everything because if anything had happened it would have been my fault, since that was my engineering. Robby Bell was standing right where he could have been jammed between two timbers if anything had happened. I measured the big log with a level each time we jacked it up because it had to be all exact. If one side was lopsided it could have started to slide so I made sure it was absolutely even. So we kept jacking one end and then the other, back and forth. The end of the log would go up about four feet, but the little jack was only going about six to eight inches up. There were five boys working underneath it at all times, stacking those eight-by-eight timbers under it as it was going up. When we had one end jacked up it would just be balanced there in the middle while we cribbed it and then moved the jack to the other end. When the log was just high enough to be level with the cross beams that it was going to rest on, we put a little wedge under the last eight-by-eight so that they slanted in towards the cross beams about an inch. When they were all under the log and the jack had been taken out I had the two boys who were holding the guy lines let go of them and that big log just rolled into the grooves that we had made for it. It was really quite easy and we did both of those logs inside of a day.

About that time I ran out of money to pay the boys that had been working with me. I told my boys that I didn't have any more money but that if they wanted to stay on working for me I would just keep putting their time down and maybe someday we would get some money. I told them, "when that money comes I can pay you but it might be a week, it might be two months from now, or it might be two years from now." I was going to tell them straight because I didn't want them to think that I was just trying to hang onto them for nothing. So some of the boys quit but some of the others stayed on. I made a special trip to Vancouver and talked to Mr. Boys, the Indian commissioner, and told him that we were running out of money. "Well," he said, "this is right at the end of the fiscal year for the government and the books will be closed and we don't know what will happen. It might take two or three weeks to get some special funds but I'll get them for you because I want you to finish that house. I know you are going to finish it because you have been on schedule and you told me that you would finish it." So when I went back to Alert Bay I told the boys what he had said and about four of them stayed and helped me. I had to use some of my own money because some of them came to me and said, "Jimmy, I need $25 or so," and I had to give them some of my money. I had faith in the government that they were going to give us the money and we got it about a month later.

We had planned to finish that community house by June since we all had to go fishing in July, and it was all finished right on schedule by the first week in June of 1965. If it hadn't been for Mr. Roach, the Indian agent, I don't think we would have finished that house because he really encouraged me. After it was finished he came to me and said, "Jimmy, I'd like to congratulate you for this building because a lot of people told me that you would never finish it. Now it is finished and I want to tell you how happy I am because you know that I have been coming around every day to talk to you and encourage you on this building." When it was done we dissolved the building committee and I called all the members of the Kwakwala Arts and Crafts Organization together for a general meeting. At that meeting we elected our board of directors to look after the business of the big community house and the work that we were going to do there making and selling things. There were about twelve on that committee and I was elected chairman and Henry Speck vice-chairman. We began to make plans about how we could encourage the people that knew something about the arts and crafts of the people to do them and teach the young people.

During May, Chief James Knox of the Fort Rupert people had approached me about putting on an Indian dance and potlatch in the community house during the June sports days when all the people came to Alert Bay. I told him that would be fine if we got the house completed. It wasn't to be the official opening of the community house because my idea was to open it during the 1966 centennial year. Chief James Knox asked Henry Speck and me to get the community house ready and the singers ready and all the other arrangements made. We made a big screen to put up at the end of the house where the hamatsa was going to get behind. We hired all the good singers from the different villages because

Chief Knox was giving this potlatch and paying those people to take part in what he was doing. The purpose of that do was to have James Knox' son become a hamatsa. Dave Martin, the boy's father, had died quite a while before that and I suppose James Knox felt that he should do something because he was one of the leading men of the Kwakiutl nation.

Late in June on the night before the sports days all the people came and gathered in that community house at about eight o'clock in the evening. There were over five hundred people there and some white people were visiting too. We didn't have enough seats and people were just standing all around the house with the big fire in the middle. After everybody gathered in there I got up and made the first welcoming speech. I told them, "I want to thank all of you for coming into this new community house. I am very proud of this house and I'm proud that it was finished on time for Chief James Knox to use. This is not the official opening of the community house but we thought that we would just let him have it because he wanted to use it. This house isn't ours but it belongs to a large group of people who are members of the Kwakwala Arts and Crafts Organization. Now we are going to have the dances and Chief Bill Scow will be interpreting them for you over this microphone." I explained all that because there were a number of white people visiting us. Everyone was really surprised at how beautiful that building looked because it was the only one of its kind in the whole world. I went over to the end of the house and sat down in front of the hamatsa screen with the singers, and Bill Scow began to announce the different dances and the names that Chief James Knox was giving out that night.

Young Peter Knox was the first dancer to come out because he was the new hamatsa, and he had quite a few old hamatsas dancing with him. Old Herbert Martin, his grandfather, was dancing and his brother was there teaching him how to dance. He didn't run out of the house or do anything real wild that night. Then there were all sorts of others who were related to James Knox who danced that night, and a lot of the chiefs from the other villages made speeches but I couldn't hear them because I was down with the singers. Chief Sandy Willey from Kingcome got up and made a speech and referred to the fact that Chief Knox was part-Kwiksutainuk. Toward the end of the dancing Chief Knox came over to me and asked me to dance the feather dance. "Jimmy," he said, "it won't be right if you don't dance and I'm going to have your friend with you." Charlie Peters, my friend from Cape Mudge, was there so they asked him to dance it with me. We put on our regalia and I asked Sandy Willey who was leading the singing to use my grandfather's song that he had received from the Bella Coola. Of course, Sandy Willey announced that it was my grandfather, Chief Sewid's song and that James Knox was very closely related to me so therefore he had the right to use anything that I had.

Chief James Knox was very happy to have me dance for him because it was always the feeling of our chiefs to get all their relatives wherever they were from. It didn't matter how many dances you put on but it was important to use all your relatives that you could. That showed that you were a prominent man, you were a big man, and you were related to all the different tribes. That's what it meant. That was when the people could witness that you were a very important man when you had relatives from all over. Some people used to just claim that they were from this village and that village, but how could you tell when they had never given a potlatch to prove that? That was the way that the people could recognize you and knew that you had relatives from all the other villages. They had a lot of dances that night. My wife Flora danced and my daughter Dora danced because we were all related to Chief Knox.

About midnight when all the dancing was over they served coffee and sandwiches and nice cakes. Everybody was busy eating and everybody was happy. As soon as they had eaten their refreshments they brought out all the articles that they were going to give away. Chief Knox came to me and said for me to go ahead and look after everything, so I went around with Henry Speck and saw that everybody got their present because I was supervising it. There were a lot of people helping and we just started passing out money and articles but we didn't give the presents out in any special order. I guess we were past that stage. I was the one that was giving away the cash and I gave ten dollars to the leading chiefs and five dollars to the older persons and two dollars to the young men. I passed out about three hundred and fifty dollars. After that everybody went to where they were staying because the next day we had some sports going on.

The British Columbia centennial year was 1966 so we thought it would be a good idea to have the official opening of the community house during that year. That was also the time that the government of British Columbia returned the foreshore to the Nimpkish people. The Nimpkish village was right on the waterfront and the tribe owned the land in front of the houses right down to the water. Somewhere around 1932 the provincial government wanted to put in a paved road all along the waterfront of Alert Bay, and it was to run right along in front of the Nimpkish reserve as well as the white end of the village. That would make it possible for cars and trucks to go along that road when they delivered freight to the St. Michael's School which was at one end of the village. So the Nimpkish people in those days told the provincial government that they could use that strip of land to put in a road. They had a good heart and faith in the government that was in power at that time and so they said they could have the road, but they didn't know that they were going to lose their rights to the land between the road and the water which was called the foreshore.

In one of my early years as chief councillor I had looked into that because the government had taken over the lease from Alert Bay Shipyards, which was situated on that foreshore. That shipyard had leased a section of the foreshore from the Nimpkish people for one hundred and twenty dollars a year. At one time when the social credit government took over, the law was changed somehow and the government went to the man who owned the shipyards and said, "You don't have any more dealings with the Indian people here. You are going to deal directly with us from now on." So this man stopped paying the Indians for leasing the foreshore and began to pay the government about three or four hundred dollars a year, which was three times more than he had been paying the Indian people. It was quite a while before anyone knew about it, but when I found out about it I called my council together and told them that I didn't like it. Mr. Findlay was the Indian agent at that time and he wrote some letters but nothing much happened. Sometime after that one old man who had an old house on that foreshore property came to me and showed me a letter that he had received from the provincial government. The letter was addressed to his brother who had died quite a few years before, and it said that his house was too old and just a wreck and it had been condemned. It said that they were going to burn that house along with some others and they gave him so many days to get out of it. So I asked that old man, "Did any of your neighbors who live along there get any letters like this?" "Oh, yes," he said, "they got the same kind of letter as me." So I gathered up a few of those letters and I got busy and went into the Indian Office and I told them to write a letter and tell them not to come and interfere with us because that was an Indian reserve. It wasn't because I wanted those old houses to remain there, but my idea was that I was in a fight and I had a fighting spirit to ask the government to renegotiate with us for the foreshore.

Then I authorized Mr. Findlay to write to the government and tell them to send a man up so we could talk the whole matter over with him. I phoned Guy Williams, the president of the Native Brotherhood, to come and sit in on that meeting because that was only one of many foreshores that we had been fighting for among the Indians on the coast of British Columbia. So when that deputy minister in the land business came I phoned around and got my council all to come to the Indian Office for a meeting. That man from the government told us that in the early days the Indian people had agreed for the government to take over both the land for the road and the foreshore. So I demanded that he show us a copy of any kind of lease or agreement or anything at all concerning the taking over of the foreshore. The first thing he showed us was a letter that had about a dozen names on it. So I said to him, "In those days there was no elected councillors but only Old Joe Harris was the hereditary chief. Anytime the government wanted to talk to any group of Indians about getting any portion of land that was going to be relinquished, they had to have a general meeting and the majority ruled. All the people had to meet on a certain day and vote and it wasn't the council that decided those matters like we are doing today. I think there were about one hundred and thirty people in this Nimpkish village then and you only have twelve names. There must have been at least half of the people that could vote.

And I don't like this because these twelve men that you have here were very, very low ranking men according to my estimation."

So he looked all through his papers and brought out one that was signed by Mr. Halliday, who was the Indian agent in those days. It authorized the government to have the road anytime they wanted to use it. He was the one who was writing back and forth to the government and telling them that it was all right for them to take over the road and all that kind of thing and that it was all right with the Indian people. So right away I said to him, "Look here, this is between you and the Indian agent. The Indian agent doesn't have any business to speak for the Indians. He is just our mouthpiece but he should ask the consent of the Indians before he makes those kind of remarks or makes those kind of letters. That Indian agent was more or less speaking for himself. I don't know whether he was speaking for the government too, but at least he was speaking for himself in that letter you showed me. You people are supposed to come and talk to us about what you want with us, not the Indian agent. He just is our servant as far as I'm concerned. He is just working for us. So that means that we don't know anything about it." So anyway he said, "Well, I'm going back to Victoria and I'll write to Ottawa and see if they have any other agreements and I'll talk to my ministers and see what can be done. I'll let you fellows know."

The minister of municipal affairs, Mr. Dan Campbell, was a friend of mine and every time that he came here I would get hold of him and tell him that I wanted to get together with the government and take up that foreshore problem. So finally in February of 1966 they asked us to come down to Victoria and have a meeting with the minister of lands. I went down with Mr. Roach and George Alfred who was on my council. There was quite a group of people there that were representing the government's side. Of course, I was the spokesman and I told them, "I want to thank you, Mr. Minister, for giving us your time to discuss this way overdue problem between my people and the government. At the time that my people gave the road to the government they didn't know that they were going to lose their rights to the foreshore. The government didn't let the Indians know that they were going to take everything away, the foreshore and everything. That was not the understanding of

my people because we still thought that we owned the foreshore
and that we could have the say there if anybody wanted to lease it
from us. We have no objection to the public using that road. It is
all right because we use it with our own cars now and I think it is
quite in order. What we want is that strip of land outside the road
so we can have control over it. In the early days when there was no
wharf my people used to have places all along the foreshore where
they kept their canoes in front of their big community houses. We
used to use that foreshore in the early days and I can't see why they
just all of a sudden took it over from us." Of course the minister
said right away, "Well, we have to give it back to them. It's theirs
and it was only a mistake of the government that was in power in
those days." One of the deputy ministers spoke up and said to the
minister, "That is going to be awfully hard to do because it will
have to go through the Order-in-Council." The minister answered
him, "That's fine, just tell them to put it through the Order-in-
Council. It is theirs and we might as well settle it now, and the
shipyard that has been paying the government for their lease, you
tell them to go back to paying the Indians for the foreshore." So we
came home quite happy and I thought it was quite a nice victory for
our people and for the Indians all over British Columbia.

In March Dan Campbell phoned me and asked when the best
time would be for them to come and present the rights to the foreshore to my people. I told him that the end of June would be a
good time because we had our annual sports days then and the
people from all the other villages would be in Alert Bay. So he
called me back and said that he had made arrangements for the
lieutenant governor of British Columbia to come up with him and
that the lieutenant governor was going to invite the prime minister
of Canada to come also. So I called my council together and told
them what was going to happen. I wrote a letter to the minister of
Indian affairs, Arthur Lang, and told him that I felt he should come
and witness what was going to take place that day, the giving back
of the foreshore to the Indians because it had been taken away from
us. My council said that I would have to look after all that we were
going to do when the lieutenant governor came, so I formed a committee with some of the leaders from the other end of the village
and some of our Indian people. I told them what was going to

happen and that it was going to be quite a heavy weekend for the people of the whole island. So we started having meetings and planned everything that we wanted to do when the representatives of the government came.

On June 18 the lieutenant governor and his wife and Dan Campbell and his wife arrived on a destroyer. The prime minister wasn't able to come. We had the school band down there to meet them, and when they came ashore I met the lieutenant governor, George R. Pearkes, and we both got into the backseat of an old 1926 Model A Ford and Ray Rosback drove us around Alert Bay and we stopped at the Canadian Legion Hall for a few minutes with the whole party. Then we drove back to the Nimpkish council hall and had a luncheon that had been prepared by all the young girls of the Nimpkish band. We had a wonderful time and all the members of my council and the chiefs and their wives and the prominent men of all the villages were there. I made a little speech to welcome the lieutenant governor and then he said a few words. After the luncheon was over, I got into the old car again with Lieutenant Governor Pearkes and we drove to the field in front of the community house. There was a big crowd of people there waiting for us from all over the coast. We had built a platform in front of the community house and I went up there with the lieutenant governor, Dan Campbell, and Mr. Boys, who was the Indian commissioner. Mr. Boys got up first and explained why the foreshore had been taken away and why the Indian people wanted to get it back. Then he had Dan Campbell explain why the foreshore was going to be given back. Then Dan Campbell asked the lieutenant governor to do the honor of signing the Order-in-Council and give back the foreshore to us as a representative of Her Majesty, the Queen. There wasn't enough room on the platform for all my council so they were standing beside it. When he had signed it I got up, and he made a little speech when he handed that declaration over to me.

This is the little speech I made: "On behalf of my people, the Nimpkish people, I will gladly accept the giving back of our foreshore. This is a victory not only for us but for all the Indians of British Columbia because there are many more reserves and foreshores that we would like to settle with the government. We are not treaty Indians and have not given up the ownership of British

Columbia to the white man." Then I told a little joke. "I remember that there was an old Indian man who went up on a high hill with his young son. He said to his son, 'Look around you, my son, at this beautiful country. One day this all belonged to the Indian people and someday it is going to be all ours again. The white man is going to give it back when they all go to the moon.'" As soon as I had received the foreshore from the lieutenant governor, I made an announcement on the microphone: "We are going to officially open the community house and I would like everybody to go inside and make yourselves comfortable. There are so many people here, many of you are visitors from all over, that I don't think there will be enough room, and so I would like to have all the small children stay outside and leave the room for the grownups. This is a very historical occasion and this ceremony will be different from any other you have ever seen. You can all go in now."

I had Henry Speck in the back room in charge of all the people who were going to dance, and they were getting ready with their regalia. I told Dan Campbell and the wives to go on in to the special seats they had for them and I asked the lieutenant governor to stay outside with me. So they all went in and just me and the lieutenant governor were there and the commander of the destroyer who was to be with him at all times. Then we went around to the room at the back of the community house and I changed into my regalia and we put a nice Indian robe on the lieutenant governor and put a cedar bark ring around his neck and a cedar bark crown on his head. Then we went out of that little room in the back and came around to the front door with all of the dancers and singers. We had the chiefs from all of the different tribes go in first, and they were chanting one of the chants that had been used in the early days when the people welcomed the victory and happiness that had come among them. I was last with the lieutenant governor and we all marched around in the big community house. Then after we had gone around, all the dancers and singers gathered by the door and the lieutenant governor had a long stick with a torch on the end of it, which he lit. Then he put the torch to a pile of logs that were in the center of the dirt floor and watched the smoke rise through the hole in the ceiling from that fire which was a symbol of the first fire in the house. Then he made a little speech and declared the community house was officially opened. It was very impressive and I think it was the only ceremony of its kind. We had planned that quite a few weeks ahead of time because we wanted to make it different and authentic. We thought of having the lieutenant governor go and cut a ribbon the way the non-Indian people open a bridge or a building, but I suggested to my committee that we should have him put a torch to that wood and start a fire to open the house.

Then I asked the lieutenant governor to take his seat and the singers from all the different villages started singing and the dancers began dancing around the fire. They were singing a victory song and the dancers were dancing with joy and everybody was happy. When the dancing was over, I went to the microphone and made a little speech. "I want to thank you, Lieutenant Governor Pearkes, for officially opening this community house because we are very proud of this big house. When I was a little boy I used to live in this kind of house and I am very proud of it because I was the architect of this building. We would like to use it to revive the arts and crafts of my people because they are so beautiful and we don't want them forgotten. You are an honorary member of the Nimpkish people and you can come back here anytime you retire. I want to confirm to you the name that was given to you two years ago at Gilford Island, Yakuglas, which means a 'person with wealth to share.' If you will come up here now I want to present you with this carved Indian paddle. This is a token of the Nimpkish people." I presented him with a nice beautiful paddle made by our young carvers. Then Dan Campbell came up and when I presented a paddle to him, I said, "This is the kind of paddle we used to use in the early days before there were any power boats and we just used to paddle our canoes. Now we don't use it anymore because we are living in the modern world. These are the only paddles we have left and when you get back to Victoria, remind them that we have no paddles left and that now we need a ferry. This is a reminder to you that we need a ferry." You could hear that building just roaring with the people laughing because we have been after the government for a long time to give us a ferry. Then I called some of the Nimpkish women forward who presented the wives with some carved copper bracelets. At that same time, Billy Cook presented the lieutenant governor with another small carved paddle from the Nimpkish Athletic Club. Then Mrs. Arthur Dick, my wife's younger sister, came up and took her blanket off and presented that beautiful Indian robe to the wife of the lieutenant governor. Of course the lieutenant governor and Dan Campbell both made a speech and said they were very happy to be with us that day and that it had been a wonderful gathering and they really enjoyed every bit of it.

After everything was over Dan Campbell announced that he would like to make a little presentation to the lieutenant governor and me. I was very surprised because I didn't know anything about it. He made us both members in the Loyal Order of the Whale's Tooth and said that the only others who had had that honor were two mayors from Quebec. He explained that the whale's tooth was recognized as a symbol to honor outstanding chiefs and government officials. He took an engraved whale's tooth and placed it around the neck of the lieutenant governor and then said, "I am bestowing this honor on you because no other lieutenant governor ever took so much time to visit the small communities of British Columbia. Of particular note are the times and the occasions that you have visited the Indian people of the province and through your interest in their culture you have brought new meaning to the life of these people." Then he took the other whale's tooth and placed it around my neck and said, "Chief Sewid, during the past several years you have worked to uplift the lives of the people who live on Cormorant Island, be they white or Indian. With great energy you have sought to encourage your people to maintain their culture and their arts. The flourishing crafts industry which resulted in the creation of the community house is a tribute to your leadership. Alert Bay and British Columbia are therefore better places because you took the leadership you did." We both thanked him for the honor and then we all went out of that house.

It was about 4:30 and the women had prepared some barbecued fish outside in the field beside the community house. So everyone came and got some potatoes and barbecued fish and other things and then went into the big house and sat down and ate. The lieutenant governor was quite pleased and he sure enjoyed that barbecued fish. And the day was getting quite strenuous for me because I had spent most of my time going around with the lieu-

tenant governor. Everything had run very smoothly and I had never
seen the likes of it. After the dinner was over I went around and
checked with the people because we had an Indian dance that night,
and we made about $300 for our Kwakwala Arts and Crafts Organi-
zation. The next day they had all the sports and everything and all
the people had a good time.

I had gotten my Kwakwala Arts and Crafts Committee together
and we talked over what we wanted to do that summer for the
tourists who came to Alert Bay. We thought we could sell our arts
and crafts and perform our dances for the tourists, because that was
the reason why we built that Kwakiutl house. I felt that a lot of my
people, especially the older people, had no jobs that they could do,
but they could make something to sell to the tourists. That was
always in the back of my mind. A steamship came through and
stopped at Alert Bay for a few hours on its way up north during
the summer, and at that time the tourists would look around Alert
Bay. We decided that we should do something but we didn't know
how to go about it. I decided to bring it up to the Board of Trade
and see if they could help us.

At our next meeting I brought it up to them and told them
straight that I would be away most of the summer fishing and there
was none of our people that could manage it. I said I could be there
when it started, but I didn't want to just start something and then
have it stopped when I had to go out fishing. If we didn't get some
help from them I would be the only man there that really cared to
be there and get things ready. So the Board of Trade talked it over,
and they decided that they could take it over and manage it because
it would mean a lot of tourist business for the white end of Alert
Bay. They decided to prepare the publicity for nothing because it
would be worth it to them and then find someone who could help
me look after it during the summer. The first thing they did was to
print up little folders with the killer whale on the front and the
program of dances on the inside. They got in touch with the C.P.R.
people who ran the steamship and were able to have the programs
sold to the passengers as part of their fare. They cost $1.75 each
and there were three tickets on them which allowed them to get a
taxi ride to and from the boat and admission to the community
house.

So that summer there were fourteen cruise ships that came into Alert Bay and we put on a program for all the tourists on each ship. There were over three thousand people who came into the community house and saw our dances. When the ship arrived there were a lot of cars and taxis waiting to transport them up to the community house, and it took about twenty minutes to get them all up there. I was working at the microphone and as soon as the first bunch came in I said, "You have freedom to walk around and take all the pictures you want while you are waiting for the rest of the tourists to come ashore. Some of our Indian arts and crafts are on display and you may buy them if you want." As soon as everybody had arrived we began our program, which used to last about thirty minutes, and I announced and interpreted all the dances. When I was out fishing later in the summer some of the other leading men took over that job. All of the people were dressed in their regalia and it was a very colorful dance and they were all very impressed with it. When it was over, they all just looked around and some of them bought little totem poles, straw mats with Indian designs, pottery, and bracelets that had designs on them. I don't know how much was sold because all of that was a private thing. The people who had anything to sell just put it on that table and we hired a couple of women to look after it.

The money we got for the admission price was used to pay all the dancers and anything that was left over went into our Kwakwala Arts and Crafts Organization. I talked to Drew Oswald when it was time for me to go out fishing, because he was going to be in charge of managing it. "You have to take it," I told him, "because if you give it to one of our people it won't work. I would like you to look after all the money and as soon as each performance is over to pay all the people." And he really carried out what I wanted him to do. He got all the statements and paid all the people before they left and the balance went to the bank. The way I saw it was that it would work fine as long as a non-Indian looked after it. If you gave it to one of the people here they would just make a mess of it because nobody was capable of that. All the performers got different wages. We priced it the nearest we could. If a dancer danced for about five minutes we gave him six or seven dollars. If a man was performing twice he would get twice as much. I was on the mike for the first few times and I got fifteen dollars for that. I would tell the whole story of how we built that house and then announce the dances and the singers. All of the singers got paid for singing.

When the day came for the last ship of the summer to come in, Henry Speck came and asked me to stay because I had been planning to go out fishing. He told me there was going to be some kind of presentation to the captain and the officers of the ship. So when the performance was over that day I called the officers to come forward because we had a little present for them which was a token for their cooperation and advertising what we were doing in the community house. Then I said, "I am very pleased with this community house. I'm not thinking just of my people but I'm thinking of the island as a whole. I don't care what race you are, whether you are white, Japanese, Chinese, or Indian, it doesn't matter. We have had people from all over the world this summer, some as far away as England and Hawaii. They come here and they see no difference between the different races. This is what I have been working for all these years and I think we have proved to ourselves that it can be done." Then that ship pulled out and it was the last one that summer. We are planning to do the same thing next summer but we want to put on different dances. I would like to build another little community house next to the big one and make it just the same but only about twenty feet by twenty feet and use it as a store where we could keep all our stuff.

Early in December 1966 I made a trip down to Vancouver and when I returned I decided to put on a special kind of potlatch. When I was a little boy my parents and grandparents had told me about how they sometimes used to have a *gwomiass*, which is a play potlatch. I didn't actually see one but they used to talk about it and say that it was more or less like a social gathering with friends. It was different from the real potlatch where a big chief would give a lot of things away. The smaller the amount that one gave away the bigger he was in this play potlatch because it was just for fun. It was just a play. After I was married my wife's aunt and mother used to tell me about it and that anybody could give small things away to each person, such as a lot of candy, buttons, or nickels. They had little names that they gave to people, such as a fish, a rapid of a river, a tree, a bird, or a duck. They were not like the real chief's names but they were inherited from their ancestors to be used in the play potlatch. They also had songs which were handed from generation to generation which had pretty bad words in them. At the play potlatch they would divide up with the men on the one side of the big house and the women on the other, and they would sing these songs and give things away, and each side would try to beat the other side.

So I talked to some of my people and asked them if there was anything going on the day before Christmas Eve. They said that there was nothing going on and so I thought it would be good to have something going on for my people and for the non-Indians as well. I talked to some of the older people and some of the younger people to see if we could put on a play potlatch since it was Christmas time and everybody was happy together. Well, we sent word around in Alert Bay but we didn't invite any of the outside villages and it wasn't advertised too much. So we all gathered in the community house and there were about one hundred people there that night. The men were on one side and the women were on the other and the women started it off. Each side had their own master of ceremonies who announced what they were going to do. One of the older women got up and announced that a great chief was going to give a potlatch. Then a young girl got up and they mentioned her name, it was a funny little name, and they all started singing a funny little song. The words of that song were more or less calling the men's side down. After they sang that song someone danced and then that young girl gave away little pieces of candy to everybody that was there. Her friends were helping her give away those little presents.

When she was done then one of the men on our side got up and announced that a great chief, a non-Indian, was going to give a potlatch. We gave him a funny little name and then some of us helped him give out his presents. Then it just went back and forth from one side to the other and some of the people were dancing some of the time. Flora gave away a lot of little five-cent candy bars but I didn't give anything away that night. I danced the feather dance to show some of my non-Indian friends how it went. Some of the others danced the hamatsa dance and tried to imitate the regular hamatsas making noises and singing like the hamatsas do. The speeches that they made that night were more or less a joke, telling how great the person was and that they were going to sing the great songs of that great chief. It was all in our language but there were some who were interpreting it to the non-Indian friends of ours. We didn't measure who was the highest that night, but the women beat the men because there were more women that gave away than men. It went on until about eleven o'clock and then we all went home. It was quite a nice gathering and everybody was happy and laughing and dancing around all that evening.

That is the end of my story. As I think back over my life I think it was a full life and a wonderful life. I realize that I have gone through many things in my life and I think lots of my people can learn from my experiences. As a little boy I grew up in the Indian way and now our life has turned to the modern way. Many times I have talked to my people at gatherings on how to go about their own business and how to go about their family life and how to carry on the work for their tribe. I don't like to brag about anything that I have done because I'm not the judge as to what I have done. I have always tried to live up to all the things that I have done and I think that others can learn from hearing about my experiences. I thought that if I could put my life story in a written book then even people that I know in distant places could read about it and it might be a help to them. That was why I thought it was necessary to make this book.

As I look forward to the rest of my life there are some things that I am hoping for. We have had many problems that have been solved. I'm quite satisfied with the education system now because our children are going to the public high school. I do want to see the Indian day school closed down and all those children who live at St. Michael's Residential School going to the public school. I'm quite satisfied with the old age pension and the family pension and the housing that my people are getting. I never did agree with some of our people that wanted their houses for nothing. I think they should pay at least half and maybe the government could meet them halfway. I always say that if you are going to give anybody anything for nothing that it will spoil the person by doing that. If you pay for what you have, then you will be much more careful in looking after it. I'm satisfied that we are allowed to go to the beer parlor and sit there like any other person, and also that we are allowed to go to the liquor store and get what we want instead of going and buying it from the bootleggers at $35 a bottle.

I think the biggest problem to be solved and the most important is the land question. We are nontreaty Indians on the coast and I think we should be compensated for our land. When the Europeans came here and settled, they just took all our mineral and timber and salmon and everything that we rightfully owned and they have never settled it with us. We have been pounding and pounding on the doors of the government because we would like to settle it so we can satisfy the minds of the Indians. I would also like to see my people get ahead and have their own industry, especially in a place like Alert Bay where the population is growing all the time. I think we should have an industry of our own where the people can work all year around instead of only two and a half months' fishing the way we do. That was one of the main reasons that it came to my mind to build that community house, so that the people could have some work to do. Instead of going to the Indian Department for help my people can go in there and carve and make a little money to get by. I think that the best thing for the Indian people is for them to help themselves. I think the worst thing that ever happened to us was when they took our pride away.

For myself I don't want to slow down. I think I would be lost if I ever quit what I have been doing because I started very young. I would like to keep on fishing because that is my life. I like fishing and I don't know if I am qualified to fit into anything other than fishing. I would like very much to get some other job somewhere where I could settle down and work twelve months a year because I am unhappy about working only thirty or thirty-five days a year fishing when we have a short season. But since I am a man without any education and don't know what I would be fit for at my age, I will just keep on until they tell me that I am no longer useful. I would also like to travel and go to some strange places where I have never been. I have always wanted to go to England where the head of the Anglo-British Columbia Packing Company is so that they could see what the Indian people are like. I belong to the Church of England, and they sent Mr. Hall here all the way from England to teach my people the gospel and to live among my people. There is no doubt that the people where he came from who sent him over would like to see the result of his work, how he did and whether it was all wasted or not. I sometimes think about building a smaller house for Flora because I built my house for the large family that we had. I always say that I should build a small house for her, but then again, what do I do with all our friends and relatives and the people that come and visit us? Our table is usually full all the time with our family and friends coming in and sitting down to have dinner with us.

I have always felt, ever since I lived with my old grandmother, Lucy, as a little boy, that someone was looking after me and I am very thankful for that. I want to end my story now with the sermon that I preached in 1966 on Harvest Thanksgiving Sunday at Christ Church in Alert Bay:

On this morning we can look around us, especially the young people, and we can find many good things in our church. I know it is tempting and I would be tempted if I was a youngster, but I am not tempting you to take some with you. Canada is a big country and it is a beautiful country. North America and South America are much the same; they have rich country. We happen to live in a very prosperous country such as Canada. I have been through right to the other side of Canada when I went back east. Each province has their own way of living as I found out when I was back east. The Parliament buildings in Ottawa are all made out of stone and they are still working there carving today. What I found most interesting was that they had carved everything that is in Canada, animals, fish, birds, flowers, and trees. The walls of that great building are covered with those carvings.

Now today we celebrate this most beautiful harvest of the year when we can all say to one another, especially to our children and our friends, "We should come to church and thank God for what we are doing and for what He has done for us in 1966." Some of us might have been sick in 1966 and then were cured and became a new person again and we should be thankful for that. Some of you children come from afar off from Alert Bay, places like Bella Bella and Bella Coola. I recognize some of you from those places. And you should be thankful that there is room in our schools because we are having a rough time not only in Alert Bay but all over Canada. We should be thankful there are schools because education is needed among our people.

Canada has everything. We have fruit and wheat. When I went back east we were flying on a jet plane and I could see wheat fields for miles and miles. I'm sure our minister and his wife, Rev. and Mrs. David Rogers, know all about that country, more than I do, because they came to us from Montreal. I went from Ottawa to Montreal by train and there were little farms all along the railroad tracks. While I was there I studied the lives of the people there because I like to study the lives of people. I like to study how they live. It's none of my business and if anybody had come out and said, "It's none of your business," I might have just run very quickly and come back to British Columbia. And after seeing all those things back there I appreciated very much that I am from British Columbia after I returned, because British Columbia is a very wealthy province. We have everything here. And that is something to be thankful for.

Now my text this morning is from Luke 17 and I'm going to read it to you:

> And it came to pass as He went to Jerusalem that He passed through the midst of Samaria and Galilee. And as He entered into a certain village there met Him ten men that were lepers which stood afar off. And they lifted up their voices and said, "Jesus, Master, have mercy on us." And when He saw them He said unto them, "Go show yourselves unto the priests." And it came to pass that as they went they were cleansed. And one of them when he saw that he was healed turned back and with a loud voice glorified God, and fell down on his face at His feet, giving Him thanks and he was a Samaritan. Jesus answered and said, "Were there not ten cleansed? But where are the nine? They are not found that return to give glory to God save this stranger," and He said unto him, "Arise, go thy way, thy faith has made thee whole."

Now there are a lot of us fishermen in our village here on this little island that understand what a fisherman's life should be. We go to the net loft when it is time to get our nets ready and our boats ready because we know this is our harvest. The land of British Columbia is all rocky and there isn't much of any place to plant

seeds on this rocky coast, but we have another harvest from the
seed. The fishermen paint their boats, mend their nets, and get
ready for the fishing season. Don't you think some of us trust God
to do the things we need? We hope for a good year and some
years are good and some years are bad. But as a fisherman I think
God will look after me what He thinks is best for me. If it is a poor
year it is not up to me to complain what happens. I think it is up
to every fisherman to look toward his Maker because He can provide. The lesson this morning was taken from the Gospel of Luke
and it tells there how a man should live in this world. The lesson
that was read in the earlier part of this service told of a man who
built himself a big barn and he was going to store everything he had
and then he said he was going to relax and retire. We hear a lot of
people talking about retiring these days and a lot of them ask me,
"Jimmy, when are you going to retire?" And I tell them, "Never!
As long as I have breath in me, I want to work even if I have to
crawl." Well, this person must have felt like those people who
want to retire. He wanted to take it easy and have a good time, but
he forgot that his life was just borrowed. His life wasn't going to
last more than a few hours after his barn was finished. God had said
so. He was going to use his barn, and then he was going to lose
everything he had in this world because everything belonged to
this world. We came here naked and we are going to go away
naked because we were made by God and He made everything for
us on earth so that we could use it.

We are to use what God has given us sensibly and not abuse it.
Sometimes I think about the grapes and many of the other fruits
that they make liquor from. A lot of my people abuse that. There
have been some people coming from the United States to see me
and they ask me, "What can we do with our people in order to
teach them how to use this stuff?" My answer was, "Teach them in
school where they are taught everything else. The young people are
taught in school and I think it is about time now that we ask the
government to teach the youngsters how to take a drink the way
you are supposed to use it." It is good for you in some ways but if
you take too much of it, what is going to happen? It is just like anything else. Suppose that you take my challenge this morning and
eat a couple of dozen apples, what is going to happen to you? You

are going to get sick. Now my Indian people in the early days used to go up the rivers at this time of year and reap the harvest of the sea. There were not nets or sailboats or gill-net boats in those days. And the Indian people used to go to those little rivers and dry enough salmon for the winter. Many of them used to go across the way here to the Nimpkish River, and I used to go there as a young man and help the people out by gathering wood for them, and their harvest was the fish. That was the time when they thanked God for everything they received from the sea. And at those places up the river the salmon used to come to spawn and I used to go after those salmon with my grandparents. We used to have fifteen hundred or two thousand smoked fish. We used to use all different kinds of fish and we even smoked the heads. They were used not only by our families, but my grandparents used to give it out to the people and share their fish with the people who couldn't go. And that was the thing that made the people understand that everything came from God.

Now this year, my friends, is a big year and next year we are going to celebrate the birthday of Canada all across our land. When they discovered this land there were only Indians living in this beautiful rich country of ours. Now we are going to celebrate with the white people because we can see all the help that came with them from Europe to show us many things. This is what we are going to be thankful for. I think it's a wonderful thing that we are working together and that we join our hands with the non-Indians in Canada to work together for the good.

I'd like to tell you a little story about the harvest, especially for the young people that are here. Harvest Thanksgiving is the time that you can give something back to God. How are you going to give something back to God? There are many ways. We know that God's work is on earth here because He loved us. He loved the people and it is up to us to help in order to bring some of our people that never come to church and to teach them that they should give something in return. Now let me say that as rector's warden and as a member of the church committee for many many years we have been struggling with this church. It takes money to run the lights and the heat. Because of the few people that give something towards the work of the church, we sometimes wonder where we are going to get the next few dollars to pay for the light bill next month. Some of us today can say that here is something that I'd like to give toward the work of the church in return and to say that I'm thankful for what God has done for me. The story I want to tell is about a preacher and a little boy. The preacher was preaching in his church the Sunday before Harvest Thanksgiving and he said that the next Sunday was going to be Harvest Thanksgiving Sunday. He went on to say, "You can give money; you can give food if you have a farm. You can make some jam or some canned fish and bring it to the church, but if you haven't got anything you can offer yourselves to God." It happened that one of the people there was a little Negro boy. This poor little colored boy didn't have anything to offer so he really listened when the preacher said, "You can give yourselves to God. You can offer yourselves to God as a thanksgiving. He needs you more than your money. He wants you." So on the day before Harvest Thanksgiving Sunday there were some ladies bringing in fruit and vegetables and putting them on the altar of the church. So the minister came in late to check his church and see if everything was all right, and here was this Negro boy lying on top of the vegetables. He had come and offered himself to God. He really felt that he should come and offer himself to his Maker.

Our lesson this morning was one of my favorite texts in the Bible. Let me pass this on to you young people because I learned this when I was a little boy. "Seek ye first the Kingdom of God." That's the last part of the lesson this morning. "Seek ye first the Kingdom of God." Come to church and worship together with God's people. "Seek ye first the Kingdom of God," and this is very important, "and everything will be granted unto you." God will help you and God will bless you, but you have to seek His Kingdom first. It is very simple and anybody can do it if you can make up your mind. Nobody else is going to make up your mind but yourself. "Seek ye first the Kingdom of God and everything will be added unto you." Now let's bow our heads for prayer.

Oh, most merciful Father, we humbly thank Thee for all Thy gifts so freely bestowed upon us; for life and health and safety; for power to work and rest; for all that is beautiful in creation and in the lives of men. We praise and magnify Thy holy Name but above all we thank Thee for all our spiritual mercies in Christ our Lord, for the means of grace and for the hope of glory. Fill our hearts with all joy and peace in believing through Jesus Christ our Lord. Amen.

Now to God the Father, God the Son, God the Holy Spirit, we ascribe all the majesties, dominion, and power, for now and forevermore. Amen.

AFTERWORD

by James Spradley

James Sewid's Adaptation to Culture Conflict

Although it would be possible to embark upon a comprehensive analysis of James Sewid's personality, the focus of this postscript to his own story is on the dynamic situation of culture conflict. The clash of cultures which resulted from the interaction of Indians and Europeans was the most outstanding feature of his experience. During his first year of life he was the object of a large potlatch held in violation of the white man's law. At seven he witnessed his relatives and friends being jailed for the crime of practicing their traditional culture. His schooling, marriage, initiation into the hamatsa society, and attempts to become economically independent all revealed different facets of the culture conflict situation. Most of his adult life was spent in efforts to better the conditions of the Indians, correct injustices they experienced, and help them surmount the difficulties brought about by culture conflict. His life is a record of the extent and meaning of this conflict for one individual. A description of different cultures and the manner in which they are at cross-purposes can never be so vivid as the individual's experience of such discord.

James Sewid's life provides a much needed corrective to the widely held idea that the effect of culture conflict is primarily negative. The negative effects may certainly be seen in the lives of individuals and in the disappearance of a once-flourishing cultural system. Yet the positive side also exists. Examination of Sewid's response to culture conflict illustrates successful adaptation in the detail of one man's life. Since he was effective in meeting the challenge of the new cultural conditions, a study of his style of adaptation may add to our understanding of an important human problem.

Before the Europeans arrived, the Kwakiutl of course had knowledge of other groups whose cultures differed from their own. During long-distance trading expeditions they interacted with such people, but their relationship with them was a kind of stable equilibrium. Hostilities were expressed in periodic warfare, whereas cooperation appeared in trading and ceremonial life; however, what we mean by culture conflict was almost nonexistent, in part because their technology and social life were at similar levels of development. With the appearance of Europeans, the Kwakiutl encountered for the first time people whose culture contrasted radically with their own. In spite of this, until nearly 1850, they were able to maintain a relatively stable equilibrium. While cultural changes did occur, they were integrated into the existing Kwakiutl way of life. Europeans accepted their dependence on Indians and considered them a valuable source of labor and trade goods, and the Kwakiutl were likewise dependent on the Europeans for various trade items. Kwakiutl culture was actually more effective for adaptation to the Northwest Coast environment in technology, social life, and health practices (Hawthorn et al. 1960:58–60). Furthermore, contact was infrequent between the two groups; the Indians were in the majority, and they maintained their political autonomy.

The more or less stable relationships between these two contrasting cultural groups soon deteriorated, and by 1850 (Duff 1964) the increase in the number of Europeans, their technological superiority, and their political power brought the two cultures into open conflict. (There is a large body of literature on the history and nature of this conflict which is beyond the scope of this work: Codere 1961, Drucker 1958, Hawthorn et al. 1960, Wolcott 1967.) Missions, schools, and Indian agents all began to exert a powerful influence upon the Kwakiutl, and with their introduction, the Europeans, because of their status and power, became an important reference group. An Indian's very life came to depend upon how seriously he considered the white man's evaluation of Kwakiutl practices. Individual Kwakiutl had maintained their sense of identity and well-being from the knowledge that their values, beliefs, and behavior were appropriate and were thus recognized by other members of the society. Since the Kwakiutl shared the same cultural definition of the situation, there had been a high degree of consensus on such matters. But now they began to experience culture conflict as European attitudes came to be considered significant. The Europeans, on the other hand, did not feel that their culture was being called into question even though it was to some degree scorned and disapproved of by the Kwakiutl, because they were politically, numerically, and technologically in control of the contact situation. This conflict, which James Sewid experienced along with the rest of his people, may be considered in three areas of life.

First, the Europeans held a stereotyped definition of the Indian as inferior. What has been said about ethnic relations between the Indians and whites in British Columbia was also generally true for the Kwakiutl (Hawthorn et al. 1960:58–59). Whites saw the Indians as a threat because of violent behavior, a nuisance because of contrasting morals and institutions, a vanishing race needing no permanent solutions to their problems, and a group to be Westernized under programs administered by whites. Although there have been changes in the direction of greater tolerance of the Indians, the feelings of white superiority have continued. Implicit in much of James Sewid's autobiography is the awareness of this definition of inferiority (pp. 118, 199). It posed a constant threat to the Indians' sense of identity and security and was one of the reasons for Indian avoidance of whites. While some Indians accepted this loss of status and respect or sought escape from the resultant anxiety, others denied or rationalized the loss. Both in action and thought, James Sewid sought to understand and correct this definition of the Indian.

Second, James Sewid was confronted with different beliefs, practices, and values which whites considered good for everyone. A great many features of his own culture were condemned as evil. This seriously called into question the daily behavior of the individual and further undermined his security and positive sense of identity. To be a good Kwakiutl, James Sewid learned that he should respect kinship ties, obey his elders, give away his money, but at the same time to conform to white values he should acquire and save his money for personal possessions and refuse to participate in the ceremonies that validated traditional privileges and positions. The number and types of cultural differences that James Sewid experienced as conflicting can be glimpsed in his own story. Role expectations and the use of money and material possessions were the most significant and illustrate this conflict.

An important function of every human culture is to structure interpersonal relationships so that interactions between members of the society become predictable as a result of the shared definitions of cultural roles. One set of role expectations that James Sewid found to be in conflict with Western culture involved age. A great many roles were based on the premise that one should respect, obey, and show deference to all older persons within the clan, village, and tribe. The inheritance patterns of the Kwakiutl favored the eldest child, often to the exclusion of younger children, and being the eldest, James Sewid received preferential treatment from his relatives, while learning from the whites that he should not do the same with his children.

During his life he experienced great conflict over decisions between obeying the elders and conforming to demands made by members of the white society. Legally he was supposed to go to the residential school at Alert Bay, but his grandparents kept him from doing so. The Indian agent tried to prevent his early marriage but he went ahead, almost against his own desires. His motivations indicate that this tension was not just interpersonal but involved internalized values (pp. 66–67). Similar conflicts took place when his grandfather wanted him to become a member of the hamatsa society. The problems he encountered at Village Island and later at Alert Bay because of his progressive ideas resulted in part because he was not obeying the elders of the village.

The roles an individual enacts within any society may be assigned to him at birth or they may be achieved through some action. Most roles in Kwakiutl society tended to be assigned on the basis of sex and birth order, whereas roles in white society were based largely on achievement. Nowhere may this conflict be seen more clearly than in the problems James Sewid had over the role of chief. The traditional status of chief was acquired through inheritance, while the office of modern chief councillor was acquired more through achievement. All his life he interacted with others who were chiefs in some sense, as well as enacting the role of chief himself. He has discussed at length the different cultural definitions of this role and some of the conflicts involved. While some aspects of culture conflict may result only in personal stress, the multiplicity of definitions of the chief role also led to serious interpersonal stress for James Sewid.

As these differences in role definitions began to pervade the life of the Kwakiutl, anxiety, stress, and insecurity became part of every human interaction. The traditional basis of village and tribal membership was torn between the criteria of kinship and a vote by village members. James Sewid was caught between the values of being a quiet, soft-spoken leader of traditional importance and being an aggressive, hard-driving skipper of a seine boat who shouted orders at his crew. Such events as funeral ceremonies led to tension because of different cultural definitions regarding how one should show respect for the dead. Even the relationships within the family were not free from the problem created by culture conflict. Husband-wife and parent-child relationships were no longer easily predicted on the basis of their traditional culture.

The most overt clash of cultures probably resulted from differences in the use of money and other material possessions. In both cultures wealth was one of the most important symbols of high status. In both cultures there was a great emphasis upon the acquisition of large amounts of money and other property. The similarities ended here, for whites achieved their status positions through simply acquiring wealth, where the Kwakiutl demonstrated the validity of their inherited status positions by giving away wealth, a practice so incomprehensible to the Europeans that they passed laws and took coercive action to eliminate such outrageous behavior.

It was no easy matter to enforce these laws although many attempts were made, such as the one James Sewid witnessed as a child when his school was used for a courtroom. The net effect of such direct action against the Kwakiutl was that the potlatch distributions were done secretly. It was possible to carry on the potlatch custom in isolated places such as Village Island, but even here the Royal Canadian Mounted Police might come to enforce the law, as they did at the time James Sewid was initiated into the hamatsa society. The revised Indian Act of 1951 omitted the sections which prohibited the potlatch, and after that date potlatches could be given without fear of the police.

The strength of Kwakiutl commitment and motivation to give things away must be understood in terms of their status-prestige system. James Sewid was profoundly influenced by his grandfather, who was a respected chief in Kwakiutl society because he gave things away. Not only did he have this ego model, but those who were unable to give, or refused to, were publicly rebuked in speeches. Although privileges and positions of high status in Kwakiutl society were inherited, they could never be assumed without a distribution of money or other goods.

Another conflict resulted from the different beliefs about the use of wealth. Those who wished to pursue European economic goals were encouraged to do so by individual whites, but in order to do this they had to ignore the traditional responsibility to help those who requested money, goods, or services. James Sewid faced this problem in trying to operate a store in Alert Bay. Children and adults alike would purchase goods on credit and even come to the store for loans of money; the business venture was finally discontinued because of such conflict.

The third area of life where James Sewid experienced culture conflict resulted from his activities directed toward the achievement of Western goals. In addition to his Western business ventures, he accepted and pursued other values which brought him into conflict with more traditionally oriented Kwakiutl. His actions in bringing about the change in the Nimpkish band government from the traditional system to an elected council were interpreted by some as a repudiation of both Kwakiutl culture and those individuals who held traditional leadership positions. During all the years that he was a member of the village council he worked to improve village conditions, but along with others who adopted Western values he was sometimes cast in opposition to more conservative Kwakiutl, for example, when he attempted to collect village water bills, use band funds for community projects, accept new members into the band, and create a new function for the traditional dance ceremonies. When he moved to the Industrial Reserve at Alert Bay to escape this conflict and develop a community of progressive Indians from all over the province, the Bureau of Indian Affairs amalgamated this group with the nearby Nimpkish band, thereby thwarting his plans. Thus he found the pursuit of Western goals for himself and the Indian community a difficult venture. Not only were these goals foreign to his Kwakiutl heritage, but pursuing them meant conflict with more tradition-oriented Kwakiutl.

James Sewid did not adapt to culture conflict by being committed to Kwakiutl values to the exclusion of Western values. He did not reject his traditional heritage and move into the dominant society, nor did he seek to escape from the conflict through passive withdrawal from the goal-directed activities of both cultures. Instead, he actively pursued the goals of both cultures in spite of the contradictions in these two ways of life. Although he was more Western-oriented and participated in Western institutions more than most other Kwakiutl, at the same time he was more committed to the traditional culture and social institutions than many of his peers. His way of adapting to the conflict was to become *bicultural.*

This type of adaptation must not be confused with the sequential acquisition of two cultural systems. Learning a native culture and subsequently learning to live in terms of Western culture is significantly different from simultaneous participation in two cultural systems. James Sewid is important for what he can teach us about this style of adaptation. All too little is known about bicultural individuals, their related personality characteristics, and socialization experiences.

BICULTURAL ADAPTATION

In order to make clear the nature of a bicultural way of life it must be distinguished from two similar but distinct ways of living with two cultures. One involves a temporal separation of conflicting norms. Thus, a person who has been socialized into one culture may, through migration or some other process, later be confronted with a different way of life and learn to live in terms of the second culture for the remainder of his life. This task, though difficult, is facilitated by the fact that often those who shared the first cultural heritage have been left behind, and thus there are few if any social pressures to conform to the first culture, giving relative freedom to conform to the second. In fact, one motivation for migration from societies undergoing culture conflict is to escape from these conflicting pressures. This was undoubtedly one of the reasons why James Sewid moved from the Indian community of Village Island to Alert Bay, where white culture predominated. While certain periods of his life tended to be oriented more toward one culture than the other, he has lived his entire life in the context of both.

During the first six years of his life he lived primarily in remote villages where Kwakiutl culture was dominant; he was one of the last Indians to grow up in the traditional community house. From seven to twelve his experiences were more influenced by whites. During this time he went to school, visited Vancouver, and came to know a number of whites. This did not prevent him from returning to the remote villages for periods of time with his relatives, where Kwakiutl ways were reinforced. After his marriage at thirteen, he lived briefly in Alert Bay and then returned to Village Island. His grandfather's influence was strong, and it was at his insistance that he became a hamatsa. When he was about twenty-five his grandfather died and he began to pursue white values more consistently. In his mid-thirties he migrated to an open reserve at Alert Bay where he could more easily adopt Western culture. He acquired land on this reserve by promising not to participate in potlatches and to conform to certain Western customs. He planned to create a progressive community of Indians who were all eager to adopt the new ways, and if the present study had been carried out at this time, James Sewid might well have appeared to be giving up his Kwakiutl heritage. Such was not the case. The amalgamation with the Nimpkish led eventually to his election as chief councillor of that band. Although the inclination to escape the conflict did not die, from then on he remained socially anchored within Kwakiutl society. In 1950 he determined to bring out his regalia and begin potlatching again, and from that time until the close of his story he simultaneously pursued the values of each culture. The close proximity of the Nimpkish reserve to the white community of Alert Bay meant that he was continually influenced by Western culture. Throughout his life then, James Sewid lived in a dual cultural environment.

A second factor which may influence adjustment to two cultures is the degree of similarity between them. If the two value systems are fundamentally similar there may be only an appearance of culture conflict. Individuals may then adopt the new culture with only minor difficulty because of their essential similarity. This argument has been used to explain the apparent rapid assimilation of the Kwakiutl into Western society. The Kwakiutl were highly motivated to acquire wealth, and their values were somewhat similar to a Western Protestant ethic. The fact that they have remained in their traditional villages and pursued traditional subsistence activities may have made Western practices easier to adopt. Yet the similarities are not sufficient to ameliorate the culture conflicts significantly. Measuring differences between institutions and cultural patterns (Codere 1961:514) seems to require that individual experiences of the conflict be considered. James Sewid, as well as other Kwakiutl interviewed, felt the conflict in contrasting cultural definitions of self, status, and roles.

James Sewid adapted to his bicultural world by striving to conform to norms of both cultures. What it meant for him to be bicultural may be seen from a brief consideration of several areas of his life. His well-equipped house is one of the most modern on the Indian reserve in Alert Bay. At the same time, it is one of the last to have a large Indian smokehouse behind it for preparing the traditional foods. Dried seaweed, smoked salmon, and olachen oil are eaten almost daily along with a variety of Western foods. Kwakiutl masks and ceremonial regalia are as much a part of his home as the television set and freezer.

The most important subsistence activity for James Sewid was the traditional one of fishing, and he made use of Western technology as well as Kwakiutl lore. His attitudes toward fish and fishing, his almost intuitive awareness of how fish behaved and where they were, and his understanding of weather, geography, and tides all came largely from his Kwakiutl heritage. The roles he played in fishing, such as engineer, were more often Western oriented. This is also evident in the way he performed as a skipper, especially in his ability to get angry at crew members and fire them, even when they were relatives. Outside of his fishing, Sewid has engaged in such non-Indian occupations as farmer, clam-buyer, and proprietor of a sawmill and store.

The acquisition of resources did not provide nearly so many difficulties as their use. James Sewid was definitely bicultural in the handling of money. He experienced social sanctions from whites to acquire and save, whereas the teaching and example of his grandfather was to acquire and give. While he may have worked harder than others to acquire money during the early part of his life, he does not appear to have acquired much capital until he was nearly twenty-five, partially because of the continual pressure to give things away. With his uncle, Robert Bell, he began his first business venture in the Western sense. Although this had been done by many other Kwakiutl, becoming a successful entrepreneur was another thing (Hawthorn et al. 1960:170–74).

James Sewid's commitment to, and achievement of, Western goals is more extraordinary when one considers that he also conformed to the contradictory value of giving things away. Time spent in assisting others and money given or loaned added to the difficulty of achieving Western goals. His commitment to Western goals appears to have grown after his grandfather's death (p. 109). His move to Alert Bay, when he did give up potlatching for a few years, may well have been an important reason for his successful activities as an entrepreneur. Throughout most of his life, he has been financially independent and in recent years quite successful in terms of both cultures.

The social environment in which James Sewid lived and interacted with others also reflects his dual culture orientation. He remained socially anchored within Kwakiutl society, living in traditional communities. His courtship and marriage were based on traditional customs, yet he was also married in the Anglican church. Most kinship roles were primarily Kwakiutl, but he has given up the custom of giving his eldest child preferential treatment. As a child he learned the importance of knowing and respecting his kinsmen; he followed this value throughout his life and taught it to his own children. While few Indians had opportunities to participate in Western institutions other than the church, James Sewid became a Mason and a member of the Alert Bay Board of Trade. In recent years, as cooperation between the white and Indian segments of Alert Bay has increased, he has been on committees for centennial celebrations, fund-raising projects, school activities, and juvenile delinquency problems. His activities with the Native Brotherhood of British Columbia have enabled him to participate in political institutions at the provincial and national level. Once in 1964, he went to Ottawa to negotiate with Canadian officials and then flew home to put on a large potlatch.

James Sewid was also bicultural in the area of religion and rituals. He appeared to be completely Westernized in his religion, but although he had a deep commitment to his Anglican faith and was more involved in the church than most Kwakiutl, he also held some traditional Kwakiutl religious beliefs. His indoctrination into both religions was simultaneous and began early. At about six he was baptized into the church, just shortly after he danced in his first secret society ceremonial; his marriage was both Anglican and Kwakiutl; his confirmation in the church took place at about the same time that he went through the extended hamatsa initiation. His understanding of Christianity was affected by Kwakiutl values. In contrast to Western individualism, Kwakiutl culture stressed submission to authority figures, and James Sewid interpreted the most important aspect of Christianity as obedience to elders (pp. 57, 235). Thus, although he appeared to be very Western in his religion, we find that he held beliefs and values that were derived from both cultures.

Two other outstanding features of James Sewid's bicultural adaptation were his roles as a *leader* and an *innovator*. His leadership activities began early and continued throughout his life. He became the informal leader of the progressive element at Village Island, and after forming a group to look after the electric power plant, he was elected chairman. He held the highest position among the Kwiksutainuk people at Village Island. On the Industrial Reserve he became the leader of the progressive Indians who had moved there, and Mr. Murry Todd, the Indian agent, came to him about the amalgamation. His leadership in the church began about this time, as some of the older people died, and he led the Kwakwala prayer meeting, becoming, in time, both rector's warden and a lay reader. As it was the only Anglican church in Alert Bay, it was made up of both white and Indian members. He was elected the first chief councillor among the Kwakiutl, and held that position almost continuously from then on. His leadership positions were too many to enumerate, but they included positions on joint white-Indian committees.

James Sewid was also responsible for many innovations, and these too began early in his life. As a child playing on the beach he constructed the first little automobile in Alert Bay from discarded items. He introduced an electric light plant into Village Island, which became the first remote village to have such a convenience, and created the "light company," a new type of social organization, to manage it. While both whites and Indians accepted the premise that schoolteachers should be paid by the government from tax money, Sewid himself paid the teacher to extend the school year at Village Island. After moving to Alert Bay he was instrumental in changing the band structure from hereditary chief to elected chief, and he created new ways to solicit and use band funds. In 1958 he developed a new kind of political structure, the intertribal council. Toward the end of his autobiography he tells of creating a new biracial committee to deal with juvenile delinquency, building the community house, and developing the Kwakwala Arts and Crafts Organization.

Seldom were his innovations simple reflections of European culture, but new ideas which had to be adapted to the realities of a bicultural environment. Identifying with both cultures, he could take those aspects which he considered valuable from each and weave them into new patterns which were often adopted by others. This style of adaptation was not free from personal or interpersonal stress, but in the midst of conflict he continually mediated without giving up his commitment to important values in both cultures.

Perhaps the most significant aspect of his response was the way in which he *simultaneously* followed both cultures, as illustrated in the hospital benefit he innovated in about 1950 (pp. 158–62). Motivated by values from both cultures, he wished to support a Western institution, the hospital, and to validate his status in an institution of Kwakiutl culture. The actual performance included such European cultural elements as paid admission, a mixed audience who were purely spectators, and a written program. The dance itself was Kwakiutl, and individuals validated their status by the traditional practices of dancing in order of rank and publicly showing their regalia. During the week or more in which this event took place James Sewid moved back and forth between two social and cultural worlds. He interacted in different groups on the basis of different cultural definitions of group processes.

His role as a leader is also evident in this same event, which took place during his first term as chief councillor of the Nimpkish reserve. Undoubtedly he was invited to be on the hospital week committee because he held this position of leadership in Kwakiutl society. The reasons he was elected as chairman of the committee are not known, but there is every indication from other events during his life that he was respected by the white members of the committee. His leadership among the Indians was based on his position as elected chief councillor and on his inherited positions in a number of tribes, while the resistance on the part of others to his ideas may have been due, in part, to his age and the fact that he was not the hereditary chief of the Nimpkish band. His eagerness to pay the expenses of the other chiefs had they gone home, and to send to their villages for their dance regalia, was consistent with Kwakiutl values; a high-ranking chief could demonstrate his prestige and social status or shame those he opposed by such an expenditure of wealth.

James Sewid's account of this innovation shows its novelty. It is safe to assume that most Kwakiutl had some knowledge of the theater or stage programs where people paid money to view a dramatic performance. Whites, on the other hand, had knowledge of practices in their own culture where giving gifts of money or goods brought recognition. These facts did not keep either whites or Kwakiutl from rejecting the customs of the other. Many whites found the potlatch an incomprehensible practice, and the Kwakiutl, at least in this event, found it difficult to think of using their dances in a pattern dictated by Western culture. To show one's masks and other privileges *without* distributing wealth was to do it for *nothing* and traditionally would have been a reason to be ashamed. If an individual showed his masks and then gave away money he validated his status, receiving recognition, praise, and an increase in self-esteem. While the resistance to James Sewid's idea was due in part to his age and other rivalries, it was also due to a fear of losing status by being prevented from giving away money. As an innovator, he was somehow able to comprehend, reconcile, and recombine the different cultural conceptions involved.

Personality

James Sewid came to terms with his world, which was characterized by reverberative conflict between his Indian and the surrounding white culture, by developing a bicultural style of life. His activities as a leader and an innovator facilitated his bicultural adaptation. In order to understand Sewid it is necessary to examine his social and cultural environment and the manner in which he was able to cope with that environment. Further, a number of personality characteristics which were central to his style of adaptation must be identified. The difficulty of assessing such inherited factors as intelligence, temperament, and physique in non-Western societies is well known. While not discounting their possible importance, the focus in this discussion will be upon personality characteristics that James Sewid acquired through interaction with his environment. Evidence from the nonverbal parts of psychological tests developed for use in Western culture suggests that he was above average in intelligence, but not exceptional. Although inconclusive, this suggests that his ability to cope with culture conflict was *learned*. The most striking aspects of his personality, and those which strongly influenced his adaptive style, involved his achievement motivation and self-concept.

The achievement motive refers to the desire to do things as rapidly or as well as possible and has been widely studied in Western culture (Murray 1938:164, McClelland et al. 1953). In every society there are standards and norms against which individuals may measure their behavior. Awareness of these standards does not necessarily lead to a desire to measure up to them, and some individuals in every society are content when they fall short of such standards. They may excuse their failure to live up to some ideal by discounting it as "unrealistic" or by blaming some obstacle. Several approaches were used to infer the strength of James Sewid's achievement motivation.

A sentence completion test was administered and he was asked to finish a partial statement in any way he wanted. A number of responses indicated his strong achievement motivation:

> *If only* I could get ahead.
> *My most important decision* was to get ahead.
> *I feel proud when* everything goes well.
> *I feel sorry about* the condition of my village.
> *It is hard for me* to get away from my work.
> *The thing I don't like* is idle time, laying around, I like to move.

Such words as "good," "well," and "ahead" indicate his concern with achievement. When his business or the village was not meeting his standards of excellence he experienced anger or sorrow. Although James Sewid often relaxed at home, observations there and on his fishing boat indicated that he unceasingly drove himself in pursuit of his goals. He constantly worked to be an outstanding skipper and had a clear idea about the characteristics of good and poor skippers: the good ones were achievement-oriented and caught the most fish for the company (p. 99). He required his crew to measure up to standards of excellence also. Interviews with others verified Sewid's statement that he was one of the highliners during most of his life, and his employer, recognizing his achievements, used him to train other skippers (p. 173). The achievement motive involves the desire to overcome obstacles with excellent performance, and most of Sewid's innovations suggest a strong desire of this nature.

One of the few tests developed specifically for cross-cultural use is the Value Orientation Questionnaire (F. Kluckhohn 1953), which is based on the assumption that there are a limited number of basic human problems for which all cultures must find some solution. While the problems are constant, the solutions vary from one society to another. The problems and their varied solutions involve ideas about basic human nature, the relation of man to nature, the significant time dimension, the most valued personality type, and the relationship of man to other men. This questionnaire was adapted for use among the Kwakiutl and given to James Sewid. This section designed to answer the question "What is the valued personality type?" relates specifically to the achievement motive. Responses fall into the categories of "being" or "doing." Some individuals and groups value the person who is oriented toward the spontaneous expression of impulses (being), while others value "action in the sense of accomplishment and in accord with standards which are conceived as being external to the acting individual" (F. Kluckhohn 1953:351). James Sewid valued the "doing" orientation. His responses are summarized below:

Question Theme	*Value Orientation*
Type of boss desired	Doing over Being
How people like to live	Doing over Being
How James Sewid lived	Doing over Being
Types of farmers	Doing over Being
Types of housewives	Doing over Being
Use of leisure time preference	Being over Doing
James Sewid's use of leisure time	Doing over Being

In recent research on the achievement motive, a projective test was developed that has been used cross-culturally to quantify different degrees of the achievement motive. This procedure, which was developed by David McClelland and his co-workers (McClelland et al. 1953, Atkinson 1958), was used with James Sewid. The set of pictures chosen were the ones used in the original validation studies because some normative information was available for a large population of college students from Western society (Atkinson 1958:834–35). Although a more valid approach would be to compare Sewid's responses with other Kwakiutl, such a procedure was not possible. With the use of a specific scoring system, it was discovered that the students had a mean score of 6.10 with a standard deviation of 4.86. The range was from a low of — 2 to a high achievement motive score of + 25. Using the same scoring system for Sewid's protocol, his score was + 25. He thus showed a higher degree of achievement motivation, as measured by this instrument, than nearly the entire group of two hundred college students. There is good evidence, then, from his response to tests, his behavior, and his autobiography that he had a high level of achievement motivation.

Several areas of James Sewid's early experience appear to have contributed to his acquiring a strong achievement motivation. Among these were the high expectations of achievement that his relatives had for him. As the only heir to elevated positions in several tribes of the Kwakiutl, he received preferential treatment and was often reminded of his obligations to live up to high standards. Another factor appears to have been the absence of a father during his early development. A study in Turkey suggests that physical removal from the father's influence was conducive to the development of a higher achievement motivation (Bradburn 1962:467). Sewid's father died prematurely of an accident and, although he had two stepfathers and lived at times with his maternal grandfather, he did not experience the intensity of paternal authority he might have had his father lived. He lived alone with his grandmother for long periods during his early years, and the most important female socializers in his experience were his two grandmothers, his mother, his aunt, and his two godmothers.

There has been much written upon the relationship between the

Protestant ethic and achievement motivation. Achievement motivation has been said to arise out of the belief that worldly success is
evidence that one is chosen and blessed by God, and moral dedica-
tion to duty out of a belief in man's sinfulness and his responsibility
to suppress sin. While most Kwakiutl are today nominally Anglican,
there is evidence that the majority have only a superficial grasp of
the values and beliefs of the church (Codere 1961:502). James
Sewid exhibited a high degree of commitment to the Anglican
religion. He learned Protestant beliefs and values early in life
through his grandmother, godmothers, schoolteacher, and ministers
in Alert Bay. He vividly recalled learning about Christianity from
his grandmother, whose wish it was that he stand before his people
as an adult and teach them the gospel. His schoolteacher had been
a pupil of the first missionary to the Kwakiutl, and he and Sewid
often discussed the Bible during the evenings when he was going
to school. During his adult life he has been actively involved in his
church and is the only Indian in his community to hold a license as
lay reader.

There is a large body of research in Western culture that has
shown individual behavior to vary with different self-conceptions.
The way one defines his body, his abilities, his values to others, and
his place in society all influence his motivation and action, and much
of James Sewid's behavior in adapting to culture conflict may be
understood with reference to his definition of himself as an actor
within a sociocultural system. His most important self-conceptions
were his sense of self-esteem and self-reliance, his social identity,
and his conception of himself as a leader. These self-concepts
become more significant when one considers his social world, where
superiority claimed by whites and the myth of racial inferiority used
to explain Indian behavior make it difficult for Indians to develop
the sense of self-esteem so important in motivation. Sewid's ability
to pursue contradictory goals from different cultures resulted, in
part, from his exceptional sense of self-esteem and self-reliance.

On the sentence completion test he responded by saying:

> *It is hard for me* to, now, let's see, what is hard for me?
> Nothing is hard for me, nothing is impossible for me. I don't

know what is hard for me. It is hard for me to get away from
my work.

This type of statement was made many times during the interviews,
and although he mentions some mistakes, problems, and failures,
there is scarcely a hint of self-hate, inferiority, or inadequacy.

Confidence in his own ability developed very early and remained
part of his personality throughout his life. As a child in school he
perceived himself able to handle conflict with other boys (p. 47).
His achievement orientation in fishing was closely linked to his
conception of himself as an adequate individual. Even before he
became a skipper he perceived himself as very competent and able
to catch fish or perform any task. Dancing was another important
area of his life, and he thought of himself as a strong and able dancer
(p. 93). This sense of self-esteem and confidence in his own resources appeared to pervade even his unconscious life, as it revealed
itself in recurrent dreams. In these dreams, where he was faced
with seemingly insurmountable problems, he neither fled or sought
help from others but was able to meet the challenges presented
single-handedly.

Near the close of his autobiography, James Sewid commented
briefly upon the importance of self-esteem with reference to his
own race and their loss of pride. He stated many times that he was
proud to be an Indian, and the data which have been reviewed
strongly support the conclusion that he had a deep, pervasive sense
of pride, or self-esteem. Early in 1967, after his autobiography had
been edited, it was read back to him. This experience was greatly
enjoyed by him and elicited many comments indicating his feeling
of deep satisfaction. When the reading was finished and he was
asked how he felt as he looked back over his life, he responded by
saying,

> I think it is a wonderful life. That's all I can say. I think it is
> a full life. I didn't realize it, I didn't think nothing of it before
> now. It's all come to me and I'm sure now, I was looking
> forward to hearing how it would sound and what it was going
> to be like and I'm sure it is going to be something to see. I only
> wish that I live another few years and then I can make another,
> what we have left out when the book closes, what happens in
> the future. (Field Notes)

James Sewid's exceptional sense of self-esteem and self-reliance appear to be closely associated with how others perceived him as he was growing up. James Sewid was highly valued and received an extraordinary amount of respect from a wide range of individuals with whom he identified. These identity models gave him preferential treatment for a variety of reasons which must be understood against the background of two aspects of Kwakiutl culture. First is the interest in social status and worth that was one of the most important and persistent features of this culture: the ranking of tribes, the hierarchical structure of each kinship group, the practice of primogeniture, the secret society ceremonies, and the potlatch were all related to a desire to maximize social status. The second pertinent aspect of Kwakiutl culture was the interest in preserving social status by the transfer of associated rights to the proper heir. The expressed purpose of potlatches and secret society ceremonies was to transfer the rights to names, positions, songs, dances, and masks as well as to more tangible property (Spradley 1963). Boas' description of Kwakiutl social organization and rules of inheritance has given the impression of a system that was both clan-based and bilateral; ideally a man was a member of either his father's or his mother's clan, but he considered himself to be half from one clan and tribe and half from the other. The principle of primogeniture required that some rights be passed from father to oldest son. Other rights, primarily associated with the secret societies, had to be passed from "a man to his daughter's son, and [were] actually exercised by the man's son-in-law" (Codere 1961:442). In the latter case, rules of primogeniture required that the rights be passed on to the firstborn son of the oldest daughter. Symbols of prestige and social status were thereby distributed to different individuals within the extended family depending on an accident of birth. Because of circumstances of birth and death, James Sewid was in a position to inherit status positions through both lines of descent. Let us examine how the interest in social status and the desire to preserve it through inheritance were significant in the development of his self-concept.

His grandfather, Chief Aul Sewid, held a high position in the Kwiksutainuk tribe. He and his uncle, Yakatlnalis, had both become known as outstanding Kwakiutl chiefs. Aul Sewid and his son were only children, both of whom died prior to James Sewid's birth, and their positions were held for him by a man who stood in a classificatory father's brother relationship to him. Because of his position in his father's clan, Sewid was treated with great respect and esteem; he was often told of the potlatch given for him at ten months of age (p. 18). Most of his early socialization took place while he lived with his mother's clan, and the rights of his mother's father, Jim Bell, which should have been passed to the first son of his oldest daughter, came to him because her children died early in life, making Sewid the only heir possible in this type of inheritance. People were aware that he would assume high positions in both the Kwiksutainuk and Mamalilikulla tribes. Through his marriage to a girl of equal social status he received positions in many of the secret societies, one of which was the basis for his initiation into the hamatsa society. The respect and esteem he received from his mother's clan members is one of the recurrent themes of his life story (p. 26). Both Sewid and his uncle remembered that he had been the favorite of his grandparents, who treated him with special respect according to primogeniture. Because of his unique position at the nexus of the chains of inheritance in two clans, he received an extraordinary amount of favor and respect from a wide group of individuals, especially those who were important identity models.

While this in itself would appear to have been sufficient, many of the other identity models also valued him in some special way. Although retrospective information cannot always be verified, it is important to point out that it is James Sewid's perceptions of the attitudes others had toward him which reveal what was significant for his personality development. When he was three his mother married again. He had some memory of his first stepfather, who died when he was five, and could clearly recall his close relationship with Dave, the man his mother married several years later. Both of these stepfathers had no other children when they married Sewid's mother and no doubt treated him with much favor because of the primogeniture custom.

James Sewid's achievement orientation, self-esteem, and self-reliance were important motivating factors in his adaptation to culture conflict and help to explain his constant pursuit of goals and his ability to overcome obstacles through innovative activity. They do not, however, explain why he chose to pursue the goals of both cultures, or why he was a leader in so many social groups. He might have channeled his energies and abilities into either Kwakiutl or Western activities. Given these qualities of personality, it is unlikely that he would ever have coped with the problems of culture conflict by passively withdrawing from pursuing the goals of either culture. His social identity and his conception of himself as a leader influenced the manner in which his motivation found expression.

An individual's self-identity refers to conceptions of *who* he is. Self-esteem and self-reliance refer more to how one feels about who he is. Features of self-identity such as "I am James," "I am a father," "I am an Indian," "I am six feet tall," and "I am honest" may be classified into two groups: features of social identity and features of personal identity. Those which link the individual to his roles within a society make up his social identity. "I am an Indian" is a feature of social identity since it refers to membership in a racial group, while "I am a father" is also a feature of social identity because it refers to a role played within a kinship group. The other features of identity stated above refer to personal identity. They may influence how one plays a role, but they do not link the individual to a role or social group.

James Sewid's behavior must be understood in relationship to two different social groups, and it is this fact which makes the concept of social identity important. One study has shown that those individuals who responded to a relatively unstructured test of self-identity with predominantly personal identity features tended to meet adult expectations at a minimal level or below (McPartland, Cumming, and Garretson 1961). Those who responded with predominantly social identity features behaved in much more socially effective ways and were more responsive to the requirements of their roles. Although little research on the self-identities of individuals living in societies undergoing acculturation has been done, it seems reasonable to suggest the following hypothesis. Acculturation leads to wide changes in the sociocultural system which are reflected in poorly developed social identities of the members of that system. In Kwakiutl society many of the roles connected with the potlatch, secret society, economic, and kinship systems have fallen into disuse. Expectations regarding the roles which remain, or new ones which have come from European society, are not clearly defined. Other changes include a shift from assigned to achieved roles and from a limited number of roles to a wide variety. The net result is that many individuals lose their anchorage within the social system. Alienated from both Indian and white society, they have a poorly developed sense of social identity, leading to conditions of anomie and greater social disorganization.

James Sewid appears to have had a very strong sense of social identity. He enacted many roles during his lifetime and belonged to many different groups; in some he was the only Indian member. When asked to indicate the groups of which he was a member, he easily responded with the following twenty-four.

1. Family
2. Village Island Mamalilikulla
3. Guilford Island Kwiksutainuk
4. Fort Rupert Kwakiutl
5. Matilpi
6. Nimpkish Band
7. Nimpkish Council
8. Intertribal Council
9. Kwakwala Arts and Crafts Organization
10. Seine Boat Crew
11. Saw Mill and Boat Shop Company
12. Executive Board of the Native Brotherhood
13. Negotiating Committee of the Native Brotherhood
14. Anglican Church
15. Church Committee
16. Church Corporation
17. Kwakwala Prayer Group
18. Youth Guidance Committee
19. St. Andrew's Brotherhood
20. Alert Bay Board of Trade
21. Hospital Board
22. Parent Teachers Association
23. Fishing Fleet of the ABC Packers
24. Masonic Lodge

His membership involved active participation and a strong sense of identification with these groups; throughout his autobiography he continually referred to "my people," and what he wanted to do for them.

Additional data on his strong social identity comes from a self-identity test which approaches the social self-conception directly (Kuhn and McPartland 1954). The following instructions were given to Sewid:

There are 20 numbered blanks on the page below. Please write twenty answers to the simple question, "Who am I?" in the blanks. Just give twenty answers to the question. Answer as if you were giving the answers to yourself, not to somebody else. Don't worry about logic or importance. Go along fairly fast for time is limited. Write the answers in the order they come to you.

He was given twelve minutes and responded with the following answers in order.

1.	Sewid	12.	Engineer
2.	Father	13.	Architect
3.	Chief Councillor	14.	Net Man
4.	Boat Owner	15.	Logger
5.	Captain	16.	Chairman of the Youth Guidance Committee
6.	Rector's Warden		
7.	Layman's Reader	17.	Vice-President of the Native Brotherhood
8.	Native Indian		
9.	Mamalilikulla	18.	Totem Pole Carver
10.	Kwiksutainuk	19.	Hereditary Chief
11.	Carpenter	20.	Brick Layer

The relatively unstructed nature of this test enables the individual to respond with features of personal identity, social identity, or other types of self-referential statements. It is significant that all of his responses refer to his social identity. The only one which may not appear to reflect his social identity is the first response, *Sewid*. Had he put James or Jimmy, this would have been a feature of his personal identity, but within Kwakiutl society names were always identified with social positions. Sewid was the name in the Kwiksutainuk tribe that went with the position held by his grandfather and father and was passed on to him.

Not only was his social identity clearly predominant, it was also dual. He was anchored in both the white and Kwakiutl sociocultural systems. The first thirteen groups listed were Kwakiutl or Indian-oriented and the next eleven were from white society. From the self-identity test it is also clear that he had features of social identity which arose from each society. Eight of his responses on this test indicated his Indian social identity: *Sewid* referred to a position in the Kwiksutainuk tribe; *Father* was a role in the Kwakiutl kinship system; *Mamalilikulla* and *Kwiksutainuk* referred to the tribal affiliations he received from his mother and father; *Hereditary Chief* referred to a number of high positions he had in both of these tribes; *Native Indian* and *Vice-President of the Native Brotherhood* indicated his social identity with native groups beyond the Kwakiutl; *Totem Pole Carver* was a role he held in Kwakiutl society.

Eight of his responses also indicated his white social identity. *Boat Owner* is a role defined by norms from European culture, and in this role he related to officials of the packing company. *Rector's Warden* and *Layman's Reader* are both roles which were part of the social organization of the local Anglican church. *Engineer, Net Man,* and *Brick Layer* are roles in the white economic system. His role as *Chairman of the Youth Guidance Committee* also appears to be related to the white social system. Four roles are difficult to categorize as either Kwakiutl or white: *Chief Councillor, Captain, Carpenter,* and *Architect.* Although the role of chief councillor is in the contemporary Kwakiutl social system, most of the norms are defined by white society. The role of captain of a seine boat is also largely defined by white society although it related him to members of both societies. Carpenter and architect involve white definitions for roles that also exist in Kwakiutl society.

The development of James Sewid's social identity was related to three early experiences. First, most of his identity models from Kwakiutl society constantly reminded him of his place in a society that gave him extraordinary respect and valued him because of his social identity. When the number of names in a kinship group are limited, and they are used repeatedly, they tend to identify the individual closely with that social group (Goodenough 1965). Sewid shared the Kwakiutl belief that each child was a reincarnation of some ancestor whose names and designated social positions would be passed on to him in secret society and potlatch ceremonies. During his lifetime he acquired a variety of names that constantly reaffirmed the importance of his social identity.

Second, he had a large number of identity models representing different styles of life and social groups, and through close association with them he acquired a capacity to identify with contrasting groups. He was not threatened by identifying with groups whose ways of life appeared contradictory. An inquiry into those Sewid perceived as important to him during childhood resulted in fifteen identity models. The following chart summarizes their relationships to him.

IDENTITY MODELS

Relationship to James Sewid	Age of Primary and (Intermittent) Contact	Identity of Model and Nature of the Relationship
1. Mother to Son	Birth–6 (6–17)	Daughter of chief of Mamalilikulla tribe. Nurturant. Mother and only son alone for some periods of time.
2. Father's Mother to Son's Son (Eldest and Only)	6–10 (Birth–5, 11–17)	High rank in Matilpi tribe. Sewid helped support her and went to school while living with her. Strong religious influence. Valued and respected him.
3. First Stepfather to Only Stepson	2–5	High rank in Tlawitsis tribe and Kwiksutainuk tribe. Respected and valued Sewid.
4. Second Stepfather to Only Stepson	5–6 (7–17)	High rank in Matilpi tribe. Logger and mechanic who taught Sewid these skills. Close friends. Great respect for Sewid.
5. Mother's Father to Daughter's Son (Eldest and Only)	Birth–3, 10–14 (4–9, 14–17)	High rank in Mamalilikulla tribe. Potlatched for him, passed on secret society position, trained him in traditional culture. Treated his heir with great respect and care.
6. Mother's Mother to Daughter's Son (Eldest and Only)	Birth–3, 10–14 (4–9, 14–17)	Wife of Mamalilikulla chief. Treated Sewid with special favor over her own children of same age.
7. Mother's Sister's Husband to Wife's Sister's Son	(Birth–17)	High-ranking Fort Rupert Kwakiutl. Due to death of his own children he asked Sewid to live with him. Cooked and ran engine on his boat; first employer. Respected and valued Sewid as eldest son.

8. Mother's Eldest Brother to Sister's Son	Birth–3, 10–14 (4–9, 14–17)	High rank in Mamalilikulla tribe. Worked on his fishing boat.
9. Father's Brother to Brother's Son (A Classificatory Brother: FaFaFaBrDaSo)	(Birth–17)	High rank in Tsawatsainuk tribe. Held Sewid's estate until he came of age. Gave potlatches for him during childhood. Valued and respected Sewid.
10. Teacher to Student	(6–17)	Progressive man of Nimpkish tribe. Trained by early missionary. Began first native labor union. Bachelor who spent a great deal of time with Sewid out of school. Valued and respected him. Treated him with special favor.
11. Godmother to Godson	(6–17)	Wife of Nimpkish chief. Progressive and active in the church. Encouraged and cared for Sewid, expected him to work for the people.
12. Godmother to Godson	(6–17)	Wife of Indian-white descent from Seattle. Raised by first missionary. Wife of progressive Kwakiutl Indian trained by missionary. Encouraged and cared for Sewid, expected him to work for the people.
13. Minister to Parishioner	(Birth–12)	Baptized and confirmed Sewid [who lived next door to the church with his grandmother for several years]. Minister and wife cared for him with food and clothing. Sewid did odd jobs for minister.
14. Minister to Parishioner	(12–16)	Performed Sewid's wedding. Took personal interest in him.
15. Wife's Father	(14–17)	High rank in Nimpkish tribe. Lived with him after marriage. Worked for him on his boat.

Third, James Sewid's bicultural identity was related to the way he learned Indian customs and the conflicts between these and the white man's way of life. Kwakiutl culture was falling into disuse

and many of his peers received less training in the traditional practices than he did. Robert Bell, Sewid's uncle, recalled,

> I was never real strong for the Indian customs but Jimmy was
> because he was taught by my dad to be like that. My people
> never forced me to learn all those things. But they were fond
> of Jimmy, very fond of Jimmy. In our Indian custom they do
> that, they always choose the oldest boy. Jimmy was chosen
> because he was the oldest. All our people work together to
> bring him into this Indian way to be respected by the
> people. (Field Notes)

His grandparents endeavored to teach him the native culture; his
schoolteacher, on the other hand, was responsible for clarifying the
conflicts between Kwakiutl and white culture, and the vague awareness that there were differences in the two ways of life was replaced
by a clear perception of the contrasts. In the security of his relationship to his teacher, George Luther, James Sewid could find the
alien ways losing their threat to his identity as an Indian.

The final aspect of James Sewid's self-concept to be considered is
his conception of himself as a leader. Although he occupied many
leadership positions during his life he might have considered
himself as essentially dependent upon others but compelled to
occupy such positions by social pressures. Since we are dealing with
self-perceptions, we must ask how Sewid perceived his relationship
to other individuals and to social groups. Was he dominant or sub-
missive, a leader or a follower, independent or dependent? His
responses to the self-identity test provide some information on this.
Of the twenty responses he made, almost half of them refer to
features of his social identity which indicate a leadership role:
Sewid referred to his position as leader in the Kwiksutainuk tribe;
Father was his position at the head of his own family; *Chief Councillor* was an elected leadership position in the Nimpkish band;
Captain referred to his position of authority over his fishing crew;
Rector's Warden and *Layman's Reader* were leadership roles in the
Anglican church; *Chairman of the Youth Guidance Committee*
was a position of leadership in an organization which included both
whites and Indians in Alert Bay; *Vice-President of the Native
Brotherhood* was a position in a group which included members

from many Indian tribes; *Hereditary Chief* was a position of leadership based on traditional Kwakiutl customs. His responses to this
test strongly suggest that a major part of his self-concept was that
of a leader.

Since James Sewid filled many formal leadership positions, it
might be expected that he would define himself in terms of some of
these. If he had actually internalized the sense of being a leader, one
would expect that this self-definition would influence his social
relationships when he did not occupy formal leadership positions.
There is a large body of evidence in the autobiography indicating
that James Sewid perceived that others were dependent upon him
or that he had authority over them (p. 57).

While he found support and help in many adults, his stepfather
and George Luther, for example, he also saw himself as a great help
to his teacher and his grandmother Lucy. Throughout his lifetime
he saw himself as a leader among his peers; as a child he led his
friends in pulling driftwood from the beach (p. 53). During the
summers he lived with his mother and stepfather at the cannery,
but some aspects of his relationship to them were not entirely
dependent and childlike (p. 56). While he lived with his father-in-
law, doing carpentry work for him and helping him in other ways,
he worked as a straw boss with a group of Indians who were tearing
down an old sawmill in Alert Bay. After moving to Village Island
he helped the two white women who were living there, and at that
time he recalled feeling the wish for further responsibility in church
work. When he moved to the Industrial Reserve at Alert Bay he
became the informal leader of that group, and when he was elected
chief councillor of the Nimpkish band he was reminded of his
favorite text in the Bible, identifying himself with Solomon when
he became king. From that time on, his identity as a leader perme-
ated most of his activities. Even during the period he was not chief
councillor he wished to continue as an adviser. His self-conception
as a leader, acquired through interacting with those who perceived
him as a leader, was probably the outstanding feature of his socialization in Kwakiutl society. As he recalled, "They were all teaching
me how to be a leader of my people when I grew up" (p. 44).

This chapter has focused upon the characteristics which were
significant in James Sewid's bicultural style of adaptation. His

strong achievement motivation, together with a high degree of self-esteem and self-reliance, helped to account for his energetic, goal-directed activity. The sense of responsibility derived from his self-conception as a leader also contributed to this. His strong sense of social identity provided a firm anchorage to his social and cultural world and included features of both Kwakiutl and white societies, which enabled him to pursue the goals of both cultures. His dual identity, achievement motivation, and self-reliance contributed to his ability to create new ways of life by combining aspects of both cultures in novel ways. James Sewid's unique hereditary endowment and learning experiences in a changing cultural environment contributed to the development of these aspects of his personality.

Bibliography

Atkinson, John W., ed.
  1958   *Motives in Fantasy, Action and Society,* Princeton, N.J.,
         D. Van Nostrand.

Boas, Franz
  1897   *The Social Organization and the Secret Societies of the
         Kwakiutl Indians,* Report of the U.S. National Museum
         for 1895, Washington, D.C.
  1966   *Kwakiutl Ethnography,* ed. and abr., with an intro. by
         Helen Codere, Chicago, University of Chicago Press.

Bohannon, Paul
  1963   *Social Anthropology,* New York, Holt, Rinehart and
         Winston.

Bradburn, N. M.
  1962   "N Achievement and Father Dominance in Turkey,"
         Journal of Abnormal Psychology 67:464–68.

Codere, Helen
  1950   *Fighting with Property: A Study of Kwakiutl Potlatching
         and Warfare, 1792–1930,* Monographs of the American
         Ethnological Society 18, Seattle, University of Washing-
         ton Press.
  1959   "The Understanding of the Kwakiutl," in *The Anthro-
         pology of Franz Boas,* ed. Walter Goldschmidt, American
         Anthropological Association Memoir No. 89, Menasha,
         Wis.
  1961   "Kwakiutl," in *Perspectives in American Indian Culture
         Change,* ed. Edward H. Spicer, Chicago, University of
         Chicago Press, pp. 431–516.

Drucker, Philip
  1958   *Native Brotherhoods: Modern Intertribal Organizations
         on the Northwest Coast,* Bureau of American Ethnology
         Bulletin 168, Washington, D.C.

Duff, Wilson
1964   *The Indian History of British Columbia: Vol. I—The Impact of the White Man*, Victoria, B.C., Anthropology in British Columbia, Memoir No. 5.

Ford, Clellan S.
1941   *Smoke from Their Fires: The Life of a Kwakiutl Chief*, New Haven, Yale University Press.

Goldman, Irving
1937   "The Kwakiutl of Vancouver Island," in *Cooperation and Competition Among Primitive Peoples*, ed. Margaret Mead, Boston, Beacon Press.

Goodenough, Ward Hunt
1965   "Personal Names and Modes of Address in Two Oceanic Societies," in *Context and Meaning in Cultural Anthropology*, ed. Melford E. Spiro, pp. 265–76.

Hawthorn, Harry Bertram, C. S. Belshaw, and S. M. Jamieson
1960   *The Indians of British Columbia*, Berkeley, University of California Press.

Kluckhohn, Clyde
1945   "The Personal Document in Anthropological Science," in *The Use of Personal Documents in History, Anthropology, and Sociology*, ed. Louis Gottschalk, Clyde Kluckhohn, and Robert Angell, New York, Social Science Research Council Bulletin 53, pp. 78–173.

Kluckhohn, Florence Rockwood
1953   "Dominant and Variant Value Orientation," in *Personality in Nature, Society and Culture*, ed. Clyde Kluckhohn et al., New York, Alfred A. Knopf, pp. 342–57.

Kluckhohn, Florence R., and Fred Strodtbeck
1961   *Variations in Value Orientations*, Evanston, Ill., Row, Peterson.

Kuhn, Manford H., and Thomas S. McPartland
1954   "An Empirical Investigation of Self-Attitudes," *American Sociological Review, 19:*68–76

Langness, L. L.
    1965   *The Life History in Anthropological Science,* New York, Holt, Rinehart and Winston.

Lindzey, Gardner
    1961   *Projective Techniques and Cross-Cultural Research,* New York, Appleton-Century-Crofts.

McClelland, D. C., et al.
    1953   *The Achievement Motive,* New York, Appleton-Century-Crofts.

McPartland, Thomas S., John H. Cumming, and
Wynona S. Garretson
    1961   "Self-Conception and Ward Behavior in Two Psychiatric Hospitals," *Sociometry, 24:*111–124.

Murray, Henry A.
    1938   *Explorations in Personality,* Oxford, Oxford University Press.

Rohner, Ronald
    1964   *"Ethnography of a Contemporary Kwakiutl Village; Gilford Island Band,"* unpublished Ph.D. dissertation, Palo Alto, Calif., Stanford University.

    1967   *The People of Gilford: A Contemporary Kwakiutl Village,* National Museum of Canada Bulletin 225, Anthropological Series No. 83.

Spradley, James P.
    1963   "The Kwakiutl Guardian Spirit Quest: An Historical, Functional and Comparative Analysis," unpublished M.A. thesis, Seattle, University of Washington.

Whiting, John W. M., et al.
    1966   *Field Guide for a Study of Socialization,* New York, John Wiley and Sons.

Wolcott, Harry
    1964   "A Kwakiutl Village and Its School," unpublished Ph.D. dissertation, Palo Alto, Calif., Stanford University.

    1967   *A Kwakiutl Village and School,* New York, Holt, Rinehart and Winston.

Index